ated pages. This
RADICAL OFFICE DESIGN

RADICAL

GEORGIAN COLLEGE LIBRARY

Library Commons
Georgian College
One Georgian Drive
Barrie, ON
L4M 3X9

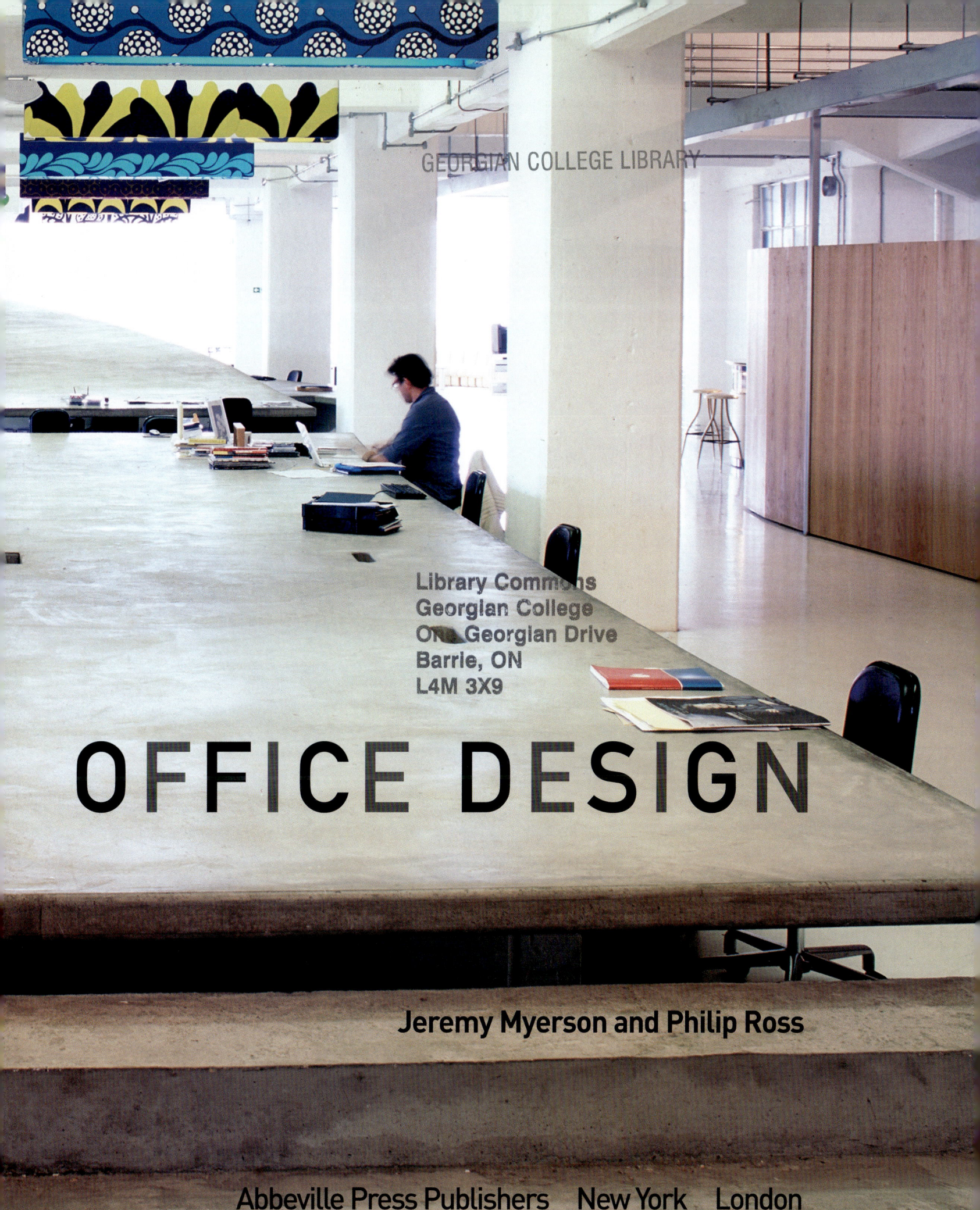

OFFICE DESIGN

Jeremy Myerson and Philip Ross

Abbeville Press Publishers   New York   London

First published in the United States of America in 2006 by Abbeville Press, 137 Varick Street, New York, NY 10013

First published in Great Britain in 2006 by Laurence King Publishing Ltd, 71 Great Russell Street, London WC1B 3BP

Text copyright © 2006 Jeremy Myerson and Philip Ross
Copyright © 2006 Laurence King Publishing Ltd

All rights reserved. No part of this book may be reproduced or utilized in any form or by any means, electronic or mechanical, including photocopying, recording, or by any information storage and retrieval system, without permission in writing from the publisher. Inquiries should be addressed to Abbeville Press, 137 Varick Street, New York, NY 10013. Printed and bound in China.

First edition
10 9 8 7 6 5 4 3 2 1

ISBN-13: 978-0-7892-0886-6
ISBN-10: 0-7892-0886-5

Library of Congress Cataloging-in-Publication Data

Myerson, Jeremy.
  Radical office design / Jeremy Myerson and Philip Ross.— 1st ed.
      p. cm.
  Includes index.
  ISBN 0-7892-0886-5 (alk. paper)
  1. Office buildings. 2. Architecture, Modern—21st century. 3. Office layout.
I. Ross, Philip, 1965- II. Title.

NA6230.M94 2006
725'.23090511—dc22
                                  2005029894

For bulk and premium sales and for text adoption procedures, write to Customer Service Manager, Abbeville Press, 137 Varick Street, New York, NY 10013 or call 1-800-ARTBOOK.

Design by Price Watkins
Jacket design by Misha Beletsky

Front cover: Kirshenbaum Bond & Partners West, San Francisco, Jensen & Macy Architects (see p. 20)
Back cover: Pallotta TeamWorks, Los Angeles, Clive Wilkinson Architects (see pp. 38–39)
Previous pages: Mother, London, Clive Wilkinson Architects (see pp. 50–51)

Contents

Introduction page 8

Academy
the learning campus
14

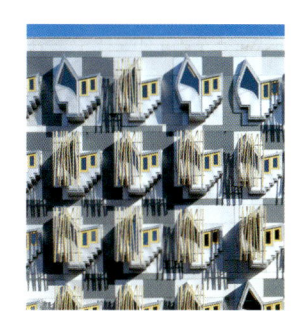

Guild
the professional cluster
74

Agora
the public workplace
114

Lodge
the live-work setting
156

Credits page 185
Index page 191

1 Academy

1.1 Kirshenbaum Bond & Partners West, San Francisco, USA
Jensen & Macy Architects — page 16

1.2 Telenor, Oslo, Norway
NBBJ/HUS/PKA/Dark Design — page 22

1.3 Sedgwick Rd., Seattle, USA
Olson Sundberg Kundig Allen Architects — page 26

1.4 PricewaterhouseCoopers, Birmingham, UK
BDGworkfutures — page 30

1.5 Rafineri, Istanbul, Turkey
Erğinoğlu & Çalişlar — page 34

1.6 Pallotta TeamWorks, Los Angeles, USA
Clive Wilkinson Architects — page 36

1.7 Norddeutsche Landesbank, Hanover, Germany
Behnisch, Behnisch & Partner — page 40

1.8 BMW Plant, Central Building, Leipzig, Germany
Zaha Hadid Architects — page 44

1.9 Mother, London, UK
Clive Wilkinson Architects — page 50

1.10 Ericsson North American Headquarters, Plano, USA
Thompson Vaivoda & Associates Architects — page 54

1.11 Interpolis, Tilburg, Holland
Veldhoen + Company — page 58

1.12 Genzyme Center, Cambridge, USA
Behnisch, Behnisch & Partner — page 64

1.13 Enjoy, Paris, France
Edouard François — page 66

1.14 EMI London Headquarters, London, UK
MoreySmith Design and Architecture — page 68

2 Guild

2.1 BBC Media Centre, London, UK
Allies and Morrison/DEGW — page 76

2.2 Parliamentary Annexe, Helsinki, Finland
Helin & Co Architects — page 82

2.3 Future Centre, Innsbruck, Austria
Peter Lorenz — page 86

2.4 Momentum, Hørsholm, Denmark
Bosch & Fjord — page 90

2.5 Scottish Parliament Building, Edinburgh, Scotland
Enric Miralles Benedetta Tagliabue Embt Arquitectes Associats SL/RMJM — page 94

2.6 ESO Hotel, Cerro Paranal, Chile
Auer+Weber+Architekten — page 100

2.7 The Royal Society, London, UK
Burrell Foley Fischer LLP — page 102

2.8 Pixar Animation Studios, Emeryville, USA
Bohlin Cywinski Jackson — page 106

2.9 Max Planck Institute of Molecular Cell Biology and Genetics, Dresden, Germany
Heikkinen-Komonen Architects — page 110

3 Agora

3.1 Coblentz, Patch, Duffy & Bass LLP, San Francisco, USA
Aston Pereira & Associates — page 116

3.2 Less Limited, Hong Kong, China
Dou Design/Bill Price — page 120

3.3 Porta22, Barcelona, Spain
Interiors Disseny — page 122

3.4 30 St Mary Axe, London, UK
Foster and Partners — page 124

3.5 Madrid Regional Documentary Centre, Madrid, Spain
Mansilla + Tuñón — page 130

3.6 Kennispoort, Eindhoven, Holland
Koen van Velsen — page 132

3.7 One Omotesando, Tokyo, Japan
Kengo Kuma & Associates — page 136

3.8 Maison de l'Architecture, Paris, France
Chartier-Corbasson Architectes — page 138

3.9 Rotterdam Chamber of Commerce, Rotterdam, Holland
Veldhoen + Company — page 142

3.10 Virgin Atlantic Clubhouse, Johannesburg, South Africa
W1 Studio — page 144

3.11 Munich Re, Munich, Germany
Baumschlager & Eberle — page 146

3.12 Academyhills Roppongi Library, Tokyo, Japan
Kengo Kuma & Associates — page 152

4 Lodge

4.1 East Union Live-Work Lofts, Seattle, USA
The Miller/Hull Partnership — page 158

4.2 Creative Lofts, Huddersfield, UK
Brewster Bye Architects — page 162

4.3 Designer's Loft, Tokyo, Japan
Toshihiko Suzuki/Hirota Design Studio — page 166

4.4 Mann Residence, Sonoma County, USA
Fernau & Hartman Architects, Inc. — page 170

4.5 Katsan Office Building, Stockholm, Sweden
White Architects — page 172

4.6 Home/Office, New York, USA
Roger Hirsch Architect and Myriam Corti — page 176

4.7 Apartment, Orio, Spain
Zómad Arquitectos — page 180

4.8 Hemingways' Outdoor Office, London, UK
Hemingway Design — page 182

Introduction

THE SPACES IN WHICH WE WORK are changing to suit the type of work we are now doing. The modern office grew out of the factory as a necessary by-product of the bureaucratization of industry. Today, however, much of the repetitive, linear, process-driven work that used to occupy vast numbers of office workers is done by computers; consequently the contemporary workplace is increasingly the setting for a new type of work that is far removed from the repetitive tasks characterised by time-and-motion studies.

The most common term for this new type of office work is 'knowledge work', and it is now the dominant mode of working in most of the world's advanced economies. Knowledge work depends not so much on formula and process, but rather on applying considerable theoretical knowledge and learning. It is based less on individuals following explicit instructions within a supervised hierarchy, and much more on the shared working practices of collaboration, initiative and exploration, in which knowledge is often implicit.

Doctors, lawyers, academics and scientists were among the first to be identified as knowledge workers. The term, which was first used in 1960 by the American economist Peter Drucker, now extends to most executive, managerial and marketing roles within organizations. Drucker has also drawn attention to a class of worker he describes as 'knowledge technologists'. These computer technicians, software designers, analysts in clinical labs, paralegals and so on are swelling the ranks of knowledge workers worldwide. Increasingly, in the early years of the twenty-first century, the world of work is becoming a world of knowledge work. Where once manual and process work fuelled economic growth, such activities are now increasingly out-sourced to developing economies. In the developed world, companies and governments alike must look to the knowledge worker for the key to future prosperity. In both the public and private sectors, ways to build, share, exchange and retain knowledge have assumed the highest priority.

Trapped on the factory floor

Most knowledge workers today, however, still struggle in outdated physical environments and organizational structures that belong to a bygone era. At a time when workers require new types of workspace and facilities to engage in the more cognitive and collaborative patterns of knowledge work, they are finding themselves on the white-collar version of the factory floor – an environment with its roots in mechanistic labour and Taylorist (after the American engineer Frederic Taylor 1856–1915) principles of efficiency.

While our recognition of the importance of knowledge work has grown in recent years, our understanding of the physical conditions in which it can flourish has failed to keep pace. So much so that 40 years after his first pioneering pronouncements on knowledge work, Peter Drucker felt moved to observe of knowledge-worker productivity: 'We are in the year 2000 roughly where we were in the year 1900 in terms of the productivity of the manual worker.'

Productivity of the manual worker increased roughly 50-fold during the twentieth century through changes in factory design, but can we be confident that knowledge-worker productivity will make similar advances in the twenty-first century through changes in office design? How much do we really know about the work settings that knowledge workers require in order to be effective? The answer, according to an influential paper in the MIT *Sloane Management Review*, 'The Mysterious Art and Science of the Knowledge-Worker Performance' (Fall 2002), is not a lot. The American authors, Thomas H Davenport, Robert J Thomas and Susan Cantrell, point out that companies today are experimenting heavily with workplace redesign, but are not learning very much in the process. According to Davenport et al, workplace design is a key determinant of knowledge-worker performance, but we are still in the dark about how to gear our offices to the demands of knowledge work.

Frank Duffy, chairman of architects DEGW plc Architects & Consultants and a leading theorist in the area, confirmed these views in a British report commissioned by CABE (Commission for Architecture and the Built Environment), in which he candidly admits that early twenty-first-century architects currently know as little about how work environment shapes business performance as early nineteenth-century physicians did about how diseases were transmitted before the science of epidemiology was established.

Against this background, *Radical Office Design* sets out to present the first overview of new office design that supports and enhances the performance of knowledge workers. We have chosen 43 case studies drawn from no fewer than 16 countries, including the USA, UK, Holland, Spain, Japan, France, Norway, Turkey, Finland, Austria, Denmark, Chile, China, South Africa and Sweden, and representing industries such as accountancy, law and insurance, technology, media and music companies, charities, car manufacturers, film-makers, advertising agencies, scientific institutions and seats of government. This body of current work tells us how such diverse organizations are addressing the needs of knowledge workers, and gives us insights into the developing trends that will shape the workplace in the knowledge economy of the near future.

Radical Office Design is the third in a series of books in which we explore the transformation of office design, from the command-and-control workplace of the industrial age to the constant connectivity of the Internet age. The first book, *The Creative Office* (1999), drew attention to the emerging practice of large, inflexible corporations emulating the more agile and responsive office design of smaller creative firms. Its message was that fixed, sterile office environments could no longer support new styles of team-based, knowledge-driven working. The second book, *The 21st Century Office* (2003), described the essential points of departure from the inflexible twentieth-century office to a new way of working in a new century that promises to be more responsive to human need, richer in narrative and less place-dependent. Its message went even further in signalling a decisive shift from the past, in which the old taboos about a faster, cheaper and leaner pursuit of office efficiency could be set aside.

In both of these books, a case study-based approach sought to place a body of contemporary practice – named organizations occupying real office buildings – within a theoretical framework. Now, in *Radical Office Design*, the third book in the trilogy, the accent is firmly on office design for knowledge work, and the approach to this subject remains the same. The case studies are set within a conceptual matrix that we have devised specifically to provide a framework for thinking about new design strategies to support knowledge workers.

Four realms for knowledge work

Radical Office Design identifies four 'realms' of knowledge work: the corporate realm ('Academy'); the professional realm ('Guild'); the public realm ('Agora'); and the domestic or private realm ('Lodge'). These realms are populated in the book with key examples of new office design projects from 2001 and onwards.

It is our contention that knowledge workers will increasingly seek to achieve a balance between four conflicting sets of relationships: colleagues within the employing organization; professional peers; customers in the marketplace; and friends and family in the home. Work itself will spread across a continuum of locations: corporate campus; city; home; and settings for professional associations and networks. In this context, organizations will need to develop workplace strategies that give their knowledge workers – who are a more mobile, self-assured and better-educated class of worker than ever before in the history of the office – more choice in where and how they work, so that they can reconcile the tensions in their working lives.

'Academy' describes a learning campus in which the employer is developing a more collegiate and collaborative approach to work. Its historical precedent, in spirit if not in terms of precise architectural template, is the university courtyard or quadrangle. 'Guild' refers to a professional cluster of peers who share a skill or specialism: its historical precedent is the medieval guild or craft society. 'Agora' describes the public workplace in which the corporation is open to the city and the marketplace: its historical precedent is the commercial and social open space in the heart of ancient Athens. 'Lodge' describes the live-work setting, the home that doubles as an office, whose historical precedent is the domestic setting, whether farmhouse or bourgeois residence, and is the hub of enterprise.

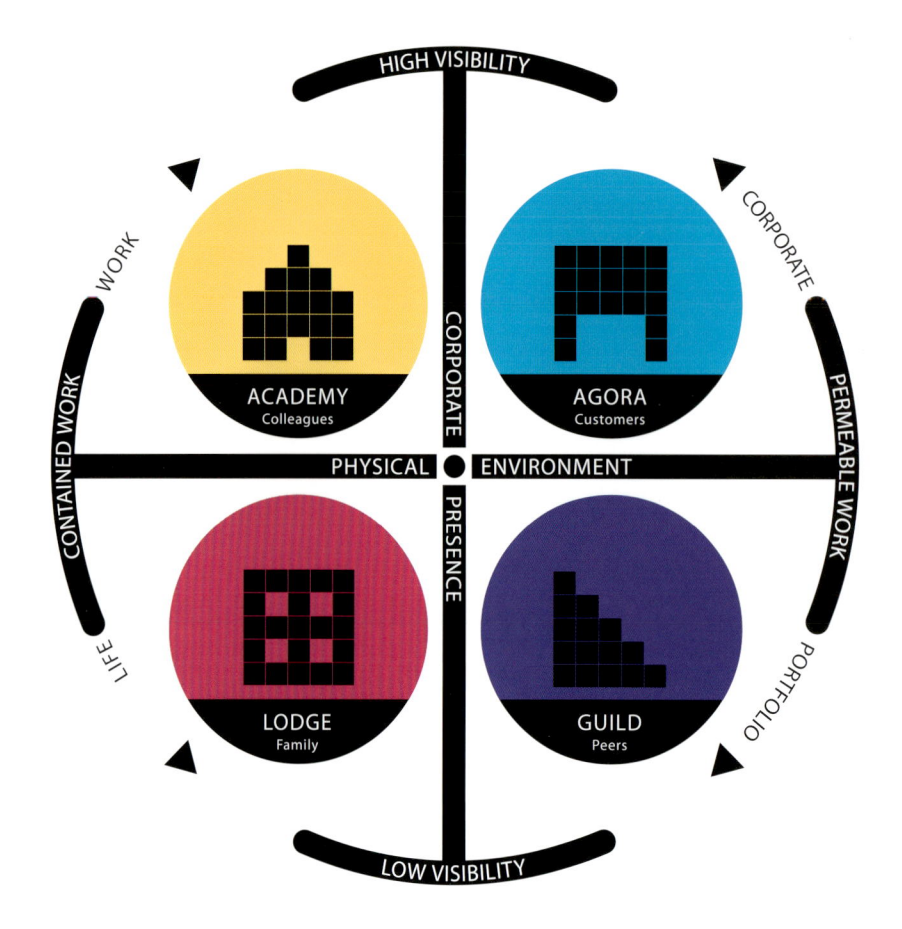

This diagram, entitled *Tensions at Work: Space Strategies for Knowledge Workers*, places all four types of knowledge workplace within a matrix. The vertical axis measures the level of corporate presence, from low to high visibility. The horizontal axis shows physical environment, ranging from work contained within a specific setting to work that is permeable across locations.

In accordance with this, Academy is a learning campus with a high level of corporate visibility contained on a specific site. Agora has a similarly high corporate presence, but is more permeable in its relationship with the city. Lodge is a contained work setting, but with zero corporate presence. Guild combines the characteristics of permeable work with low corporate visibility.

The tension between living and working – between home and office life – is shown on the left-hand side of the diagram. It identifies, in the relationship between Academy and Lodge, the challenge of achieving work-life balance, a current corporate preoccupation. Here, the tension between high and low visibility – the issue of 'presenteeism' – becomes apparent on an individual basis. Does being 'out of sight' mean 'out of mind' when the next office promotion comes along? How can people manage distributed teams that they cannot 'supervise' by watching them at work?

The tension between corporate working and portfolio working – between allegiance to an employer and reliance on your own skill or knowledge – is shown on the right-hand side of the diagram. This identifies the challenge of managing a career now that work is permeable, distributed and virtual, rather than an activity that takes place only within the corporate 'container'. It acknowledges that work is subject to freelance and short-term contracts rather than the long-term security of full-time employment. What the matrix shows is a range of alternatives for people who are increasingly managing and controlling their own work destiny. Academy, Agora, Guild and Lodge articulate a range of balances and tensions between the organization and its customers, between employment and self-employment, between working and living, and between the corporate and professional persona.

Raising knowledge-work productivity requires us to identify and reconcile these conflicting pressures. This is not about choosing which quadrant to be in, however. The four realms of knowledge work can exist in parallel, with tensions and 'opposing forces' that create equilibrium. Let us look more closely at the four realms and at the projects we have selected to describe these emerging models.

Academy: the learning campus

Academy describes a corporate office in which knowledge is more easily shared among colleagues within a collegiate learning environment. This trend signals a return to the values of the academy founded by Plato in ancient Athens, which was the forerunner of the modern university as a place of philosophical and scientific discussion.

For the formal architectural expression of the academy, however, we must look to the medieval English architecture of the first Oxford and Cambridge colleges, which organized a corporate way of life around a quadrangle incorporating hall, chapel, library, warden's lodgings and rooms for students and fellows. Architect William Wynford set the template with New College, Oxford, founded in 1379, followed by Reginald Ely's design for Queens' College, Cambridge, founded in 1448.

Today, many of the spatial principles and productivity benefits connected with training, mentoring, sharing ideas and research are

'Raising productivity requires us to identify and reconcile conflicting pressures.'

finding their way into the corporate campus. Corporations are also increasingly keen to locate close to universities and their incubator start-ups. This approach subscribes to current management theories such as those of Henry Chesbrough of Harvard University on 'open innovation'. Chesbrough sees companies as reinventing their processes from closed to open, relying more on external knowledge sources because, says Chesbrough, 'distribution of knowledge has spilled out well beyond central research labs, to other companies, customers, universities, national laboratories, industrial consortia, etc.'

The proximity of biotech company Genzyme to the Massachusetts Institute of Technology (page 64) is a clear expression of this. Spatially, Genzyme organizes its activities around a magnificent open atrium, which brings natural light and greenery from the outside in. The whole luminous space becomes a metaphor for sharing knowledge. Other corporate headquarters adopt similar tactics: Telenor in Oslo (page 22) is planned around an external plaza with illuminated pillars, and Ericsson in Texas (page 54) is organized within a village that encourages outdoor working and chance encounters along open circulation routes.

What characterizes the Academy workplace is the conscious desire for knowledge workers to cross-pollinate ideas, whether they are sitting around one continuous concrete table in Clive Wilkinson's scheme for advertising agency Mother in London (page 50), or sharing a range of unpredictable public and social spaces in the Dutch insurance company Interpolis (page 58). Giving individuals more choice in how and where they work is a key theme, vividly expressed in the funky meeting rooms and carpet-clad phone booths of Californian agency Kirshenbaum Bond & Partners West (page 16), and in the range of user-friendly settings at PricewaterhouseCoopers in Birmingham (page 30).

In shaping the Academy ideal, some projects use metaphor on a grand and monumental scale. BMW's new Leipzig car plant (page 44) has the production line running through the central administration building – it was designed by Zaha Hadid as a symbol of office and factory workers sharing knowledge. Seattle advertising agency Sedgwick Rd. uses the language of architectural salvage (page 26) to express the idea of creative advertising as a constantly recycled work in progress. Pallotta TeamWorks, a charity fundraising company based in Los Angeles, has built an office from shipping containers and tented structures, symbolizing a relief effort (page 36).

To encourage people to see things from a different perspective, as the traditional academy always sought to do, many projects have abandoned the traditional space-planning metrics that have squeezed staff, cost-effectively, into corporate buildings for decades. These new Academies are inefficient schemes by twentieth-century space standards – EMI's London headquarters, for example, is built around an extravagant glazed courtyard (page 68) – but their generous use of art, metaphor and social space make them inspirational places for people to build and share knowledge.

Guild: the professional cluster

Guild describes a new type of workplace that brings together people with a shared professional skill or specialism. This trend signals a return to the idea of the medieval craft and merchant guilds that developed and occupied the first commercial buildings in many European cities, and were in many senses the precursors of the modern corporation. From Flanders to Genoa, Cracow to the City of London, guilds or 'mysteries' represented the ancient professions and crafts, such as the Mercers, Goldsmiths, Clothworkers, Salters and Skinners. In London, the first Clothworkers' Hall was built in 1472, while the famous Goldsmiths' Hall dates from 1339.

The industrial revolution led to the demise of the guilds, and their privileges were withdrawn in England, Italy, Germany and other European cities during the nineteenth century, as the notion of 'incorporation' was introduced. However, in the age of the 'post-industrial' office, the idea of the Guild is being revived. Not only that, but new guilds are springing up, reflecting new professions such as chartered secretaries, chartered accountants, insurers, actuaries and engineers. No fewer than 25 new guilds have been created in the UK alone in recent decades.

Medieval guilds traditionally brought professional peers into regular contact, and helped to build knowledge and networks in a specific field. The Guild-style workplaces shown in *Radical Office Design* seek to reaffirm the importance of such activities. The BBC Media Centre in White City, London (page 76) and Pixar in Emeryville, California (page 106) both provide vibrant, atrium-like gathering spaces for the different experts – writers, artists, technicians, and so on – who are mutually engaged in the creative processes of animated film-making and broadcasting.

Two parliament buildings – one in Finland (page 82) and the other in Scotland (page 94) – provide innovative and accessible spaces for policy-makers and parliamentarians to work in. The thinking pods, with contemplation seats, that form the private rooms of MPs on the exterior of Enric Miralles' Edinburgh building are quite literally a stand-out feature.

A trio of projects that bring scientists together in one place – the ESO hotel and observatory in the Chilean Atacama Desert (page 100), the elegant refurbishment of the Royal Society in London (page 102) and the Max Planck Institute of Molecular Cell Biology and Genetics in Dresden (page 110) – subscribe in their creation of community to the belief that a problem shared is a problem solved. Dialogue, communication and contemplation are at the very heart of these design schemes. As for the Austrian Future Centre (page 86) and the Momentum business centre in Denmark (page 90), these are Guild destinations with a touch of the experimental and unexpected, where professionals in a particular field can come to be inspired. Indeed, many of the Guild examples in *Radical Office Design* play tricks and spring surprises in their play on the permeability between private and public.

Agora: the public workplace

Agora describes a public workplace that is integrated into the life of the city and brings the company closer to its customers and markets. This trend signals a return to civic values of work, and derives from the ancient Greek marketplace or agora. This was originally a place of congregation that quickly became the destination for trade and commerce. The agora was part of a polis, the early Greek city-state that also housed a citadel or acropolis and a gymnasium. These were the early constructs of the modern-day metropolis and defined the key spaces within a city. The Greek agora evolved into the Roman forum, which today is synonymous with the process of meeting. So this theme today represents the growth of mobile working, and the ability of knowledge workers to be effective in the marketplace and close to their customers and suppliers.

Being 'in the market' will increasingly become a feature of twenty-first-century working and, in response, new workplaces for people who need an ad hoc environment for occasional or spontaneous use 'on the pause' will become commonplace. Similarly, office buildings will increasingly take on a public face, raising corporate presence through shared or mixed-use spaces.

One tactic revealed in this book is the integration of new workspace for commercial organizations within historic public buildings. The famous San Francisco Ferry Building of 1898, for example, now has a law firm as a tenant (page 116), and a Paris chapel dating from the seventeenth century now accommodates an architectural office (page 138).

Another form of urban intervention is the corporate commissioning of landmark art and architecture. Foster's dynamic scheme at 30 St Mary Axe in the City of London for Swiss Re has created an instant icon for the capital (page 124). The Munich Re Group (page 146) has meanwhile used artists to revamp its unappealing 1970s concrete headquarters, creating a new relationship with the city whose name the company bears. In contrast, Kengo Kuma's wooden-louvred headquarters for fashion label LVMH at One Omotesando in Tokyo (page 136) seeks to blend into a tree-lined avenue rather than stand out from it.

While companies aim to shape their own Agora-style workplaces, their mobile employees are increasingly seeking out public venues that enable work. The Porta22 career information centre in Barcelona (page 122), the Madrid Regional Documentary Centre (page 130) and the Academyhills Roppongi Library in Tokyo (page 152) all fall into this category; these are projects that deliberately plan for an exchange of knowledge. Chambers of commerce are also catering for the mobile worker at large in the city: a double Dutch helping of contemporary design makes for two outstanding schemes in Eindhoven (page 132) and Rotterdam (page 142).

Agora-style workspaces are also adept at transformation, changing their mood between day and night and staying in action 24 hours a day, just like the city itself. Less Ltd in Hong Kong is an office by day and a dance/yoga studio at night; the Virgin Atlantic Clubhouse in Johannesburg allows executive travellers to work, relax or be entertained according to the hour or their whim. Most airport lounges are of course privileged, just as most libraries are public and most corporate offices are private. The Agora workplace revealed in *Radical Office Design* therefore possesses varying degrees of openness towards the city. In this, our own examples reflect the findings of the European Union-funded SANE (Sustainable Accommodation in the New Economy) research study on 'The Distributed Office', which presents a model of three phases of permeability within the city: private, privileged and public.

Lodge: the live-work setting

Lodge describes a new building type which combines living and working in one environment, reconnecting the spheres of home and work that were severed by industrialization. The earliest lodges were homes, dens, meeting halls and inns, primarily domestic but with other functions incorporated. Countless business deals in agrarian societies were made over the kitchen table and, from the early nineteenth century onwards, many banks and shipping companies started life inside the bourgeois townhouses of their owners. Only later would patterns of suburbanization and commuting to high-rise business districts emerge to drain the home of economic activity, leaving merely a place of consumption, beautification and escape from work.

A combination of factors these days is encouraging people once again to live and work in the same setting. The desire by local authorities to attract economically productive people back into run-down urban areas has relaxed planning codes and triggered the supply of live-work property. Concern over the environmental cost of commuting is another contributing factor, while the explosion of broadband technology has helped to trigger a demand for it.

To make everything work in a small space, ingeniously designed dual-function details are required: the mobile furniture of a one-room studio in Tokyo (page 166) or the flexible wall of a Manhattan home office (page 176) illustrate this. Purpose-built live-work units, such as the East Union Lofts in Seattle (page 158) or the Creative Lofts in Huddersfield (page 162) offer rather more in terms of space, and create stylish modern settings for living and working.

The Katsan Office Building by White Architects is a clever example of a workplace blending into a new dockside residential district in Stockholm (page 172), but more commonly the workspace is integrated into a single inspirational private residence. This book offers examples from Orio in Spain (page 180) and Sonoma Valley in California (page 170) to the rather eccentric, garden wigwam office of designers Wayne and Gerardine Hemingway in London (page 182).

'For the first time in a century, equipment is no longer heavy and tied to a desk.'

Enabled by technology

Quite clearly, many of the projects described in this book could not have been conceived and implemented without new technology. Technological advances mean that for the first time in a century the knowledge worker's equipment is no longer heavy and tied to a desk (adding machines, telephones and computers), but lightweight, portable and mobile, providing constant connectivity that is independent of place.

One of the key drivers of change has been the Internet – in no era since the early development of the office building has technology been so 'disruptive'. In the mid to late 1880s, the four key inventions of the time – the elevator, the typewriter, the telephone and the electric light bulb – led to the development of the twentieth-century office with which we still identify today: people trapped behind desks to which all communications and messaging were delivered.

For the majority, up until the early 1990s nothing much had changed. We were still connecting pieces of furniture together, not people, and to be away from the desk was to be 'off line' or 'out of contact'. Now, almost all of these assumptions are invalid. The explosion of mobile phones means that we increasingly call a person and not a place. Portable technology, such as the laptop, has put computing power that once filled an air-cooled room into the briefcase. Even more disruptive is the use of Internet protocols to carry out telephone calls on a global basis.

Connectivity was always deemed second-class away from office buildings, but not any more. In technology we have now reached an 'inflexion point' at which the advantages of the corporation over the individual, of office building and desk over café or home office, no longer hold true.

Demographic change

For knowledge workers, the liberated schemes in *Radical Office Design* indicate only the beginning of new work horizons in the future. For them, change cannot happen soon enough. Peter Drucker and others have pointed out that knowledge workers tend to identify themselves by their knowledge rather than by their corporate rank within an organization. They belong to a profession rather than the company, and they are always looking to add to their knowledge. In this context, inflexible and hierarchical environments are simply out of date.

Demographic change is also a factor. At one end of the knowledge workforce, entrants to employment today are the first group to have been educated in classrooms where interactive white boards, laptops and the Internet are taken for granted. They are adept at dealing with fast-paced data and information, and expect technology to enhance their lives. At the other end of the spectrum, there are growing numbers of older workers who will not retire from the workplace, but will remain at work for longer, many of them on an arm's-length consultancy basis. Several factors are driving this trend: a shortfall in pension funds; a management emphasis on retaining knowledge and experience built up over years; age and disability discrimination legislation; and the plain demographic facts of an ageing population (one out of two adults in the European Union will be over 50 by 2020).

What is clear, however, is that encouraging highly valued and well-educated older workers to remain at work for longer will require a new, more flexible and friendlier type of workplace, one that reconciles their tensions between life and work.

Beyond the corporation

Our survey of new office design also has implications for the corporation. For over a century, work has been about workers being together at the same time in the same place. Companies became an efficient model for employing people with different skills, providing apprenticeships, full-time contracts for life and generous pension benefits in retirement.

Today the rules are changing. People are disillusioned with the budgetary restraints of corporate life and have increasingly begun to rely on themselves for training and managing their own 'human capital'. A move back towards the individual's professional skill or qualification will increasingly dominate in a world where corporate loyalty becomes more fickle and full-time employment for life is confined to history. The traditional concept of the company is now under threat, and with it the traditional corporate workspace.

In his best-selling book *The Rise of the Creative Class* (2002), Richard Florida describes how the creative ethos is today starting to dominate, in much the same way as William Whyte's 1956 classic *The Organization Man* showed how the organizational ethos of that age permeated every aspect of life. If 'Organization Man' has given way to 'Creative Man', then there are clear implications for workplace design in an age of growing freelance, portfolio and temporary contract working.

Radical Office Design picks up on this challenge. It seeks to present a continuum of work settings for knowledge work, from low to high levels of permeability within cities, and from low to high levels of corporate visibility and presence. In our view it is only by finding a new equilibrium at work between the opposing forces of family, colleagues, customers and professional peers that knowledge workers in the twenty-first century can achieve the same productivity gains as manual labour did in the twentieth century.

Jeremy Myerson
Philip Ross

1 Academy
the learning campus

Offices were once designed for efficiency, based on predictable principles of hierarchy, status and repetition. They were planned by department and stacked in a way that minimized movement, thus promoting a sedentary and isolated work style that kept people in their place and impeded the flow of new ideas and information. Today, a new generation of offices is emerging that challenges this inflexible and outdated model.

'Academy' is the term chosen to describe a new type of office that encourages a more collegiate and collaborative approach to work. Academies are places where knowledge is shared more easily, where chance meetings, training and mentoring are built into the physical tapestry of the working day. They are venues where work is contained on a single site, with a high corporate presence, offering the benefits of an integrated and energized community that enables colleagues within the organization to move effectively across discipline divides.

The following selection of interiors expresses the concept of the Academy in a series of different manifestations – from banks and insurance companies (once among the most hierarchical of employers) to telecommunications and media firms, and even the nerve-centre of a global carmaker.

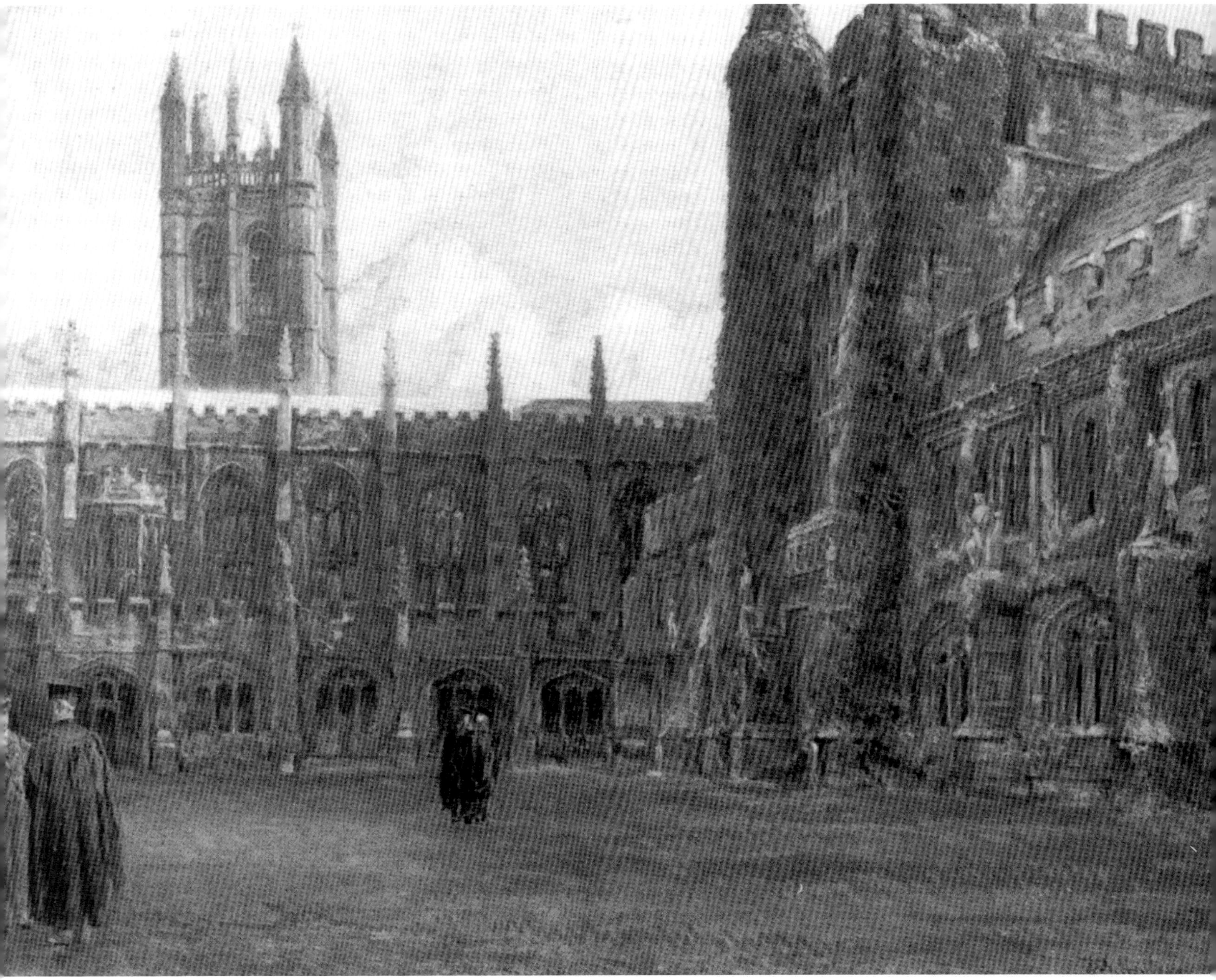

1.1
Kirshenbaum Bond & Partners West
San Francisco, USA
Jensen & Macy Architects

YOU would have to go a long way to see so many innovative design features packed into one compact scheme. This lively office interior for advertising agency Kirshenbaum Bond & Partners West (KBP West) provides an imaginative array of different work spaces that collectively owe much to the diverse project experience – in retail and residential as well as commercial – of architects Jensen & Macy.

A wealth of material and spatial experiences are contained on one floor with a mezzanine level above. This is reached by a wide staircase and used for company gatherings. In the centre of the office is a phone booth structure clad in green carpet that is used for conference calls. There are also an indoor garden with benches, trees and pebble flooring; a 5-metre (16-foot) long wooden dining counter for agency staff; a media library and various other informal meeting areas. The space planning is reminiscent of other office schemes in California that have created autonomous structures within a city plan. However, it is the sheer quality of the detailing that lends this project its distinction.

KPB West's big attraction sits on the ground floor: a three-winged conference room that contains four meeting rooms within one impressive structure. When the acoustically sealed folding doors that separate the three wings of the conference block are opened wide, a single meeting hall is created.

The symbolism of this tour de force is not accidental. This is a project that announces to staff and visitors alike that collaboration and sharing are all-important to the life of the agency. Chalkboards used for brainstorming and sketching out ideas line the conference room walls, reinforcing this message of learning together.

Location San Francisco, USA
Client Kirshenbaum Bond & Partners West
Completed 2001
Total Floor Space 2,039 square metres (21,950 square feet)
Accommodates 120

Right View of the meeting spaces within an imposing three-winged conference room lined with chalkboard to encourage spontaneous creative ideas.

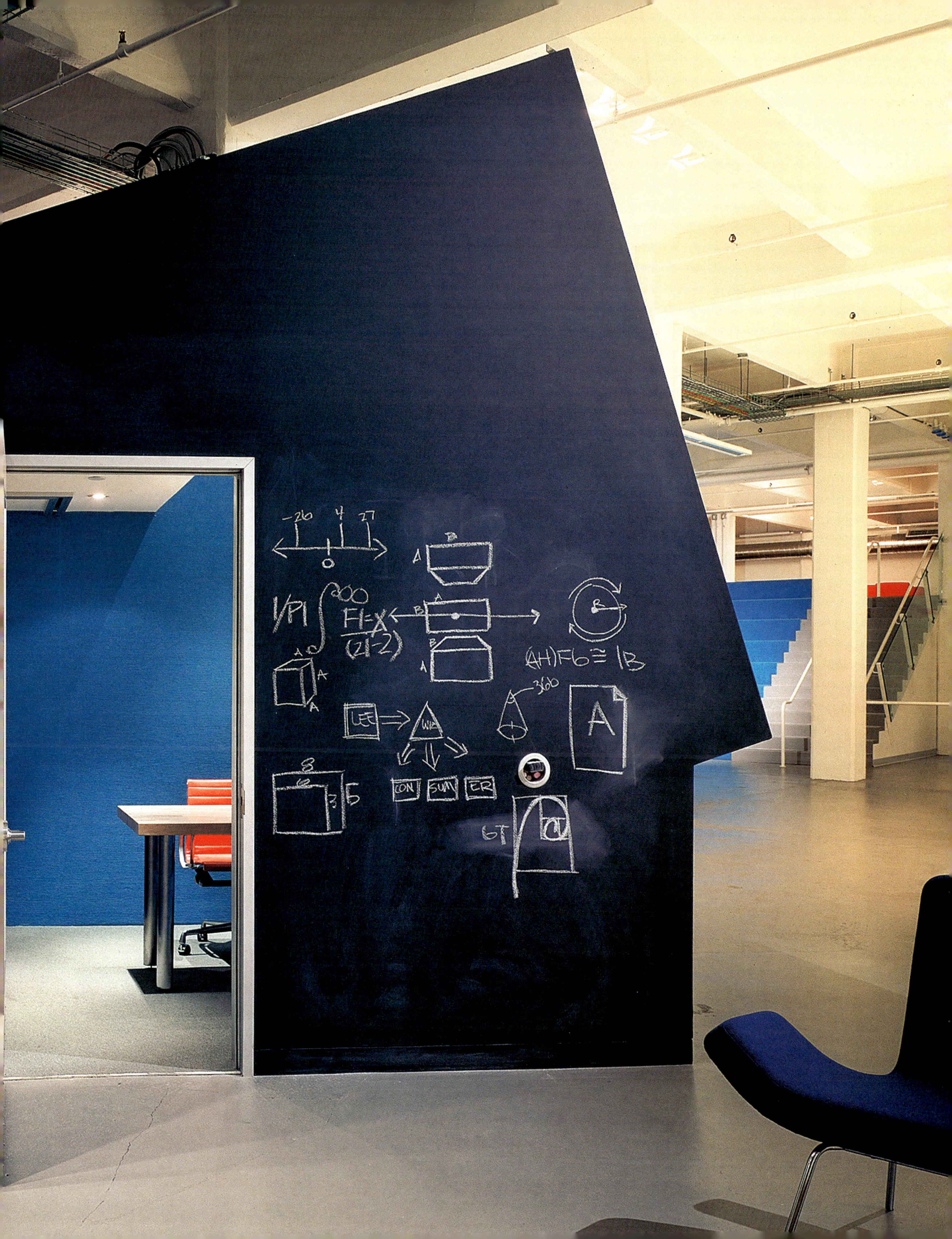

LEE
360
A
CON
SUM
ER

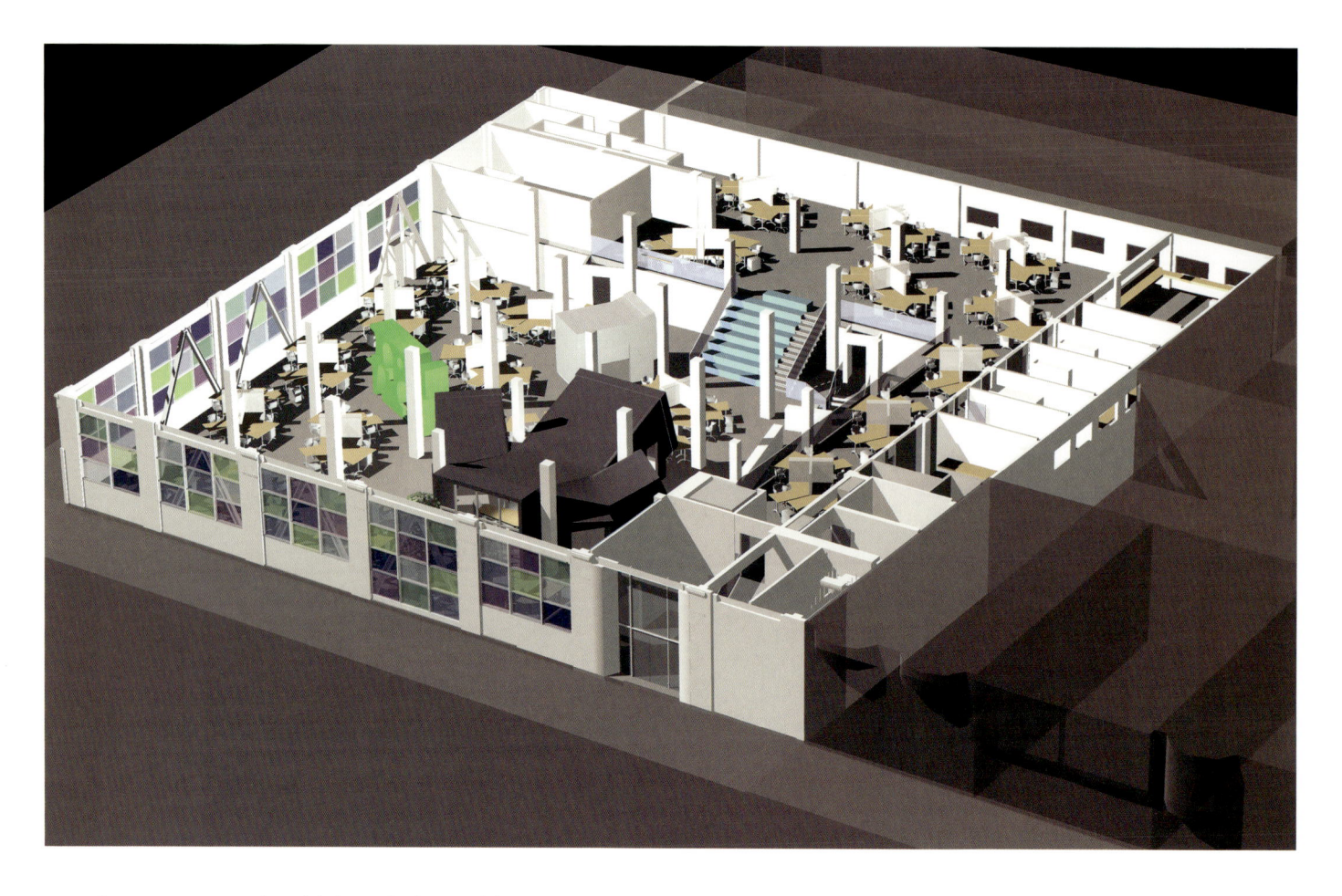

Above Computer-generated model shows the layout of the scheme. **Below** View towards large sloped windows of the meeting rooms. **Opposite** Indoor garden and meeting space. **Overleaf** Carpet-clad phone booth structure and lounge meeting area with acoustic foam walls.

18 Academy

'A unique three-wing conference building serves as the focal point of this office.' *Jensen & Macy Architects*

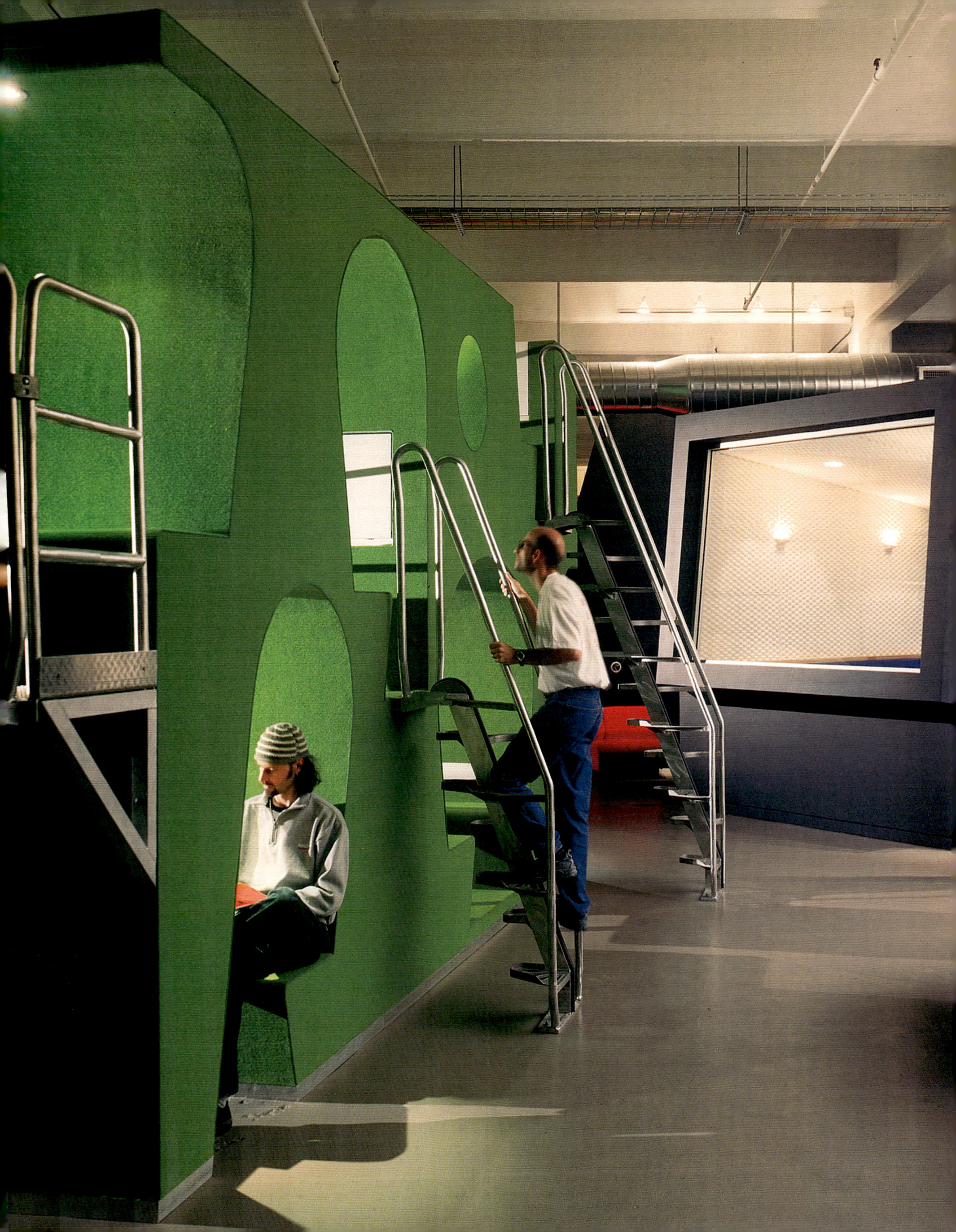

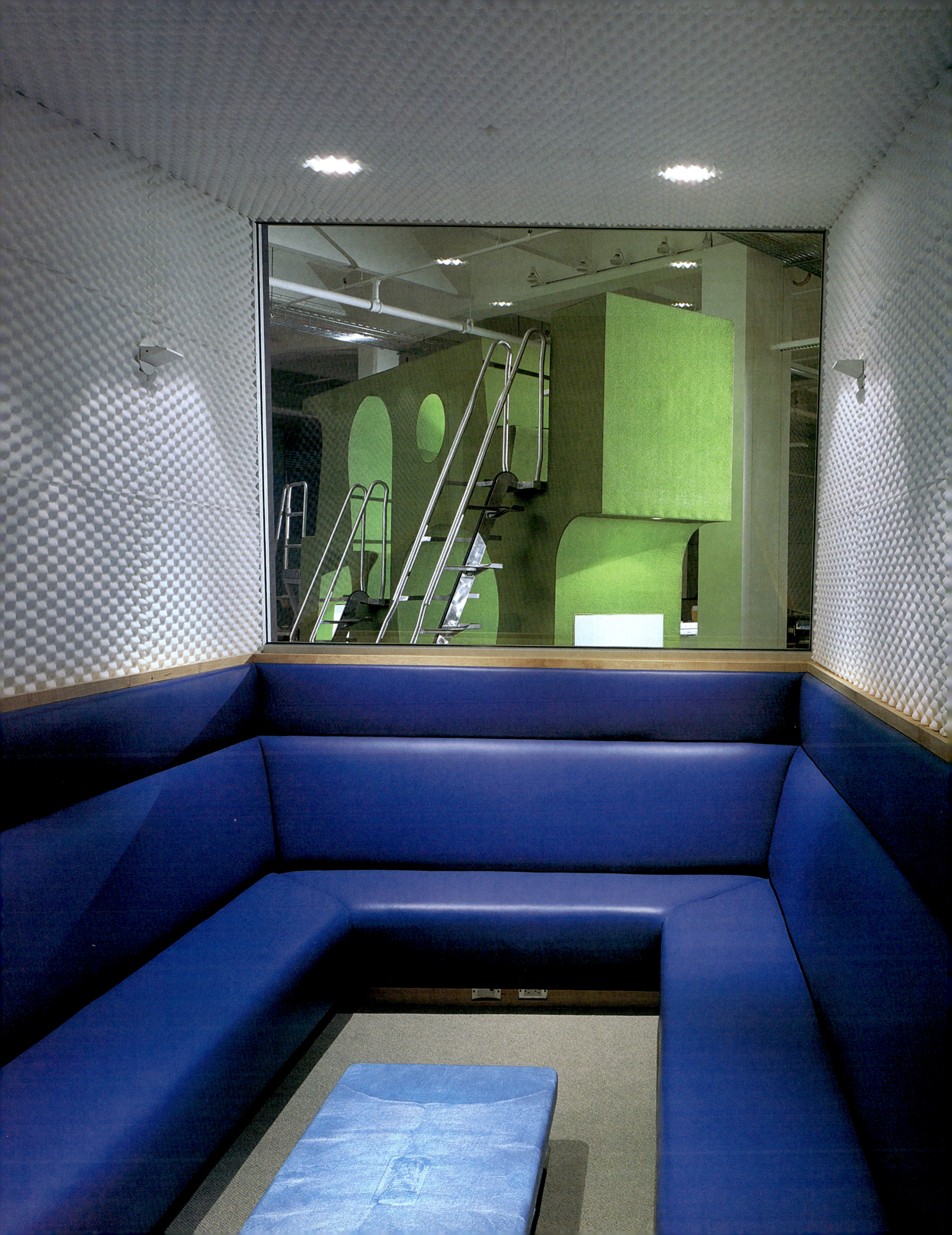

1.2
Telenor
Oslo, Norway
NBBJ/HUS/PKA/Dark Design

SCANDINAVIA'S largest office building is also its most innovative. Telenor, the Norwegian telecommunications company, has created a state-of-the-art facility, bringing together 6,000 people from almost 40 locations around Oslo into a space that provides an equitable, open and shared environment for knowledge work.

The site itself, in Fornebu, Oslo, is spectacular, facing the sea to the east and the south. The headquarters is divided into two parts around the central 'Telenortorget' or Telenor Square, which creates a dramatic outdoor meeting space and arena for art and events. This plaza, punctuated by artist Daniel Buren's 92 illuminated pillars, provides a central 'market square' for the complex.

The two main buildings gently curve towards each other and wrap around the public space. Each contains a central street that runs the length of the space, providing significant meeting places for the chance encounters that are part of the philosophy of work at Telenor. From the curved spine of each building hang four office wings where the main workplaces are located.

These office 'villages' create small-scale clusters and provide a human scale in what is a vast complex. Natural daylight, an important factor in Norwegian building codes, is provided by generous glazing. From all around the space, clever vistas and views have been created onto the landscape and water beyond the building.

Telenor's headquarters was designed to 'stimulate innovation and the rapid sharing of knowledge'. The space is divided into a series of 'zones' that suit different types of activity, from rooms for private work to a variety of spaces for informal or organized small meetings and team sessions. Among the key innovations here are project work environments, where people from different units can work together for a period of time.

Technology at Telenor is, as you would imagine for a telecommunications company, very advanced. The building has one of the largest wireless networks in the world, allowing people to connect wherever they choose to work. The 'eReady Arena' programme allows everyone to access an advanced messaging system for email, SMS and voice mail from any computer, mobile phone or hand-held device.

As in any Academy, chance encounters and meetings are a central part of the working day – this can be measured by the six million cups of coffee that are consumed each year in the Telenor building.

Location Oslo, Norway
Client Telenor AS
Completed 2002
Total Floor Space 138,000 square metres (1,485,000 square feet)
Staff 6,000

Opposite top Aerial view of the site, showing the two curved buildings.
Opposite bottom The Fornebu headquarters building.
Below Telenor Square creates a dramatic outdoor meeting space, punctuated by illuminated pillars.

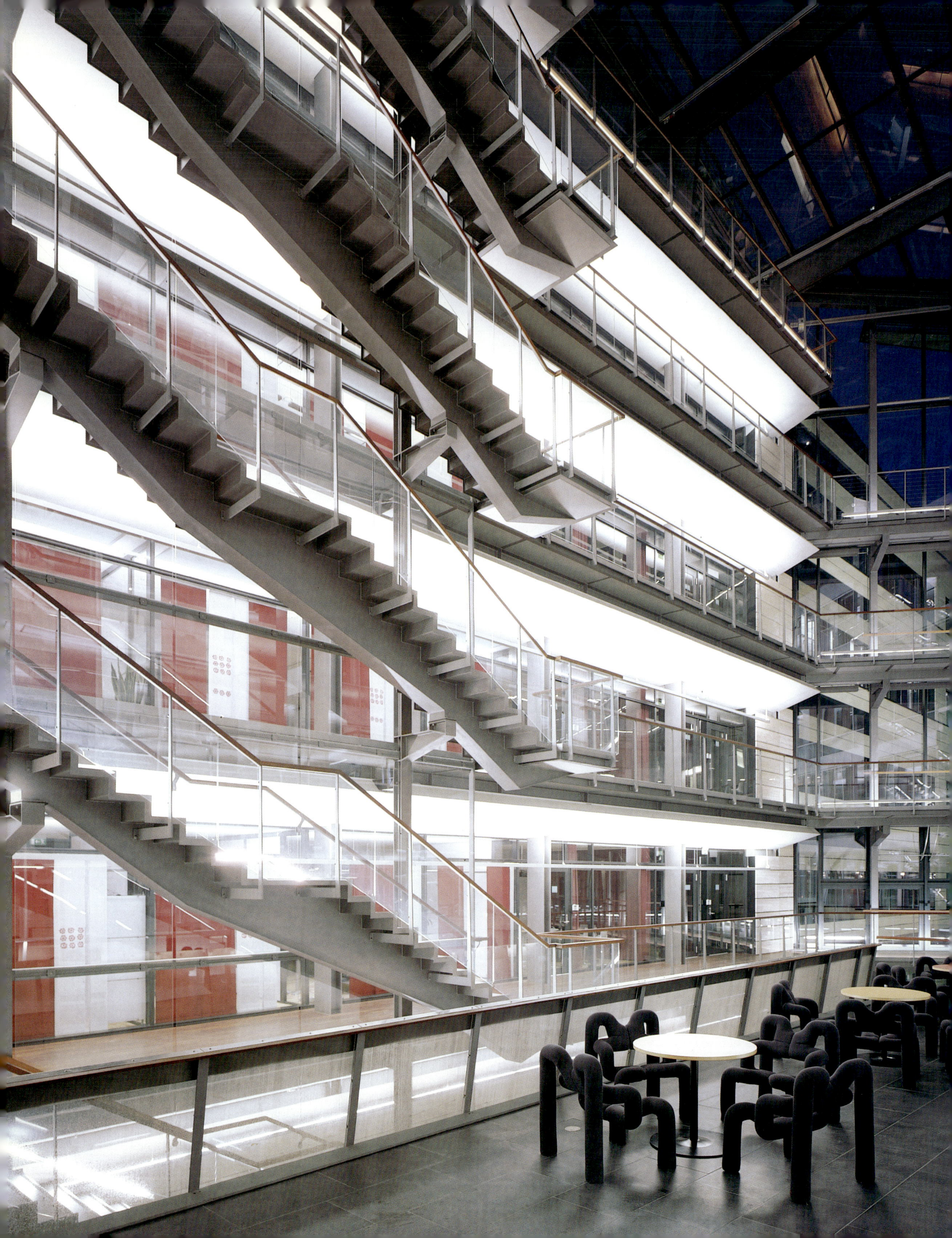

'The new building will give employees greater well-being and improve the possibilities for communication.'
Bjørn Sund, Executive President, Telenor Fornebu project

Opposite An atrium space in each office wing encourages communication and collaboration.
Top left Offices are designed to be open and democratic.
Top right The environment is punctuated by a range of more casual workspaces.
Above left A sculpture by Swedish artist Maria Miesenberger dominates one of the restaurants.
Above right One of the largest wireless networks in Europe allows people to connect from anywhere in the building.

1.3
Sedgwick Rd.
Seattle, USA
Olson Sundberg Kundig Allen Architects

THE traditional style of Madison Avenue does not necessarily go down so well in the more freewheeling cities on America's West Coast. So when the Seattle subsidiary of the New York advertising giant McCann-Erickson moved offices, it took the opportunity to completely reinvent itself, with a new name and a creative new work environment that is the antithesis of the plush Manhattan suite.

The new name – Sedgwick Rd. – reflects a tough new urban location on a street leading to a ferry dock close to downtown Seattle. The new office is a radical retooling of three floors of the Star Machinery Building, a factory that was brick-built in 1926. Within a space criss-crossed by steel roof trusses and flooded with light from clerestory-like windows, a modern work environment sits in an exposed landscape of American industrial heritage.

The key to making the project lay in the rapid reaction of the architects on accepting the commission. The first thing they did was to visit the site, halt demolition of the space and save the original beams, windows and doors for re-use. The salvaged parts were recycled to build six giant wheeled partitions, nicknamed Frankenstein, or Frankie for short. These mobile units, lit by 1950s fluorescent louvres, are reconfigured daily to form an unusual conference room and to create different meeting spaces in the old machine shop.

The Sedgwick Rd. brief emphasized the need to improve communication not just between the firm and its clients, but also between the agency's creative, media and planning teams. Breaking down barriers was essential to creating a buzz about the place. The restoring of the patina and character of the building, through the new assembly of its peeling and gnarled window frames and other components, creates a more open, workmanlike and egalitarian environment.

The largest element of the scheme is a dramatic 372-square-metre (4,000-square-foot) atrium on the open-plan second floor. All roads lead to the office hub, but this is much more than a one-trick project. The industrial metaphor extends throughout, playing on the juxtaposition of old and new. Over-sized pivoting steel doors open onto social spaces, including a media room and a bar. A wide steel staircase links the upper floors, while individual workspace cubicles are constructed of fibreglass or plywood sheet.

If the interior strategy was designed to promote the idea that advertising is unfinished business and a continual process of reinvention, then it has certainly worked for Sedgwick Rd. in Seattle. Against a background of recession in the advertising industry, the agency grew by 30 per cent in the two years following its rebranding and relocation.

Location Seattle, USA
Client Sedgwick Rd.
Completed 2001
Total Floor Space 3,067 square metres (33,015 square feet)
Staff 85

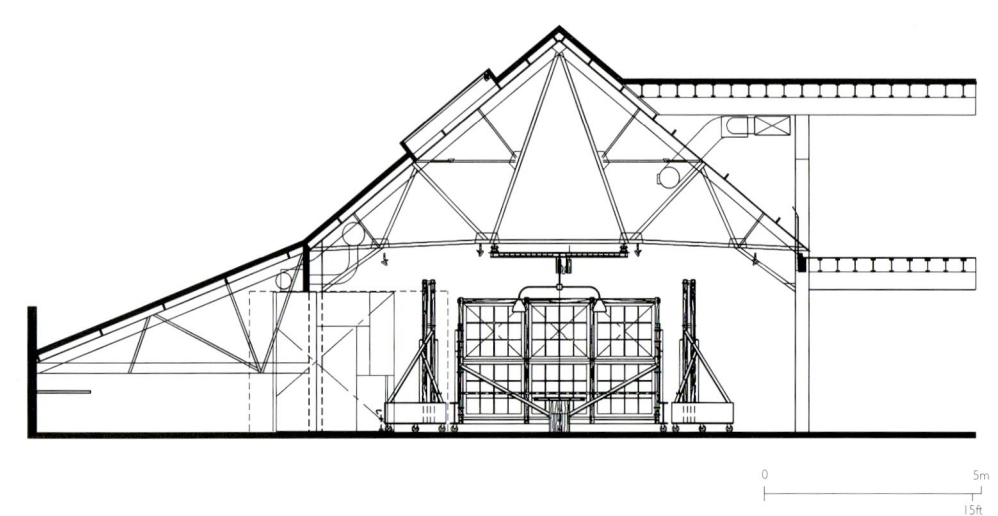

Above Section shows giant wheeled partitions, named Frankenstein, beneath steel roof trusses on the open-plan second floor.
Opposite View into the space divided by salvaged components.

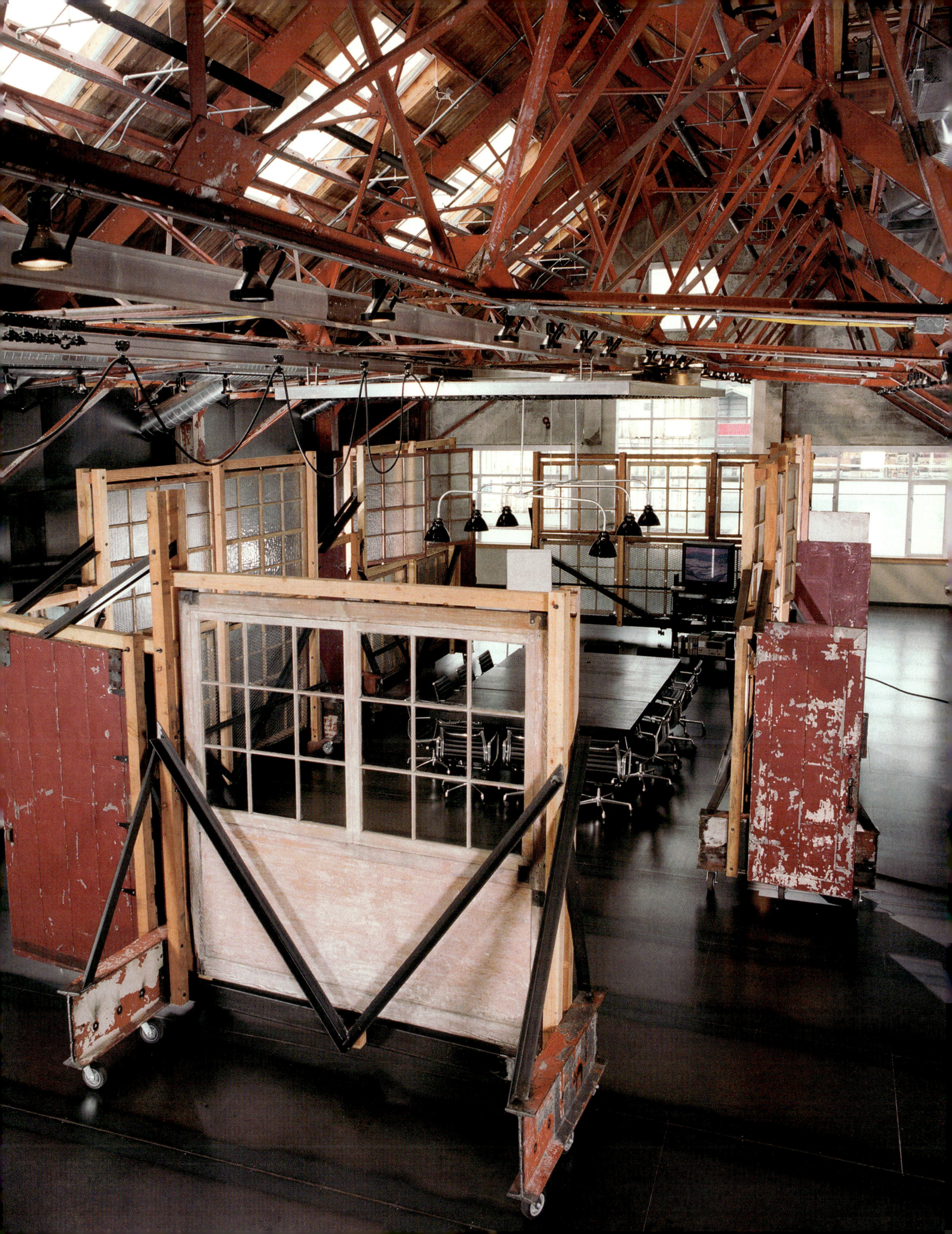

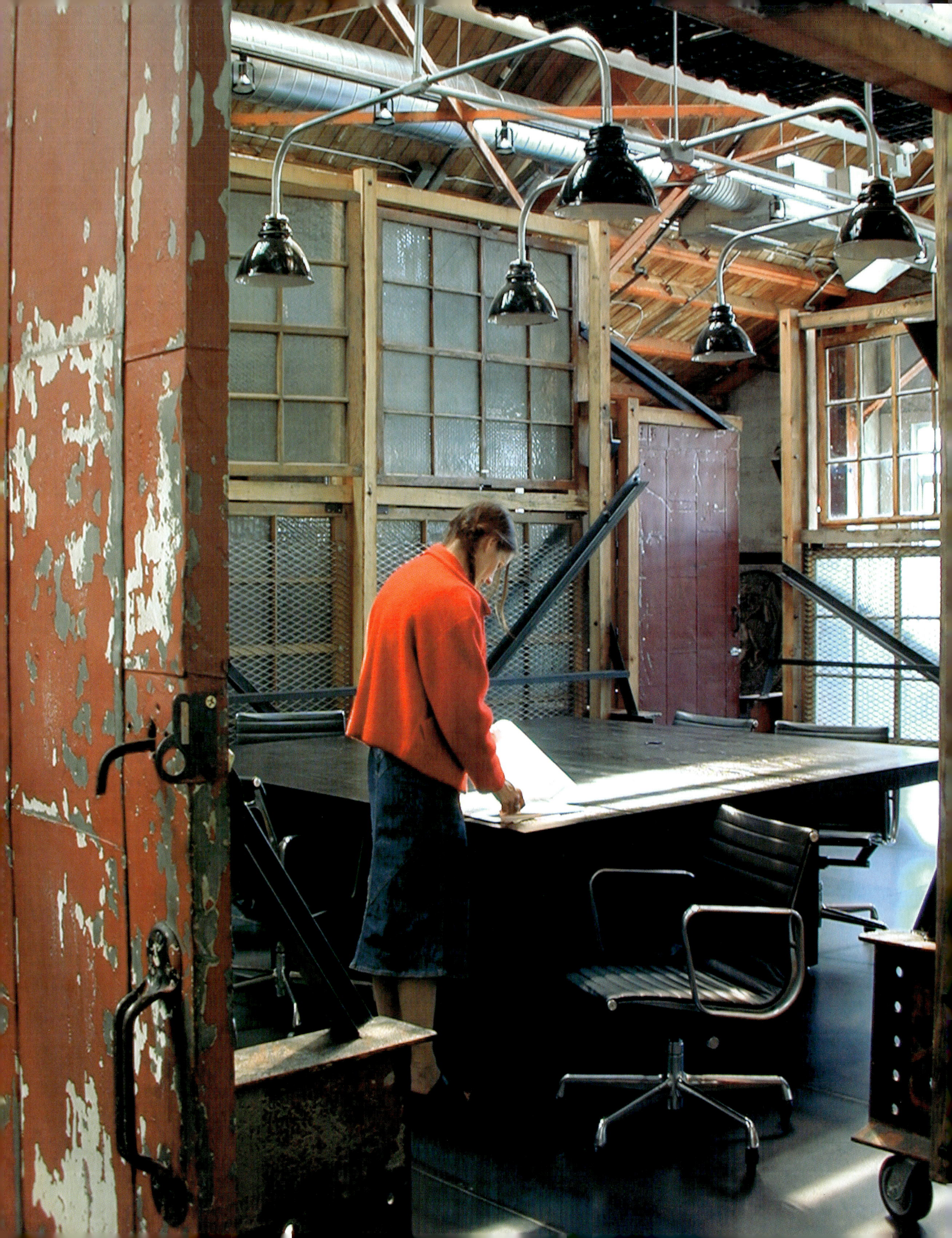

'It's unfinished and that's the essence of advertising. We don't build an end product. We just start work on the next permutation.' *Jim Walker, President, Sedgwick Rd.*

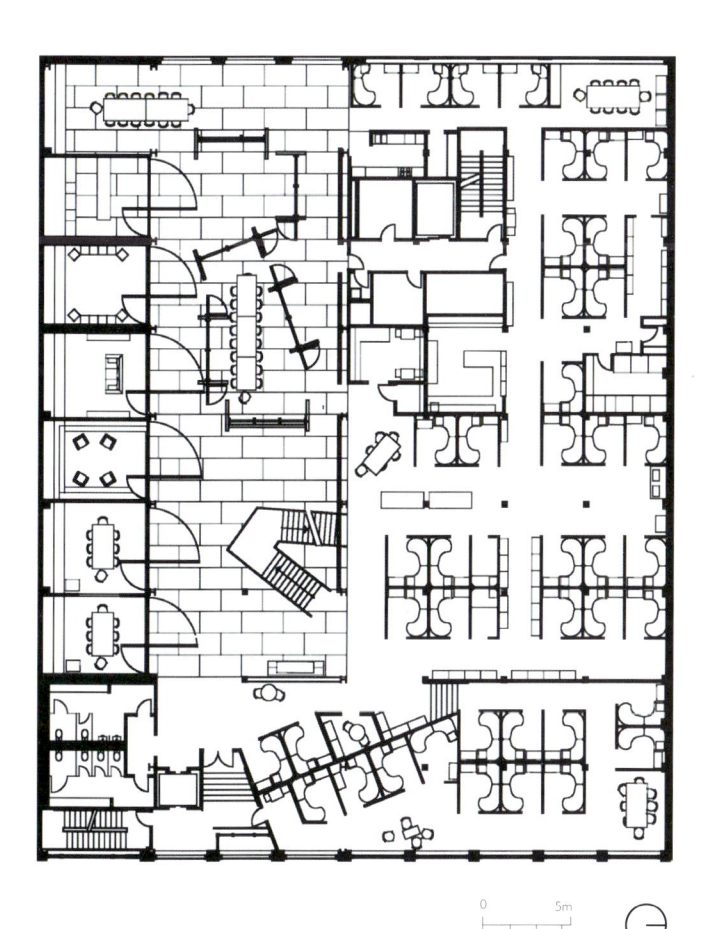

Left Plan of second floor.
Opposite Work areas encourage collaboration.
Top left Giant steel doors pivot onto social spaces.
Above Compact plywood cubicles are the same for all staff.

Sedgwick Rd. **29**

1.4
PricewaterhouseCoopers
Birmingham, UK
BDGworkfutures

MOST accountancy firms have a rather dull and grey image, but you can't accuse PricewaterhouseCoopers of blending into the background with its dramatic new office in Britain's second city. Not only does this project challenge the standard format for the professional services workplace by providing no fixed desks or offices, but does so with a visual flourish.

In fact, PricewaterhouseCoopers see things very much in black-and-white. A 'liquorice allsorts' design concept, detailing the ground-floor awnings, concierge desk and lockers, creates a clever and striking visual cohesion between the floors of the building.

The drama begins on arrival, with a vibrant reception that leads into the social hub of the building at the base of an atrium. A Starbucks café provides the buzz and ambience of a high street coffee shop, while adjacent lounges and 'touch-down spaces' provide a quieter environment where visitors can work effectively, using the wireless network to check their emails.

The office areas provide a range of work settings with well-proportioned bench desks, complete with task lights for laptop-carrying nomadic staff, and a series of semi-enclosed rooms for concentrated work. These areas are interspersed with social spaces for working, such as banquette-style booths near to the vending machines.

Cylindrical pods that house the photocopiers and the general machinery of office life punctuate the environment. By bringing these services into the middle of the work area, rather than hiding them in a corner, the designers give scale to what could otherwise be a monotonous space, and provide a focal point for spontaneous meetings during the working day. Staff can reserve a work setting through an on-line booking system, while lockers are provided for people to temporarily secure their possessions.

This scheme is an exemplar of good design for a nomadic workforce. It sets new standards for professional service firms, achieving the Academy principle of collegiate working within a highly mobile setting. The range of settings allows for choice, while the density of occupation ensures that there is always a buzz within the building. This is enhanced by a 'cross-line of service' policy that ensures people mix between departments when they book their space, so establishing a new operating model for the firm.

Location Birmingham, UK
Client PricewaterhouseCoopers
Completed 2004
Total Floor Space 7,366 square metres (79,290 square feet)
Staff 1,500

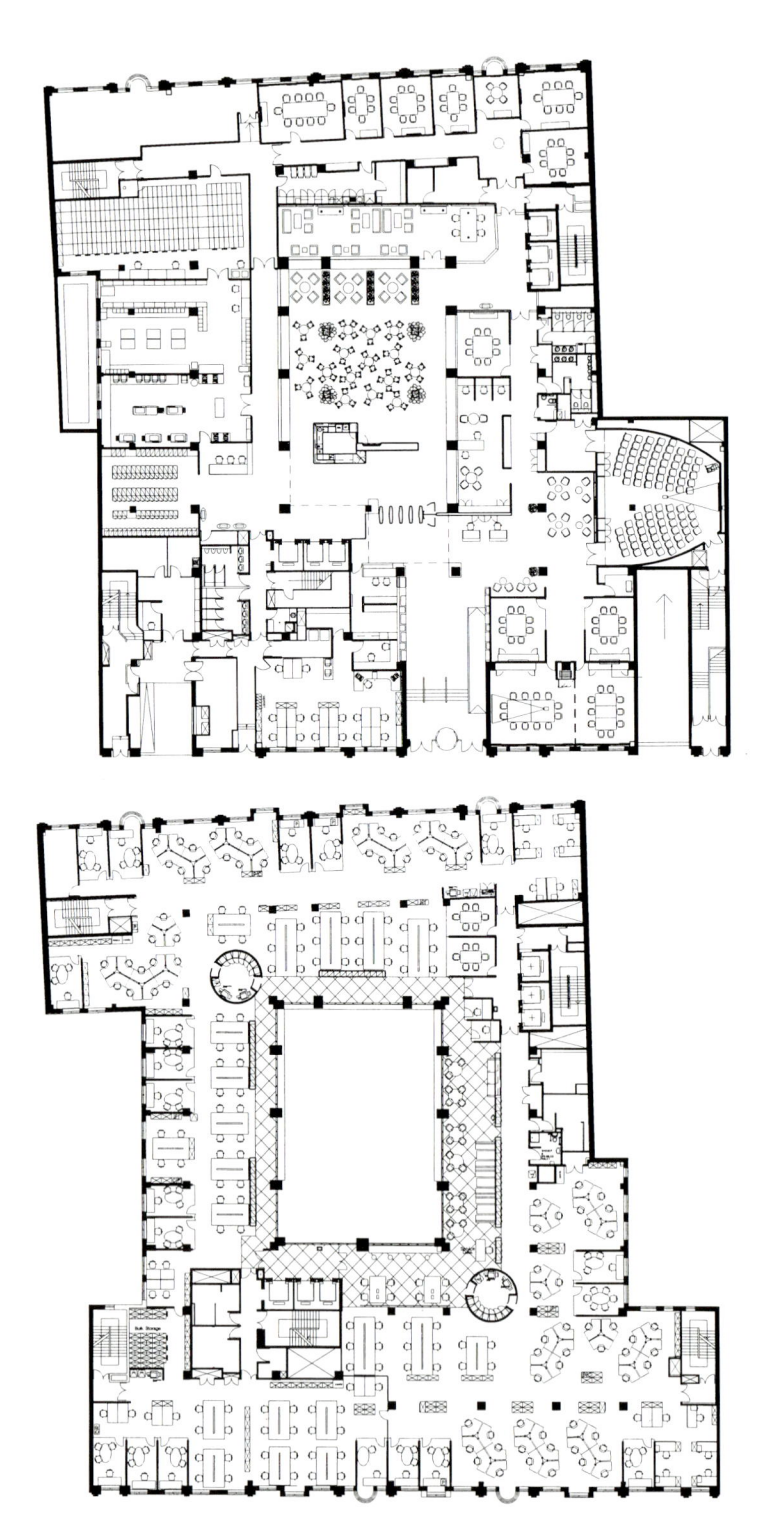

Top Plan of the ground floor, showing the central Starbucks café with surrounding facilities, including the concierge and business lounge.
Above Typical floor plan showing the shared bench workstations and cylindrical pods for office services.
Opposite View across the main atrium, showing the dramatic black-and-white design concept that is echoed on each work floor.

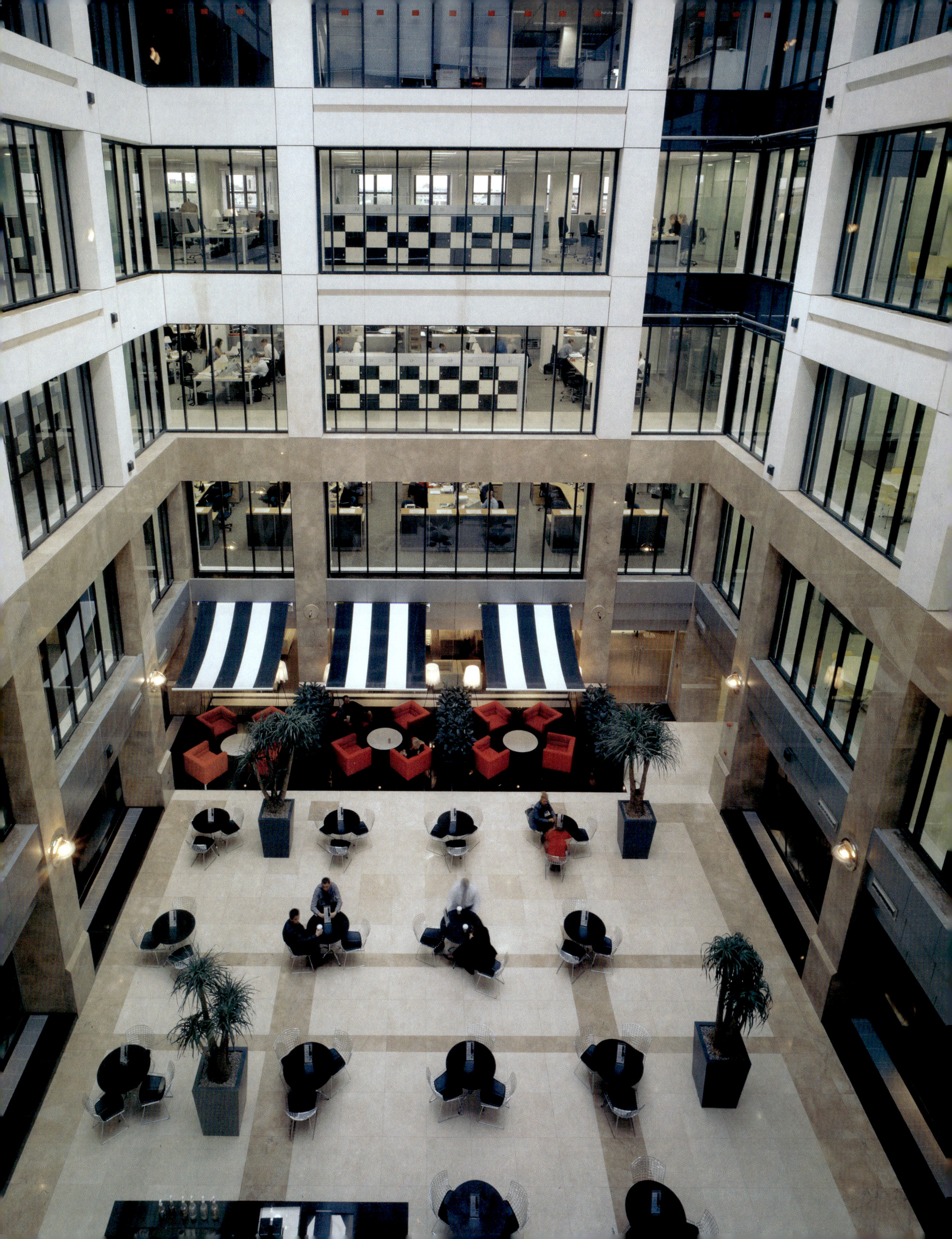

'Our working environment, particularly in terms of light, visual impact and flexibility, has supported our ambitions to recruit and retain the best people.' *David Waller, Midlands Chairman, PricewaterhouseCoopers*

Left The business lounge, adjacent to the café, provides a place for concentration and quiet work.
Middle Booths with banquette seats create an informal place for meetings or chats, adjacent to vending machines on each floor.
Right People book a workspace that provides a phone and task light, but bring their laptop and files with them for work.

Left A concierge desk provides a range of office services, and is adjacent to lockers and pigeonholes.
Middle Main workstations consist of 'variable density' benches where people are provided with a shared place for work.
Right Lockers on each floor provide a place to store personal items and files.

Examine what is said, not him who speaks*
Arab Proverb

1.5
Rafineri
Istanbul, Turkey
Erğinoğlu & Çalişlar

THREE difficult challenges were combined in the brief to create a new office for advertising agency Rafineri in Istanbul. The company name literally means 'refinery' in English and a primary aim for the architects was to create a dynamic workspace that would enable ideas to be developed and distilled, while creating memorable campaigns for clients.

The agency is owned and run by women, so there was an additional need to create a masculine design language in order to help the agency to compete in the Turkish market and to counter-balance their female-only image. The final consideration was the very short time frame available in which to architecturally renovate the office and for the agency to rethink the way in which it operated.

Given such complexities, it is to the architects' credit that the resulting scheme holds together in such a clear and robust way. The office is divided into two separate project areas, Brand 1 and Brand 2, by a system of horizontal poles and screens. Work desks are positioned on the perimeter of the space, in order to benefit from natural light, and the managers' private rooms are located close to their teams. The tough and businesslike finishes convey a youthful, go-getting spirit.

At the heart of the project is an abstractly shaped meeting room whose sharp, diagonal wooden edges project through the entire space and define the main circulation routes. Along one edge is a collapsible seat, inspired by the back seat of an old Cabriolet. This room presents the image of Rafineri to everyone who enters it.

Two additional, smaller project spaces – nicknamed UFOs – are metal cylindrical containers that can hold a meeting table and chairs and that glide on wheels within the open office space, creating temporary workshops. It is material and technical invention such as this that gives the scheme its resonance, and enables the agency to come together to generate ideas and sell them to clients.

Location Istanbul, Turkey
Client Rafineri
Completed 2002
Total Floor Space 500 square metres (5,382 square feet)
Staff 11

1 entrance
2 staff room
3 office
4 office
5 office
6 office
7 meeting room
8 head office
9 meeting room
10 lounge
11 office
12 office
13 office
14 office
15 office
16 office

Above Floor plan shows the staff workstations on the perimeter of the project.
Opposite Views of the interior reveal the sharp diagonal edges of the meeting room as well as a small wheeled metal project container – robust design deliberately conceived for a female-only agency.

'We decided to create a rough and productive place in which ideas are embodied and distilled.'
Erğinoğlu & Çalişlar

1.6
Pallotta TeamWorks
Los Angeles, USA
Clive Wilkinson Architects

THIS new headquarters for a charity fundraising company in Los Angeles creates an inspired work environment in an unconditioned warehouse-shed. A lavishly appointed office would have been inappropriate for such an organization. Instead architect Clive Wilkinson has innovated in the areas of lighting, heating and cooling to create an informal and engaging work setting that allows ideas and information to flow as freely as possible.

The project takes its main visual and functional inspiration from the mobile 'tent cities' used by the client to stage charity events. 'Breathing' tented structures are spaced throughout the scheme, providing air-conditioned areas for comfortable working without the expense of air-conditioning the entire warehouse volume. Circulation pathways are treated as external streets and left without air-conditioning.

This alternative, sustainable strategy extends to maximizing the southern Californian sunshine through skylights and reducing heat gain through the use of mainly fluorescent lighting. The total effect has been to slash energy costs in half, but this headquarters building is not simply green – its tent structures, suspended from the roof support column grid, commend themselves for a host of other reasons.

The tents provide intimate and distinct work neighbourhoods that can stretch in different directions, according to the demands of the programme. Their corners are anchored to prefabricated shipping containers that accommodate private offices and support facilities in an extremely low-cost way. Power and air feeds funnel down directly into these structures from the roof.

The shipping containers flank a 'main street' – the core element of the space plan – with plywood extensions providing bay windows and seating and giving each department its own identity. Other key features include a reception desk modelled on a Buckminster Fuller Dymaxion world map, a main square for socializing and a two-storey wooden gallery beyond the main square that houses meeting rooms and recording studios as well as other support facilities.

Building on a pre-existing office mezzanine within the warehouse, this is a scheme that has made a virtue of every economy forced on it by budget and client remit. At a cost of around $40 per square foot, it shows that money alone does not create an ideal workplace for learning and collaboration.

Location Los Angeles
Client Pallotta TeamWorks
Completed 2002
Total Floor Space 4,366 square metres (47,000 square feet)
Staff 200

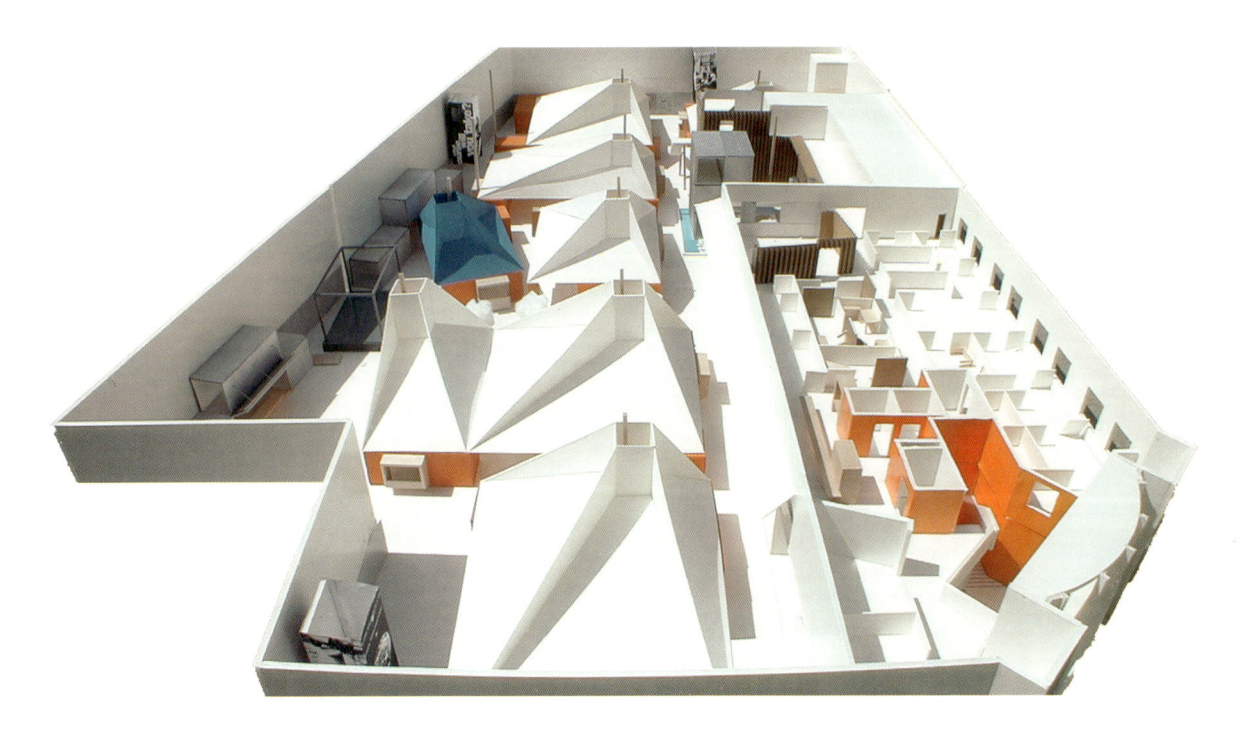

Below left Model of interior shows central row of 'breathing' tented structures. A blue shipping container forms a portal to the main volume of the building.
Below View down into street and inside prefabricated shipping container which provides intimate social space for collaboration.

Pallotta TeamWorks   **37**

'Pallotta TeamWorks is a journey – and the journey is the metaphor for the building.' *Dan Pallotta, Chief Executive Officer, Pallotta TeamWorks*

Above Stacked shipping containers link to the existing mezzanine level.
Right Reception desk modelled on Buckminster Fuller's Dymaxion world map, a projection showing continents as one continuous landmass without boundaries or states.
Far right Main street of Pallotta TeamWorks shows plywood-fronted container offices offering bay windows and seats close to the office action.

Pallotta TeamWorks 39

1.7
Norddeutsche Landesbank
Hanover, Germany
Behnisch, Behnisch & Partner

THE design for this bank's headquarters represents the office as a self-contained mini-metropolis. The architects have successfully mixed public spaces, outdoor terraces and communal social space with more traditional office environments to create an effective shared workplace that brings people together in a stimulating environment.

Before moving into its new offices, the bank had 15 separate locations spread around Hanover. Its 1,500 staff are now located in a central building that nevertheless retains its roots in discrete spaces and places. Passageways and 'tubes' link the spaces together and allow circulation between the different parts of the complex. At its centre is a dominant 70-metre (230-foot) tower, complete with a glass sculpture that changes colour throughout the day. A restaurant is provided with semi-enclosed decks adjacent to water features, and even the roof of this space has been planted with a layer of vegetation that varies by season and actually enhances the courtyard's microclimate.

The emphasis on the individual extends to the office areas, where there are windows that can be opened as an alternative to air-conditioning. Glazed partitions maintain the openness and transparency of the space. Within the office areas, 'coffee corners' encourage informal interaction and information exchange. A 'forum' offers a mixed-use meeting space that also functions as an art gallery and a lecture hall. Towards the top of the tower a 'sky lounge' provides a place for clients, alongside more traditional conference and meeting rooms.

The architect's design reaches out to the surrounding district. Its elevations face in a multitude of directions, in effect 'connecting' the bank to the surrounding community. An inner courtyard that is open to the public and a retail space provided at ground floor level strengthen this strategy. Artist Michael Craig-Martin has used murals and bold colour to enliven the space and to highlight the different places and circulation routes that define this collection of working environments. This is a scheme that carefully composes public and private, professional and social within a satisfying whole that enables knowledge work to flourish.

Location Hanover, Germany
Client Norddeutsche Landesbank
Completed 2002
Total Floor Space 75,000 square metres (807,293 square feet)
Staff 1,500

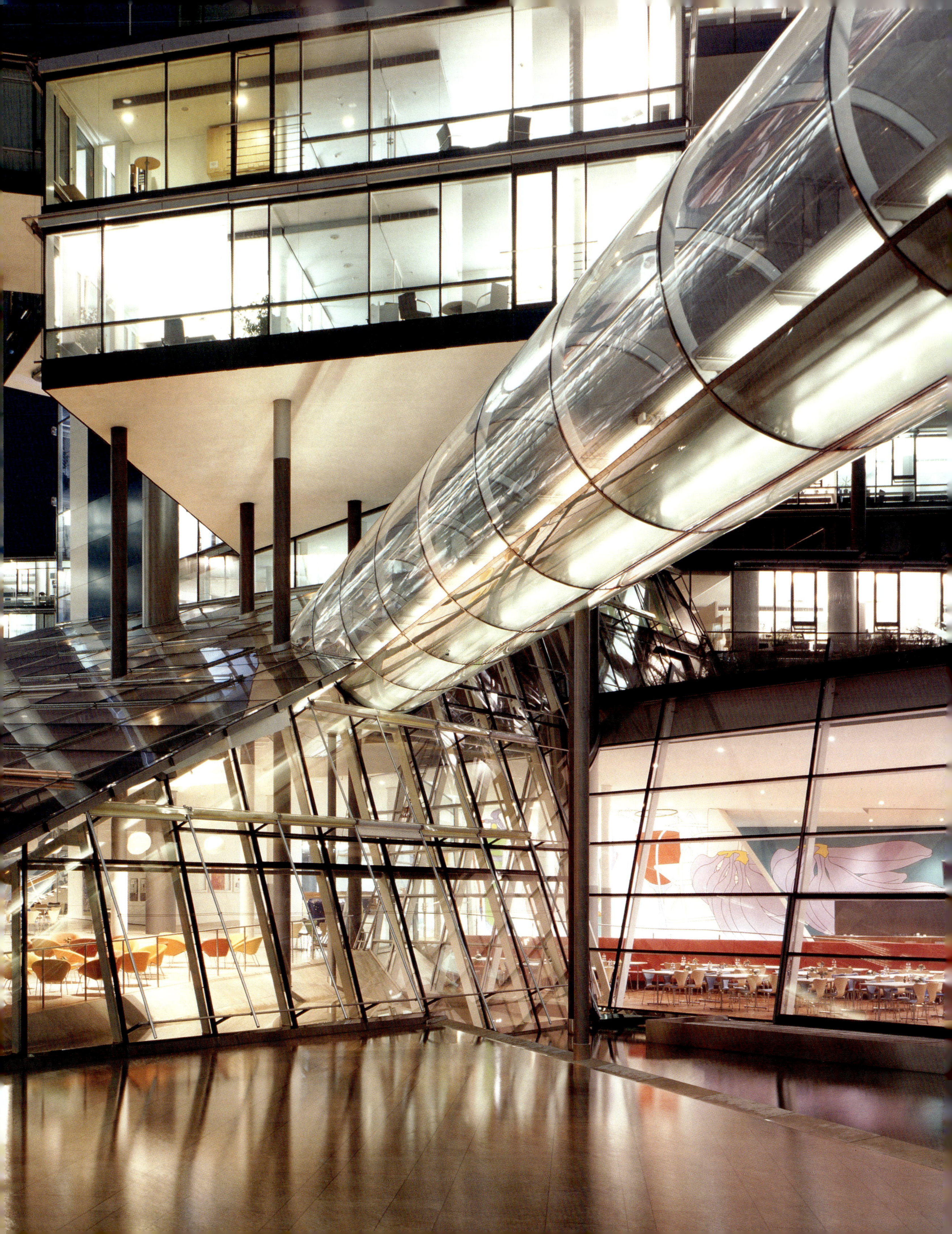

'The bank building occupies an important part of the city, and in return it "gives back" an attractive public space.' *Behnisch, Behnisch & Partner*

Previous page View into the main restaurant across the courtyard, complete with spectacular glass 'tubes' that connect the various parts of this 'mini metropolis'.
Top Artist Michael Craig-Martin was commissioned to create these murals that lend drama and colour to the staff restaurant.
Above Executive office where, with natural ventilation and opening windows, people are allowed to control their environment.

1 conference room
2 library
3 kitchen
4 roof garden
5 terrace
6 existing Siemens building

Above Plan showing the building with its mix of public spaces and outdoor terraces.
Below A historic nineteenth-century building once occupied by Siemens has been retained and now functions as the training centre. The elevation has been painted in Norddeutsche Landesbank's corporate colours.

1.8
BMW Plant, Central Building
Leipzig, Germany
Zaha Hadid Architects

ZAHA Hadid's competition-winning Central Building scheme for BMW Group's Leipzig factory does more than tie together the three main production segments: assembly, body shop and paint shop. It is also the vital nerve-centre for the entire complex, acting as the administration hub in the carmaker's vast new manufacturing plant where all the production processes converge.

Traditionally, blue-collar and white-collar workers have been kept apart in car factories, but at BMW Leipzig the two worlds collide. This is part of a deliberate architectural strategy to ensure that administrative, engineering and production staff all share the same routes and spaces through a central 'marketplace', in order to enhance communication.

The platform for this audacious piece of social engineering is the design of the Central Building, its complex geometries creating a unique large, open office. It comprises a stacked landscape of concrete terraces, above and through which runs the car production line. Bathed in an ethereal blue light, the production line is a constant reminder of what working at BMW is all about.

Two sequences of concrete terraced plates extend like giant staircases, stepping up from north to south and from south to north, occupying a long connective void. One terrace starts close to a large public lobby in the north and the other starts with offices at the south, meeting the first cascade and moving all the way up to a space overlooking the entrance. The plan thus creates three levels that overlap dynamically to provide unusual vistas in all directions.

Within these giant cascading floor plates the atmosphere is monolithic, but the patterns of occupation are also agile and flexible. Custom-designed furniture was developed by the manufacturer Bene, including specially designed workstations and a series of 'think tanks' (quite literally glass meeting bowls) that enhance the functionality of the environment. A special aluminium desk lamp, by Kai Byok of Kb Form, was also commissioned for the project.

Everyone in the Central Building has their own desk, and the lockers and social spaces of the factory workers are also located deep within this administration heartland. This indicates the desire to bring all parts of the BMW community together, in order to share experience and knowledge.

As an architect, Zaha Hadid is increasingly interested in geology and topology – in carving space as if it were landscape. This project is a key landmark in the evolution of her thinking, its lines converging to create a 'communication knot' through which a more integrated approach to making cars can be achieved.

Location Leipzig, Germany
Client BMW Group
Completed 2005
Total Floor Space 27,000 square metres (290,625 square feet)
Staff 750

Above A radical solution to bring factory workers, administrators and engineers closer together at BMW. The production line moves through the central office, bathed in blue light.

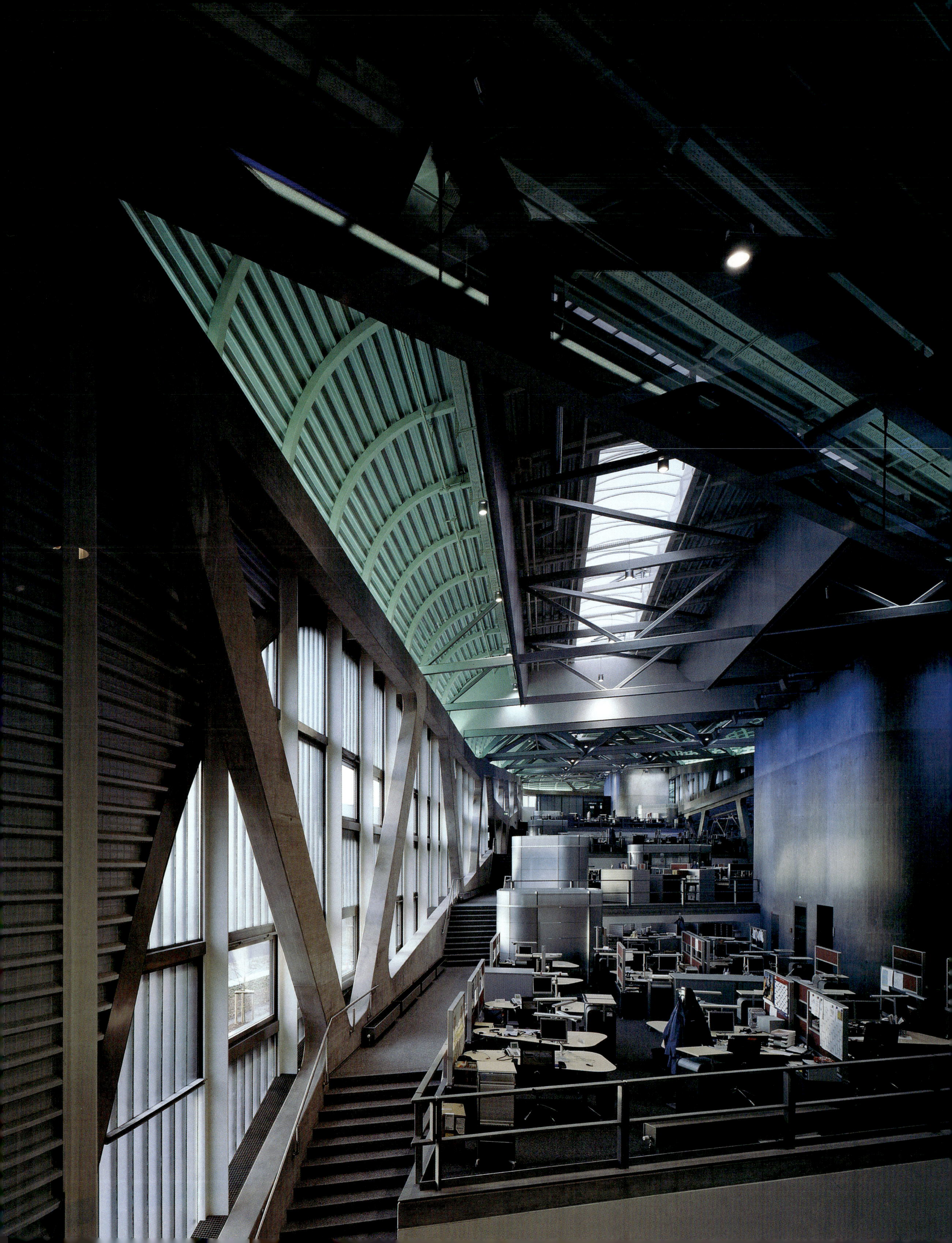

'The building's design facilitates a radical new interpretation of open office landscape.' *Zaha Hadid Architects*

Opposite and above View of the concrete terraced floor plates which ascend and descend in a series of sweeps as part of the complex geometry of the scheme, creating open-plan spaces at different levels and offering vistas in all directions.

BMW Plant, Central Building **47**

0   5m   10m
15ft   30ft

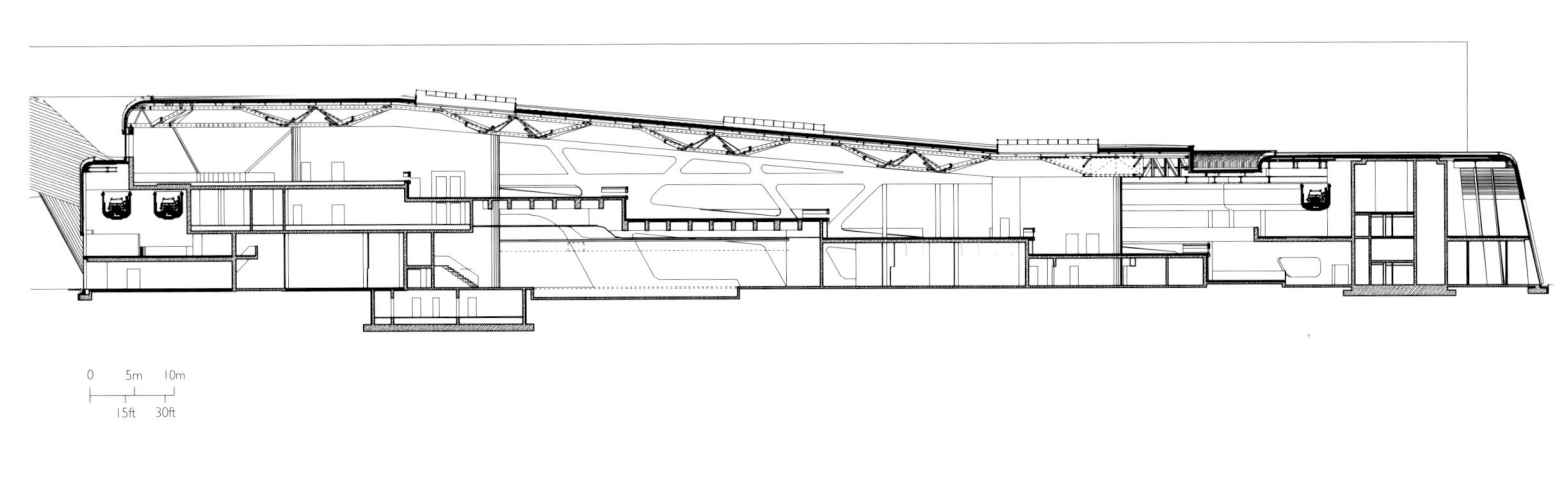

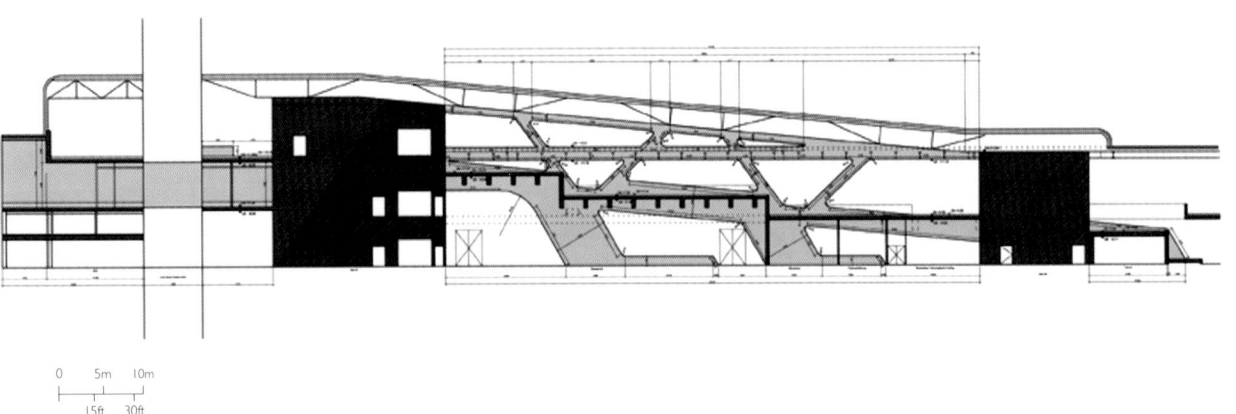

0   5m   10m
15ft   30ft

Above Sections show the idea of undulating landscape within the building interior.
Opposite A specially shaped workstation was develop for the BMW Leipzig project by manufacturer Bene to respond to the requirement for more organic space planning.

BMW Plant, Central Building 49

1.9 Mother
London, UK
Clive Wilkinson Architects

SINCE it started in the late 1990s, the advertising agency Mother has grown from a small 'boutique' outfit to one of British advertising's best-known names. Despite such rapid growth and success, however, Mother's original partners were determined not to abandon their all-for-one 'kitchen table' ethos when they moved to a new office in the Tea Building, now called the Biscuit Building, in London's Shoreditch district.

The result is an extraordinary office interior, dominated by a single continuous concrete table that is able to seat all 200 members of staff. This vast structure is a tour de force that emulates the famous 1910 racetrack on the roof of the Fiat factory in Turin. A metaphor for speed and mobility in working life – every employee moves to a new seat at the table every three weeks – it also reflects a determination to hang on to the collaborative, non-hierarchical ethos that has served the Mother agency so well.

The idea behind the scheme was simple: to increase the size of the company table as the company grew. The reason for the choice of concrete was to make a monumental statement about durability in the notoriously fickle communication industry.

The client actually wanted a wooden table, but the architect held out for the cement mixers to provide the solution. The resulting work table is possibly the world's largest table at 76 metres (250 feet) long, constructed of 7.6-centimetre (3-inch) thick concrete. At one point it takes the form of a 4-metre (14-foot) wide staircase, and at other points there are breaks in the structure to allow for circulation.

The positioning of large lampshades softens the potential brutalism of the environment. These lampshades serve the space's lighting and acoustic needs by foreshortening the ceiling height, and are decorated with vintage patterns from the 1950s and 1960s by Finnish fabric manufacturer Marimekko. Above the reception desk is a giant projection screen that transforms the entry lobby into a public screening gallery for new agency commercials.

Clive Wilkinson is possibly better known for his outstanding warehouse and factory conversions for ad agencies TBWA/Chiat/Day and Foote Cone & Belding in California. Here, however, he has adapted to the different climate and culture of London to create one of the most genuinely arresting office schemes to appear in the capital for some time.

Location London, UK
Client Mother
Completed 2004
Total Floor Space 3,902 square metres (42,000 square feet)
Staff 200

Above Computer visual shows the giant table inspired by the Fiat factory race track.
Opposite The concrete table in use.

50 Academy

'We wanted a concrete table because it's an insanely optimistic statement for such an ephemeral industry as advertising.' *Clive Wilkinson*

Above Looking down the concrete staircase to the entrance lobby.
Opposite Mother's concrete table makes a point, framed by large acoustic lampshades using classic modern Marimekko fabrics.

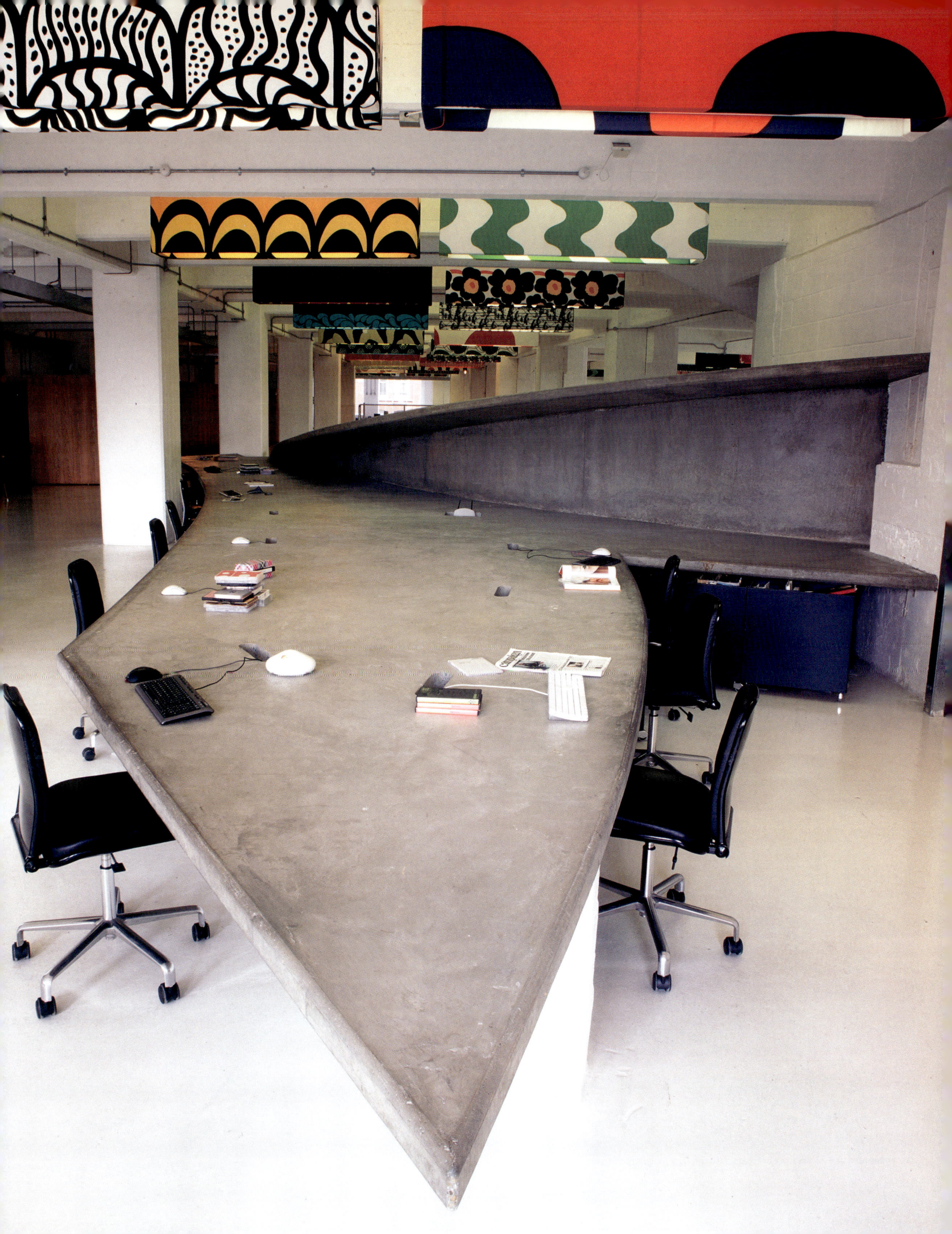

1.10
Ericsson North American Headquarters
Plano, USA
Thompson Vaivoda & Associates Architects

ERICSSON'S office 'Village' in Plano, Texas, creates a stimulating environment with outstanding public areas. It provides workspace for a community of 1,500 people, previously spread over 30 different locations around North Texas. Now that all are located within one unified campus, there is a collegiate feel to the workplace.

The first-floor entrance to the building creates a welcoming approach to what is a large complex with four office 'wings' that interconnect around a central lake. A dramatic, double-height street links the wings, and creates a clever circulation route that even includes a bridge over the lake.

Flexible floor plates were specified by the interior designers, Lauckgroup. An impressive 5,110 square metres (55,000 square feet) of flooring, with wide column spacing, were achieved through this planning topology. Called 'fabric', it offers the flexibility of a theatre set, and is designed to minimize future disruption and cost should the office layout be altered.

Furniture from Steelcase encourages flexibility with mobile pieces allowing settings to be re-configured and enabling users to create their ideal environment for concentration, interaction or other tasks. The furniture can be also be raised or lowered to allow people to work either sitting or standing. Views of the lake are achieved from all workstations by the extensive use of glass.

The 2-hectare (5-acre) landscaped grounds, including a lake and mature trees and gardens, integrates the local Texan environment with Ericsson's Swedish heritage to create a stimulating series of external settings. This cultural combination has been extended to the interior finishes which feature stone paving, vibrant coloured fabrics and light wood finishes.

Within the Village is an 'Ericsson Experience', a place to see and test the latest technologies in a state-of-the-art demonstration centre. As is only to be expected from Ericsson, wireless technology not only covers the entire built environment, but also extends across the campus to include even the lake, where remote-controlled boats are available for people to reduce stress. Workers and visitors can connect to the Ericsson network from anywhere, making the whole Village a connected community.

In its original brief, Ericsson Village was conceived as community of 'work, learning and people'. This scheme is a model for an Academy workspace, making visible the qualities that the company values in its staff in achieving a flexible, creative and team-orientated environment.

Location Texas, USA
Client Ericsson Inc.
Completed 2001
Total Floor Space 46,450 square metres (500,000 square feet)
Staff 1,500

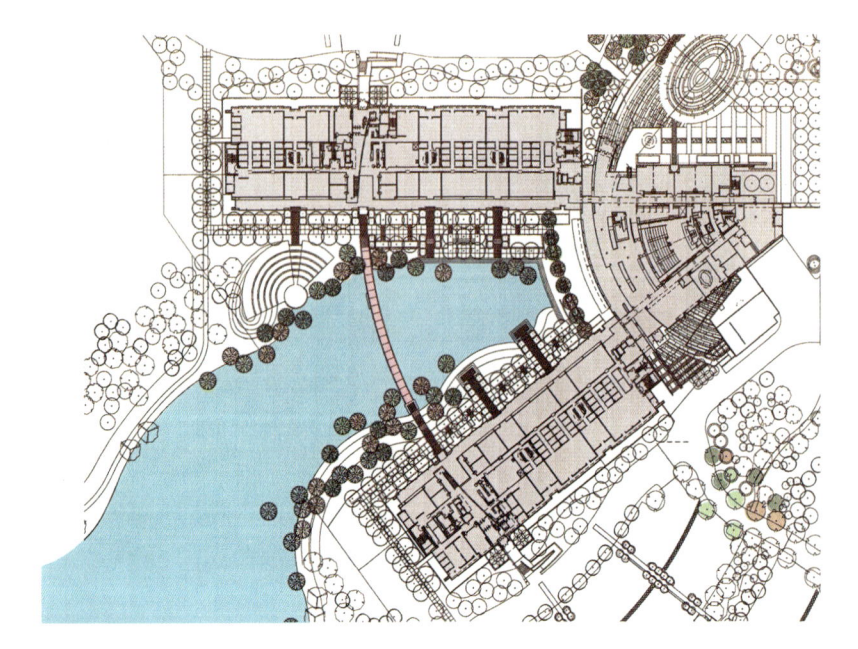

Left Site plan of the Village showing the office wings and landscaping.
Opposite Casual meeting area with view over the central lake, complete with bridge connecting the wings.

Ericsson North American Headquarters **55**

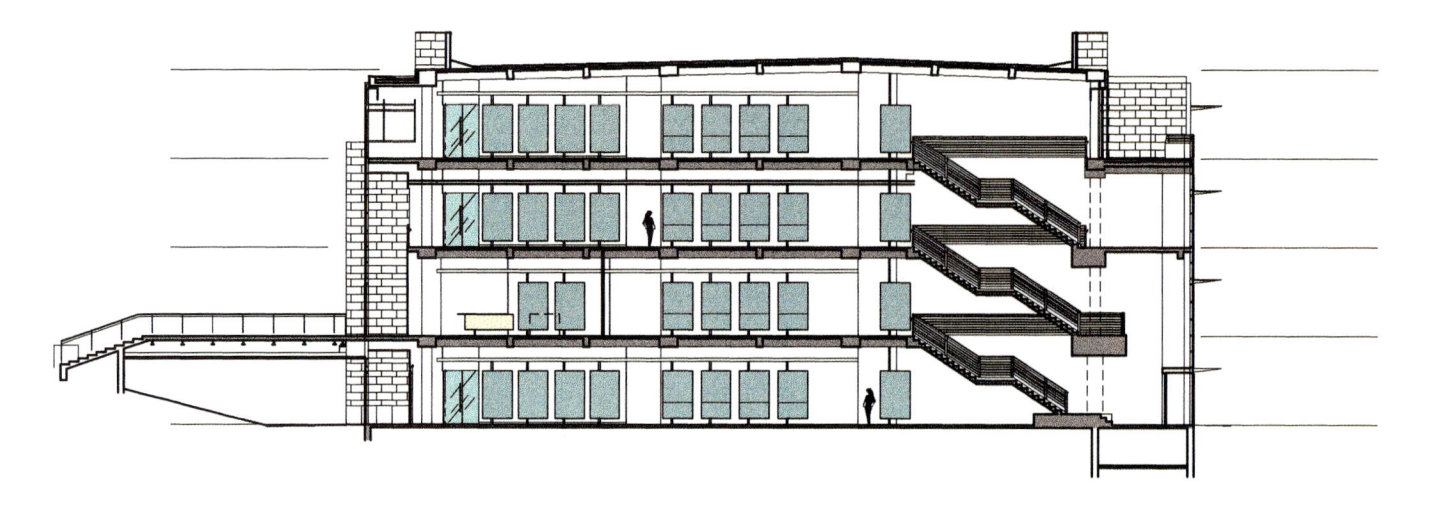

Above Section showing the main entrance bridge at first-floor level.
Below The floor plan demonstrates the juxtaposition of work areas with shared 'non-desk' spaces and amenities.

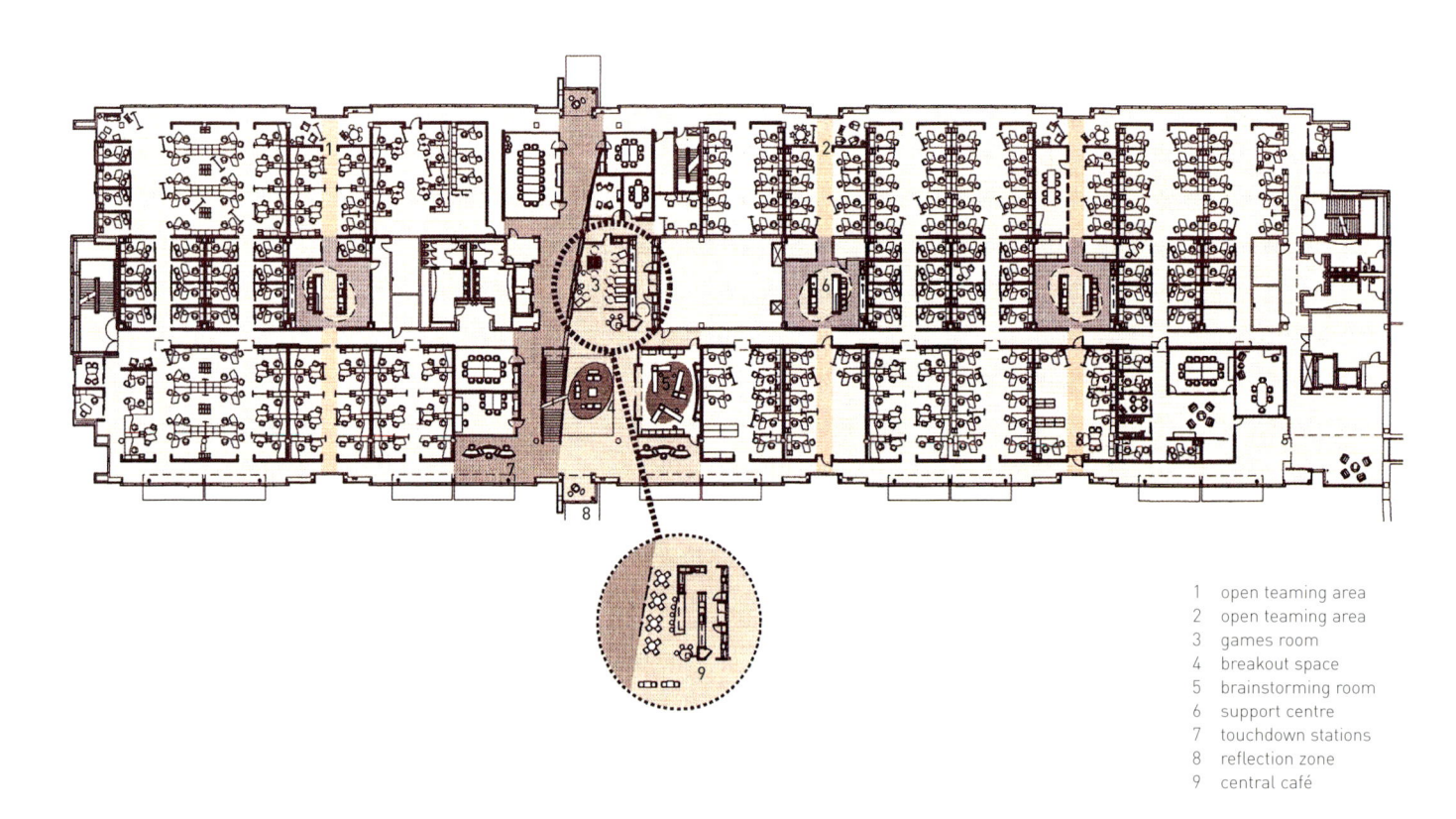

1 open teaming area
2 open teaming area
3 games room
4 breakout space
5 brainstorming room
6 support centre
7 touchdown stations
8 reflection zone
9 central café

'The overall design and functionality is an expression of Ericsson's underlying philosophy that strongly values its employees and communication.' *Brigitte Preston, Director of Design and Principal, Lauckgroup*

Above The whole Ericsson Village is a connected community: people can work from anywhere, both inside and outside the building.
Below A street at the perimeter of each wing creates a dramatic space for circulation and also encourages chance encounters.

1.11
Interpolis
Tilburg, Holland
Veldhoen + Company

THIS ground-breaking insurance company in Holland is well known for its workplace innovation, following the introduction of the first Interpolis Office Concept, with its team-spaced, wire-free design, in 1996. Seven years after the original scheme, a third project was completed adjacent to it, under the strategy of 'Clear Working'. This new project moved the ideas forward once more, creating a workspace that embodies the ideals of an Academy for knowledge workers.

Interpolis is based on the same site as the first scheme, the Tivoli site, adjacent to the original 1996 building. Its exceptional interior challenges many of the conventions of office life, with its artist-inspired spaces that break the traditional mould and provide places for people in a truly twenty-first century workplace.

One of the guiding principles behind Clear Working was the realization that, with advances in technology, the layout of buildings no longer had to mirror the organizational structure of the company. Instead, the project team decided to create a series of spaces that reflected the words 'inter' and 'polis' in a network of cities, squares and neighbourhoods.

Tivoli Plaza has thus become the heart of the Interpolis Office Network – a collection of building environments filled with neighbourhood squares, streets and pathways, shortcuts and different types of working space. These include a new vertical space that leads to interesting circulation and random meanders between floors. Within this metropolis, individuals have become the focal point rather than the buildings or hierarchies. Continuing this approach, the large floor plates were compartmentalized by introducing a patchwork of facilities, which gives a more human feel.

Avenues, streets and paths lead to a range of workspaces, some of them unpredictable. The clubhouses, for example, were each designed by a different architect and provide tranquil, warm, cosy and inspirational spaces. Interior designer Nel Verschuuren acted as a 'participating curator', selecting and guiding artists such as Piet Hein Eek and Irene Fortuyn as they created their sections of the city. A 'House of Light' was created by the theatre designer Mark Warning, while a 'Weavers' Hut' was created by interior designer Bas van Tol.

Many projects simply repeat the 'new-ways-of-working' model across all floors, but Interpolis has created a place where nowhere looks or feels like anywhere else. It is, in effect, an interior landscape of spaces for working, inhabited by a knowledge community that is in control of how it wants to work.

Location Tilburg, Holland
Client Interpolis
Completed 2003
Total Floor Space 45,000 square metres (484,375 square feet)
Staff 2,650

- streets and squares
- open spaces
- meeting rooms
- designated rooms
- clubhouses
- service centre

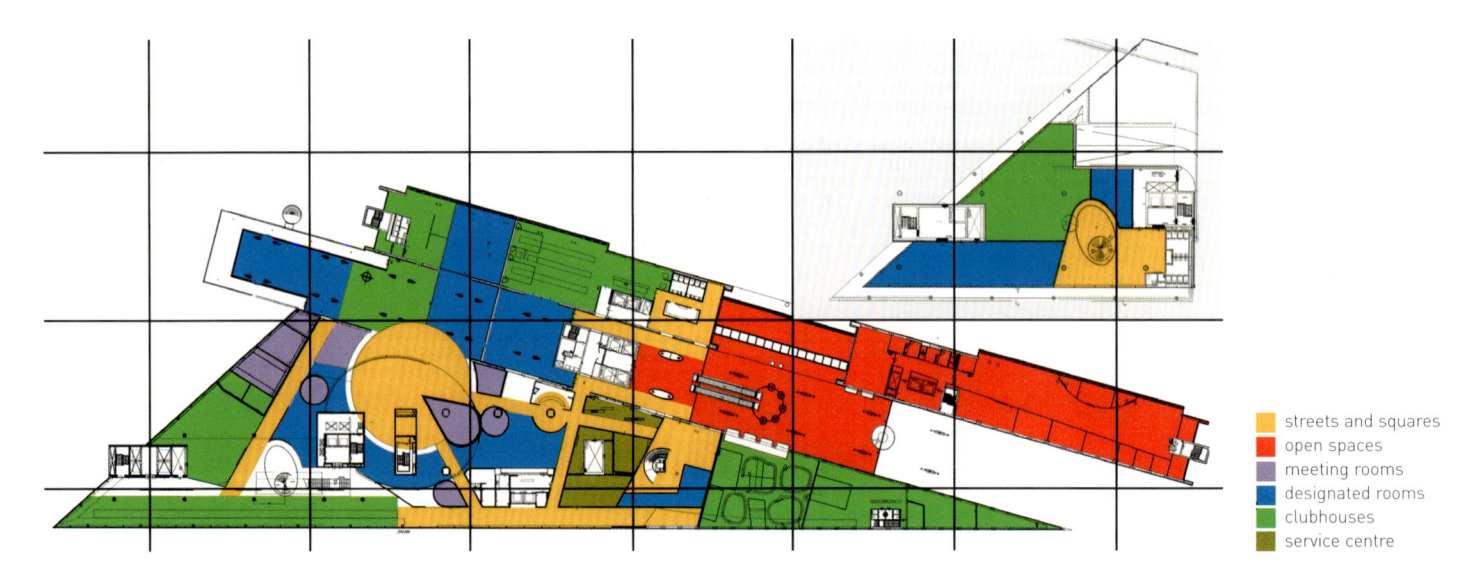

Above Block plan of the building, with ground floor detail, showing the various houses, rooms, streets and squares.
Opposite Artist-inspired spaces for people form part of the 'Clear Working' strategy in which a network of neighbourhoods, streets and pathways provides different types of working spaces.

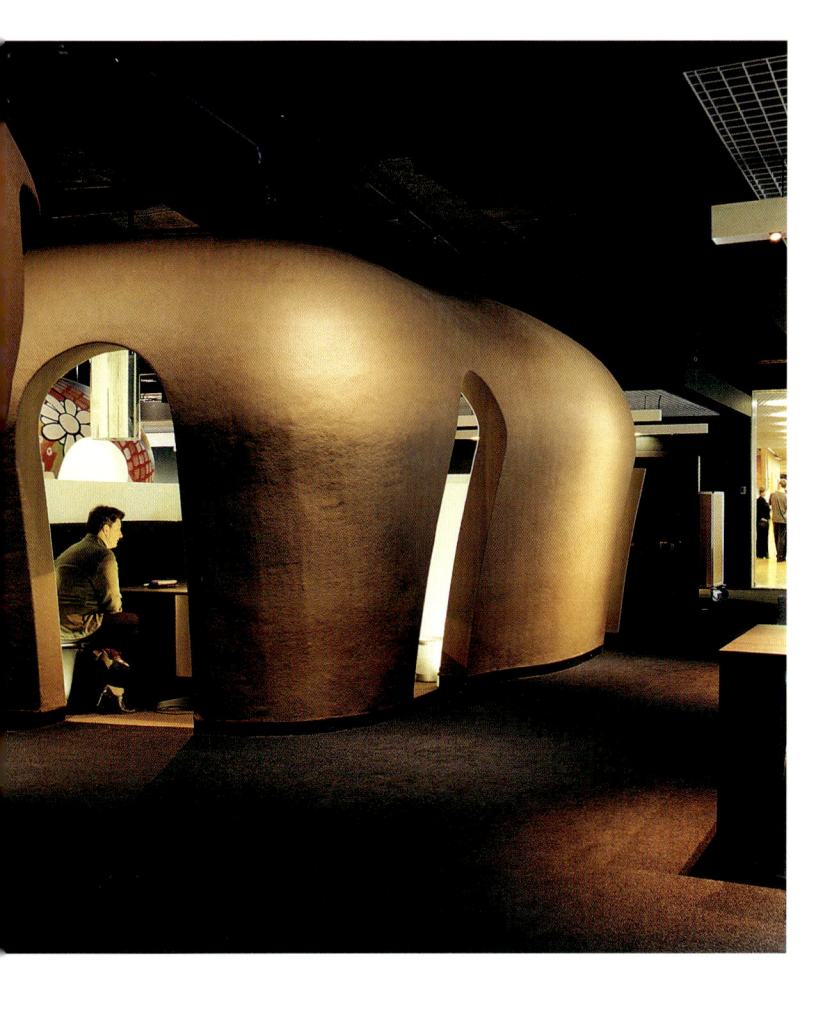

Interpolis **59**

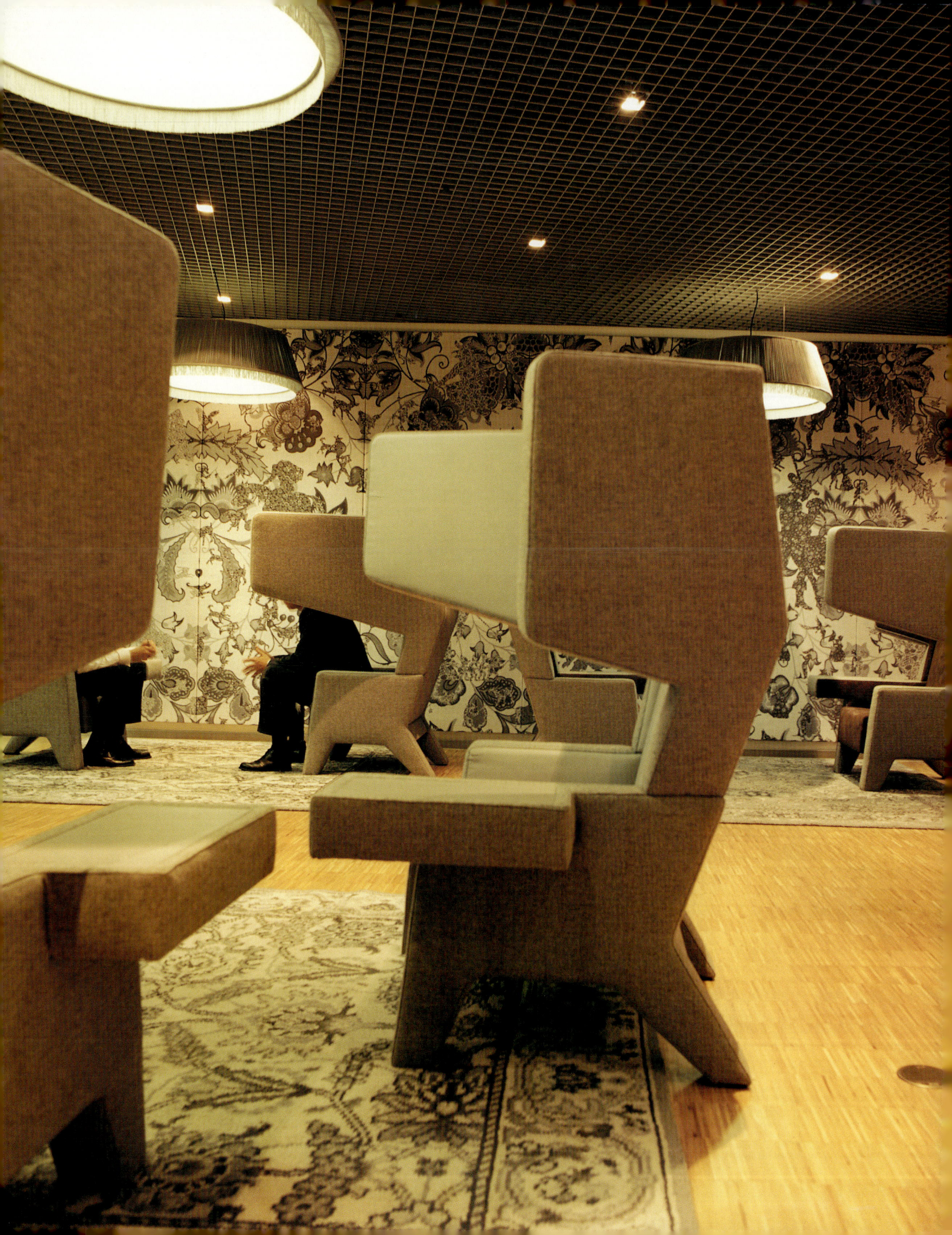

Opposite Eclectic furniture creates a sense of surprise and injects humour into one of the many meeting spaces.
Above Materials and finishes throughout the interior are innovative and uplifting, with interesting veneers, for example, applied to the front of lockers.

Interpolis 61

'It wasn't the building that changed us, the building was part of a process of change that is still underway.'
Piet van Schijndel, Former Chairman of the Board, Interpolis

Opposite 'Stone House' by Marcel Wanders creates a wonderful structure in which to meet and work.
Below 'Weavers' Hut' by Bas van Tol uses hanging cords to play on a 'networked' environment.

1.12
Genzyme Center
Cambridge, USA
Behnisch, Behnisch & Partner

THE biotechnology company Genzyme specializes in developing drugs to treat rare diseases. Its new 12-storey headquarters building in Cambridge, Massachusetts, provides something rare in office design: a dazzling selection of shared environments, full of light and space. The spaces genuinely encourage people to meet, mingle and trade ideas in an environment dedicated to exchanging knowledge.

Externally, the building projects little of its internal luminosity. With its glass curtain-wall facade, it does a solid job of anchoring an urban regeneration programme in Kendall Square, next door to the famous Massachusetts Institute of Technology. The ground floor is devoted to retail, as part of a mixed-use development, and its welcome is cordial and professional rather than inspiring.

It is only when you venture inside, passing through gardens with trees and flowing water features to the mezzanine-level reception area, that the full intent of the architects' scheme is revealed. Genzyme's innovative culture is expressed through the organization of spaces around a grand, light-filled atrium that connects all the floors and the hanging internal gardens that are attached to several of them.

The atrium is the defining feature of the project. It acts as a giant light conductor, directing and diffusing the natural light deep into the cubicle offices, meeting rooms and open work lounges of the building. Within the atrium's shaft is a large hanging sculpture – a mobile made up of reflective plastic panels that creates a kaleidoscope of light and colour. It works in combination with a series of skylights, reflective glass strips, directional louvres and solar-tracking mirrors.

With its strategy of mirrored elements to enhance the natural light and internal gardens to clean and oxygenate the air, the Genzyme Center is highly rated as a sustainable building. Key design features support savings in energy and water use and more than three-quarters of the building materials have recycled content.

Unlike some green design, this project combines environmental responsibility with social animation for staff and visitors. What matters most to a biotechnical company like Genzyme is transparency. Its new headquarters have the open feel of a glass prism. It may be eco-friendly, but it is user-friendly too.

Above Section reveals green strategy.
Below Typical floor plan.
Opposite View of the main light-filled atrium with a hanging sculpture comprised of many small reflective panels.

Location Cambridge, USA
Client Lyme Properties (developer) and Genzyme Corporation (tenant)
Completed 2004
Total Floor Space 32,000 square metres (344,450 square feet)
Staff 950

'They designed a building that is alive on the inside, where people can work creatively and productively.'
Henri Termeer, Chief Executive Officer, Genzyme

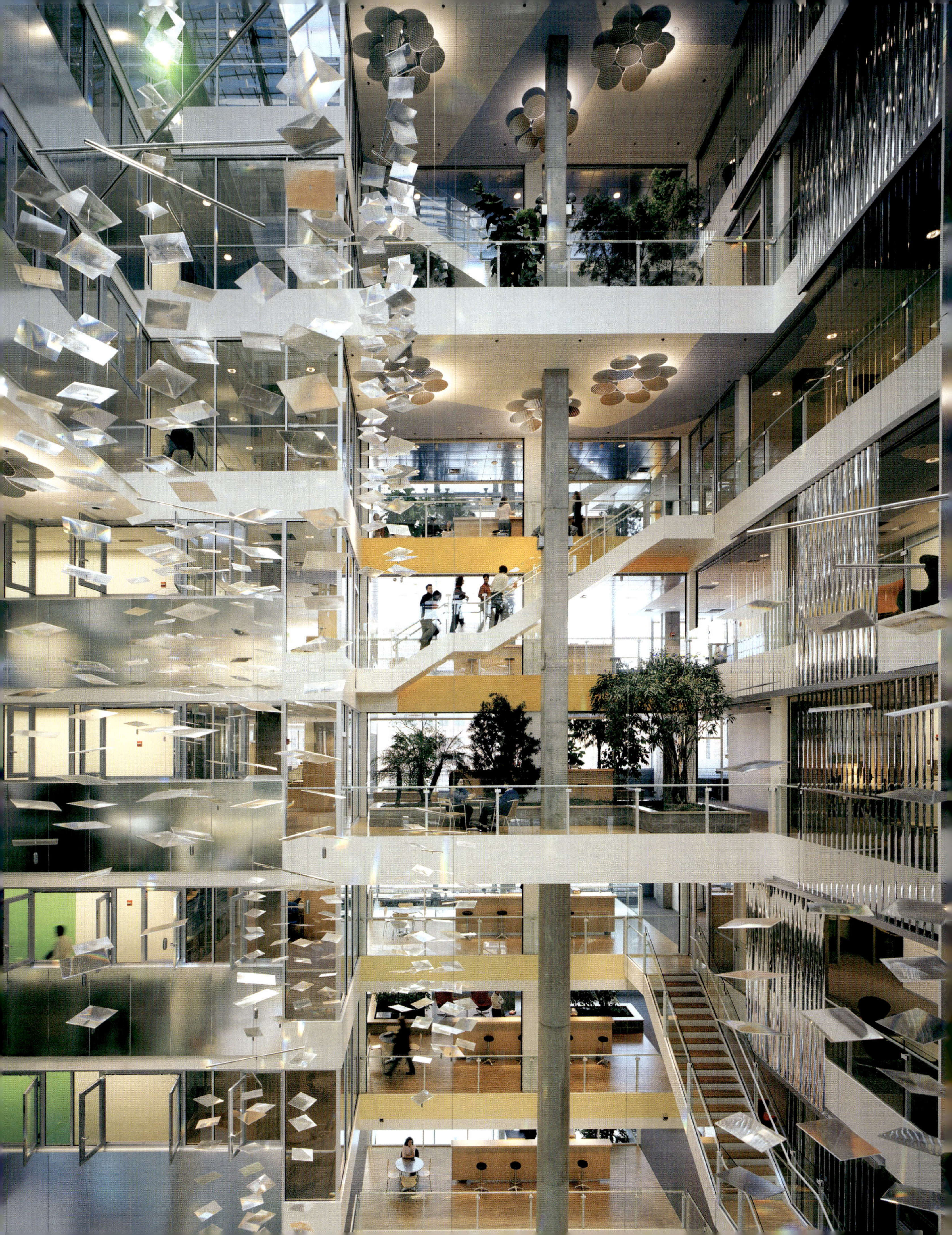

1.13
Enjoy
Paris, France
Edouard François

ENJOY, the Parisian advertising agency, has created a team space for its creative staff in a shared setting that encourages collaboration and communication. Dominating the space is 'Love', a continuous plywood table designed to accommodate the entire Enjoy team. Designer Edouard François decided that the entire 40-strong agency should occupy one room and, rather like the Mother agency in London, sit at one shared desk.

Huge cacti demarcate each work pod, which in effect provide a near 360-degree work surface. These spiked barriers provide some separation in what is otherwise a continuous surface. Two different-sized pods cluster people in either ones or twos, and access to the pods is via small cut-outs in the desks from the internal, rather than the more usual secondary, circulation route. All the pods face the perimeter, giving them views onto the outside gardens.

Storage has been carefully incorporated, with bespoke shelves and cupboards for books, stationery and filing. Functionalism is key, with natural plywood surfaces and a raw simplicity of materials. Lighting is provided from both overhead lights and bespoke desktop task lamps, giving a domestic feel to the space.

Enjoy staff all work from laptops which, together with mobile phones, keep the work surface uncluttered and remove the need for complex cable management solutions that all too often lead to over-engineered furniture. Power is provided through circular wooden 'lids' with cut-out grommets.

Formal meetings are rare at Enjoy. The clustering of employees in their 'holes' provides a novel, interactive and vibrant solution for a team of creative people who want to collaborate and spark ideas off each other.

Location Paris, France
Client Enjoy
Completed 2002
Total Floor Space 1,080 square metres (11,625 square feet)
Staff 40

Top A two-person pod, providing a clear surface for laptop-based work.
Above Plan of the table, showing the variety of cut-out pods running off the linear circulation route.
Below left The 'Love' table accommodates all 40 employees at Enjoy.
Below right Adjacent meeting rooms for privacy and concentration.

'Normally you meet around a table, but now the table is around the meeting.' *Edouard François*

1.14
EMI London Headquarters
London, UK
MoreySmith Design and Architecture

THIS award-winning refurbishment of a neglected 1970s office block, close to London's Kensington High Street, strikes just the right note as a pulsating new headquarters for the music giant EMI. However, it took the combination of a courageous client and an imaginative architect to turn a bland, forlorn-looking five-storey building, previously occupied by Penguin Books in the 1980s, into a contemporary class act in its own right.

The immediate key to the transformation is the dramatic, double-height reception space that was achieved by ripping out the slab at first-floor level. The old façade of outdated burgundy panelling and brown windows was also replaced with a smart curved glass frontage.

A central courtyard garden that had seen better days was glazed over to create a new central atrium, complete with a warehouse-style staff café and kitchen. This forms the social hub of the project, creating a dynamic environment that is overlooked by a series of open balconies which link all the floors and offer spectacular views over the interior.

From the reception, where three plasma television screens play music videos, a curved staircase rises to the first floor at the base of the atrium. This is a large, uplifting space that doubles as an arena for performances, thus enabling EMI to showcase new talent on their own doorstep.

The staff work mainly in open-plan spaces, but this is no standard office factory; each floor has its own distinct feel, owing to a varied palette of materials and colours. Domestic-style break-out areas, with rugs and sofas, are provided throughout the building. This enables people to mix and share ideas away from the structured work environment.

Graphic screens, classic furniture and lines of blue light add verve to the project. Glass walls aim to maximize the natural light within a building that has swept away the last remnants of the 1970s, the decade that style forgot, to create a community where people can come together to listen and learn.

Above EMI's imposing curved glass entrance.
Opposite View into the glazed central courtyard, the spectacular social heart of the project.

Location London, UK
Client EMI
Completed 2003
Total Floor Space 9,012 square metres (97,000 square feet)
Staff 300

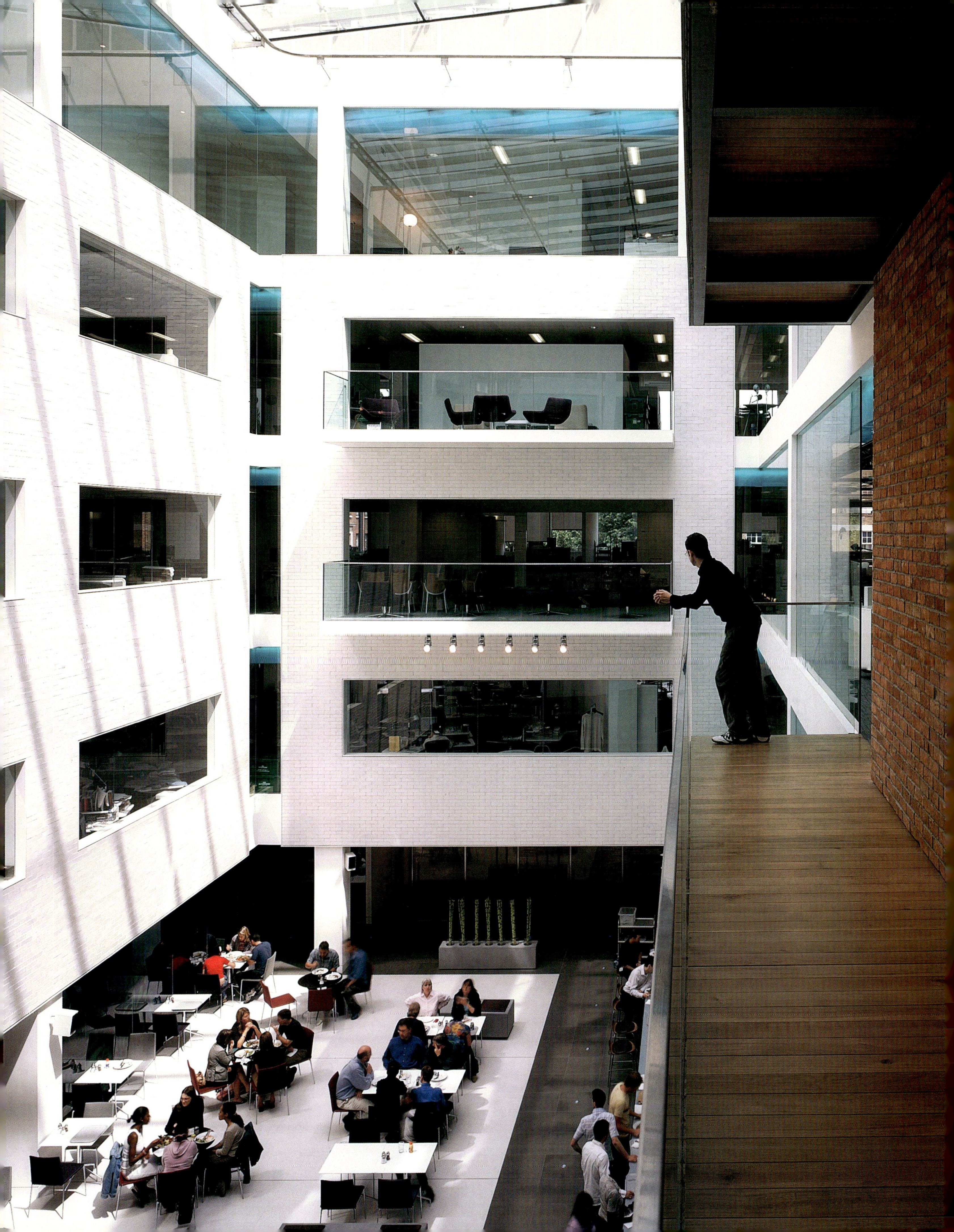

1 entrance
2 atrium
3 open-plan work space
4 open-plan work space
5 studio
6 gymnasium
7 bar

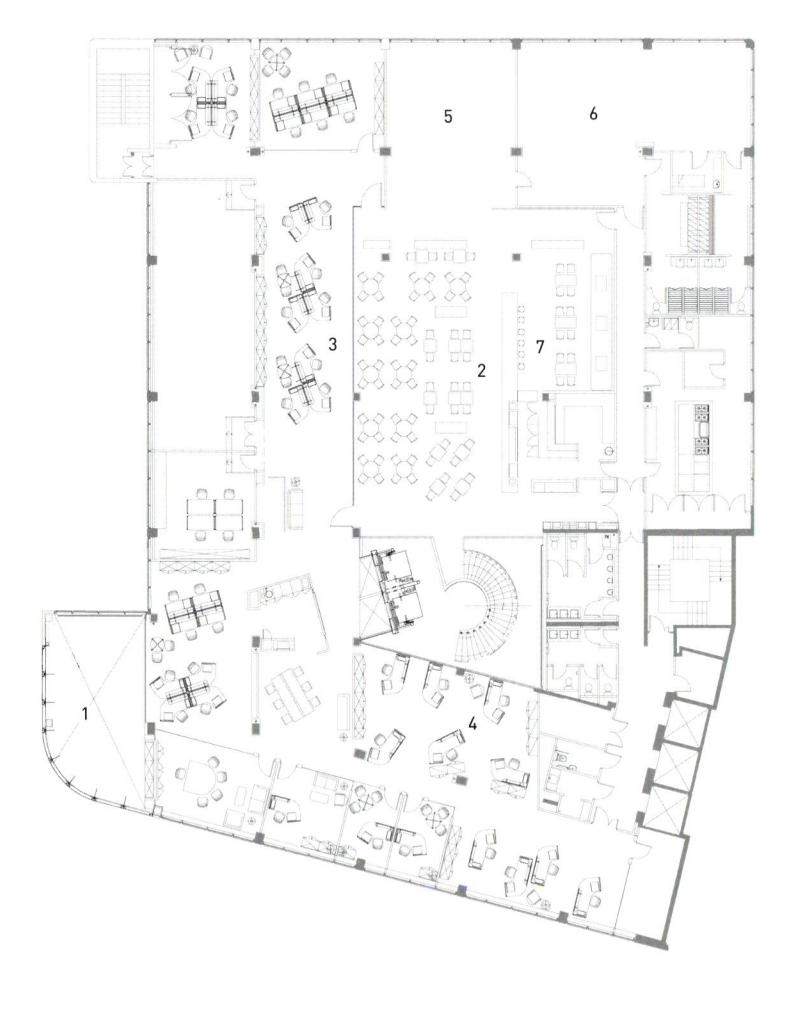

1 atrium
2 open-plan work space
3 open-plan work space
4 meeting room
5 meeting room

Far left First-floor plan shows void over the entrance and central courtyard café.
Above Upper-floor plan shows workstations around the atrium.
Centre Interior view reveals animation at every level.

EMI London Headquarters 71

'This place has a real buzz – the staff love it, but so do our visitors, whether they are artists or shareholders.'
Eric Nicoli, Group Chairman, EMI

Left The EMI project encourages an informal, relaxed work style with colour and graphics playing a key role. Here, large photomural panels refresh an individual workstation.
Above Social breakout area.
Right View towards an area for viewing music videos.

2 Guild
the professional cluster

Offices used to physically cluster together people with a diverse range of professional skills, within the organization that employed them. There was no choice in this matter: it was deemed to be the most cost-effective model, minimized interaction costs and eventually formed the basis of the modern company as we know it. Today, however, a new trend is emerging that allows people to cluster according to their professional skill or specialist area, and that recognizes the growing importance of peer group interaction within a knowledge-based economy.

The term 'Guild' describes a new type of work setting that facilitates collaboration and knowledge building between peers. In one sense it represents a high-tech return to the idea of the medieval craft guilds, who were among the first creators and occupants of bespoke buildings in the city. Guilds are venues that are characterized by a low corporate presence and a high degree of professional mobility. What matters most with this model is the proximity, at least for part of the working day, of those with similar attitudes and ideas to share.

The office interiors in this section express the concept of the Guild, as film makers, policy makers, scientists and entrepreneurs seek out their counterparts in settings that support their shared agenda.

75

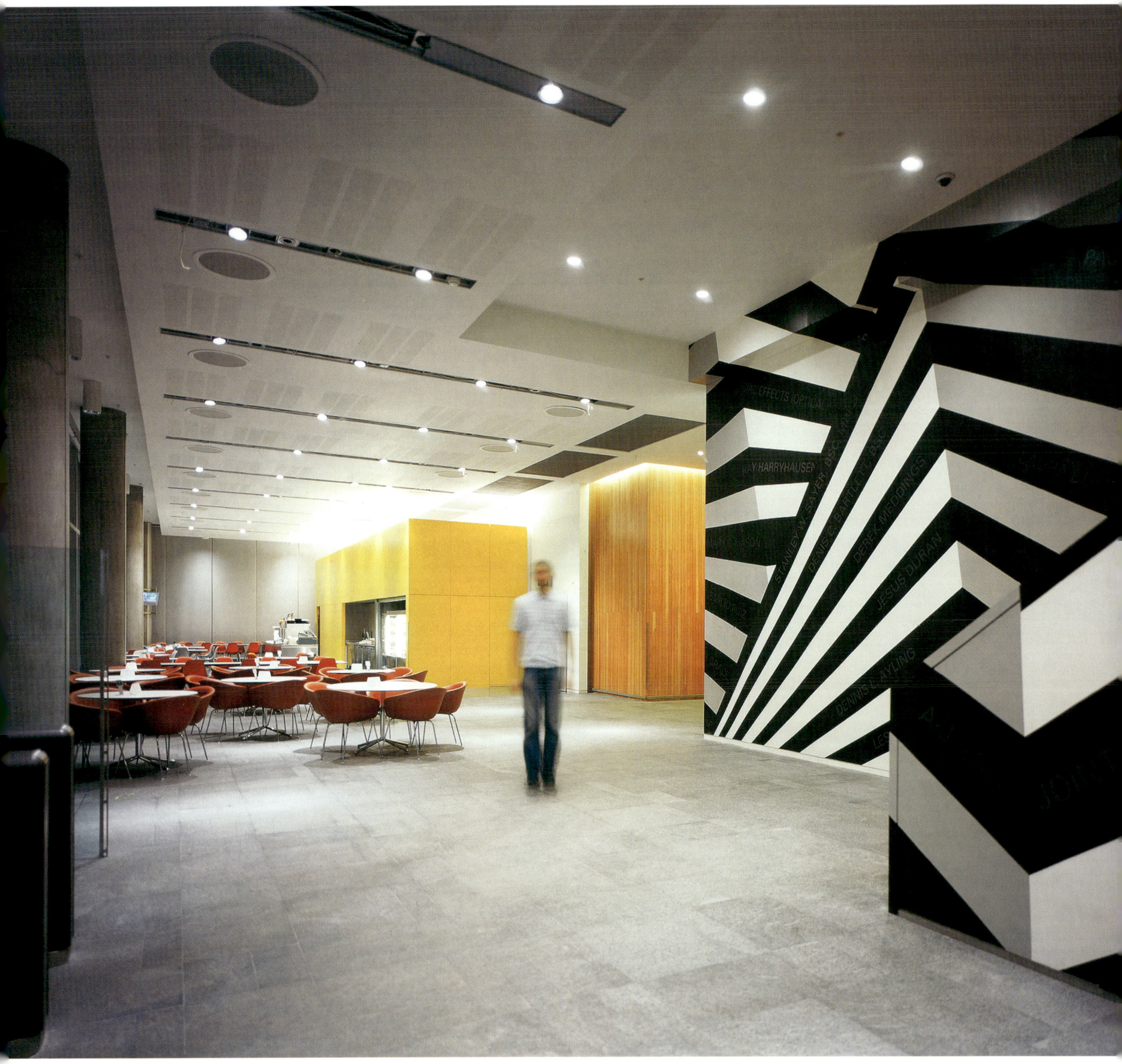

Above Media Centre reception space with dramatic artwork by Yuko Shiraishi.
Left Interior enlivened by a mural painted by Simon Patterson.
Below Group space framed by the atrium staircase.

BBC Media Centre **79**

Above View across the atrium into work areas animated by colour and graphics.
Opposite Club-like environments provide relaxed work settings for BBC staff.

'The new environment introduces a sense of openness and transparency that will radically alter the current perception.' *Allies and Morrison*

2.2
Parliamentary Annexe
Helsinki, Finland
Helin & Co Architects

THE extension to Eduskunta, the parliament of Finland, has been achieved on a historic site adjacent to Sirén's original imposing Parliament House. The extension consists of a triangular building, clad in dark brick, juxtaposed with a lower, cone-shaped block that fits in with the existing surroundings and echoes the shape of the neighbouring buildings.

The new extension houses the offices for 295 MPs and their assistants, as well as the Grand Committee Meeting Room, the Foreign Affairs Meeting Room and other collective spaces, including an auditorium. A restaurant, sitting under the dramatic glass-covered atrium, dominates the lower ground level and provides a focus for the workspace.

Natural materials, such as bedrock and wood, have been cleverly incorporated throughout the building to reflect Finland's resources and provide a nomenclature for the space. Different woods, some felled on the site, are used to panel the spaces that surround the atrium and also tie in with the name of each of the wood-lined meeting rooms – Ash (Saarni), Maple (Vaahtera), Birch (Koivu), Black Poplar (Mustapoppeli), and so on. Unusually, all the furniture has been designed by the architects, and as a result it blends into the space, echoing the serenity of the wood floors and panelling and creating a unified workspace, where clean minimalist surfaces combine with soft furnishings to create a functional set of spaces for work.

The ground floor of the building houses a visitor centre, bookshop and information centre. The public are permitted to engage in the interior spaces of democracy as the glazed façade allows them to see their MPs at work.

Below ground, volume is created in what would otherwise have been a constrained space, with a vast auditorium and the largest committee rooms. Geometry has been used imaginatively here to create an impression of space and grandeur.

This Guild project is designed as a place for individual work by MPs in private offices, and as a public space and a range of meeting environments and information resources. A clear and thoughtful theme, evoked by natural, local materials, creates an atmosphere of understated elegance and simplicity.

Location Helsinki, Finland
Client Parliament of Finland
Completed 2004
Total Floor Space 10,560 square metres (114,635 square feet)
Staff 300

Above Model of the annexe, illustrating the two elements of the building.
Opposite The atrium space provides a focal point for MPs and the public as well as a central café.
Opposite right CAD visualization of the main atrium.

Parliamentary Annexe 83

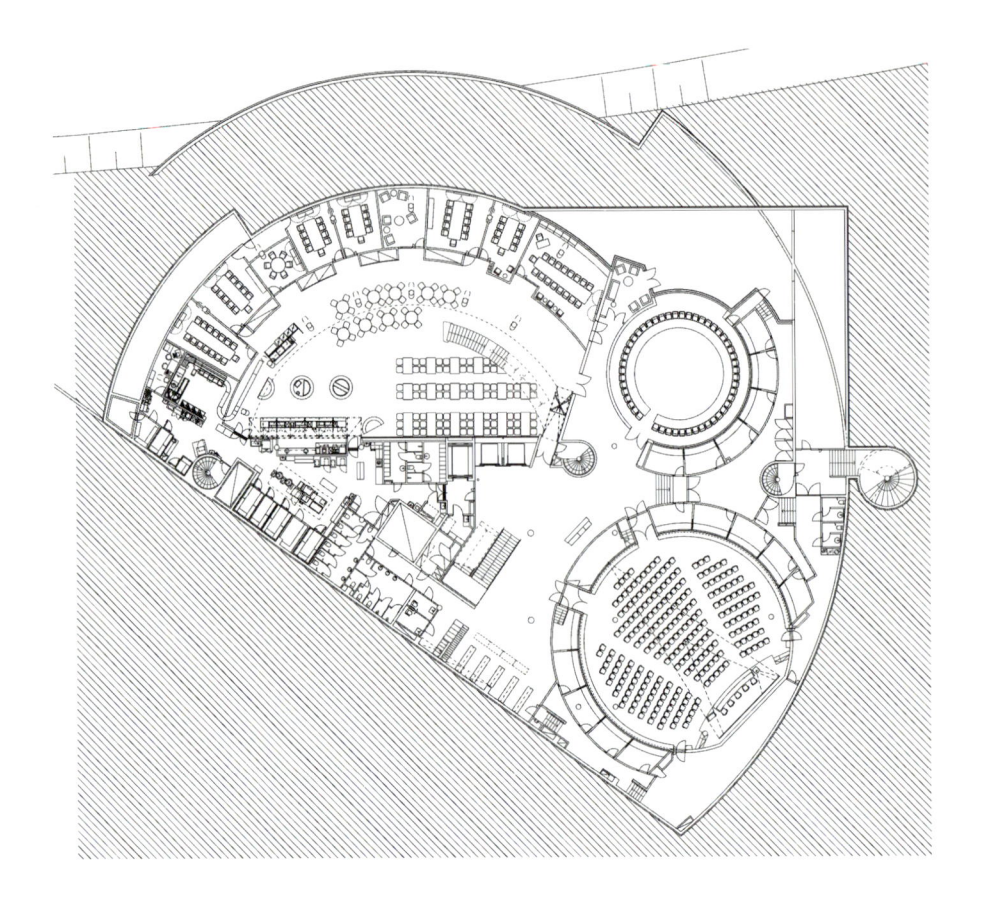

Top Floor plan showing the unusual form of the building and the extensive subterranean facilities, such as the auditorium.
Left Natural Finnish materials have been used extensively throughout.
Above One of a series of places for work and parliamentary meetings.
Opposite left One of the wood-panelled committee rooms, each named after a variety of local timber.
Opposite right A typical example of an MP's office, designed with bespoke desk furniture as well as, out of view, more informal 'soft' seating.

'The Parliament building is articulated into two parts, with an atrium as the heart of the building.'
Pekka Helin

2.3
Future Centre
Innsbruck, Austria
Peter Lorenz

PETER Lorenz's solution for an adventurous workspace plays on new materials and raw finishes to present an environment in which people can discuss and understand future work trends and technologies. Designed for Austria's Labour Association, the space was created to provide resources for life-long learning, so that its members can keep up to date with emerging work methods and media. It was also intended to spark creative thinking, new ideas and inspirations through its play between the predictable and the unexpected.

The space has been kept open to allow clear orientation and to provide for easy reconfiguration and change. The project is designed as an 'experimental work in progress', so the space has a combination of variable and permanent elements. Three discrete areas provide the visitor with different environments, based around work processes and technologies. The 'working zone' is arranged rationally while the 'study section' has a more organic design. In between these two spaces, a 'public square' has been created as a place for communication, discussion and presentation, with a café and multimedia virtual reality arena.

Lorenz has used materials to create a sense of the unexpected, exposing services that are usually hidden, such as the blue chilled-beam system on the ceiling or the uncovered tinted raised-floor system. In a similar vein, a central orange translucent box has been built to house the washrooms. Elsewhere, red acoustic felt has been used as a wall covering and green outdoor sports surfacing has been chosen for floor coverings.

This Guild environment helps people who are involved in the creation of workplaces and the management of people to think about the future together, by providing them with an inventive space in which to gather, share ideas and develop new concepts.

Location Innsbruck, Austria
Client Association of Employees/Workers
Completed 2003
Total Floor Space 2,200 square metres (23,680 square feet)
Staff 15

Above The Future Centre provides a place for creative thinking and new ideas about the future of work. Here, floor-to-ceiling virtual reality displays immerse people who gather to consider future ideas in a 'public square'.

'We do not know anything about the future, but we will arrange it nevertheless.'
Peter Lorenz

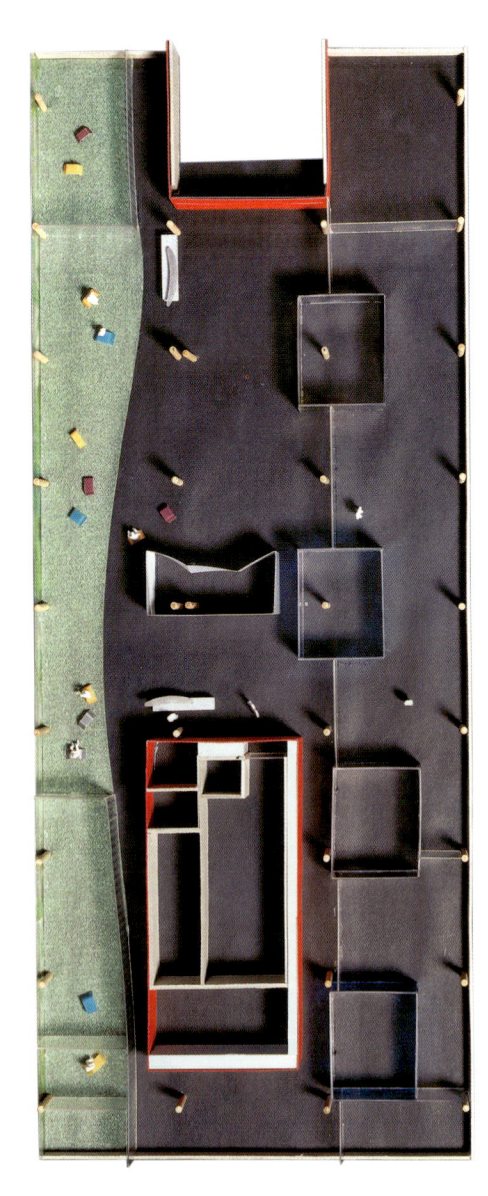

Top Looking across a presentation area into the translucent box that houses the washrooms and other facilities.
Above Aerial view of the Future Centre model.
Right View into one of the experience zones. Images are displayed on vertical plasma screens around the space.

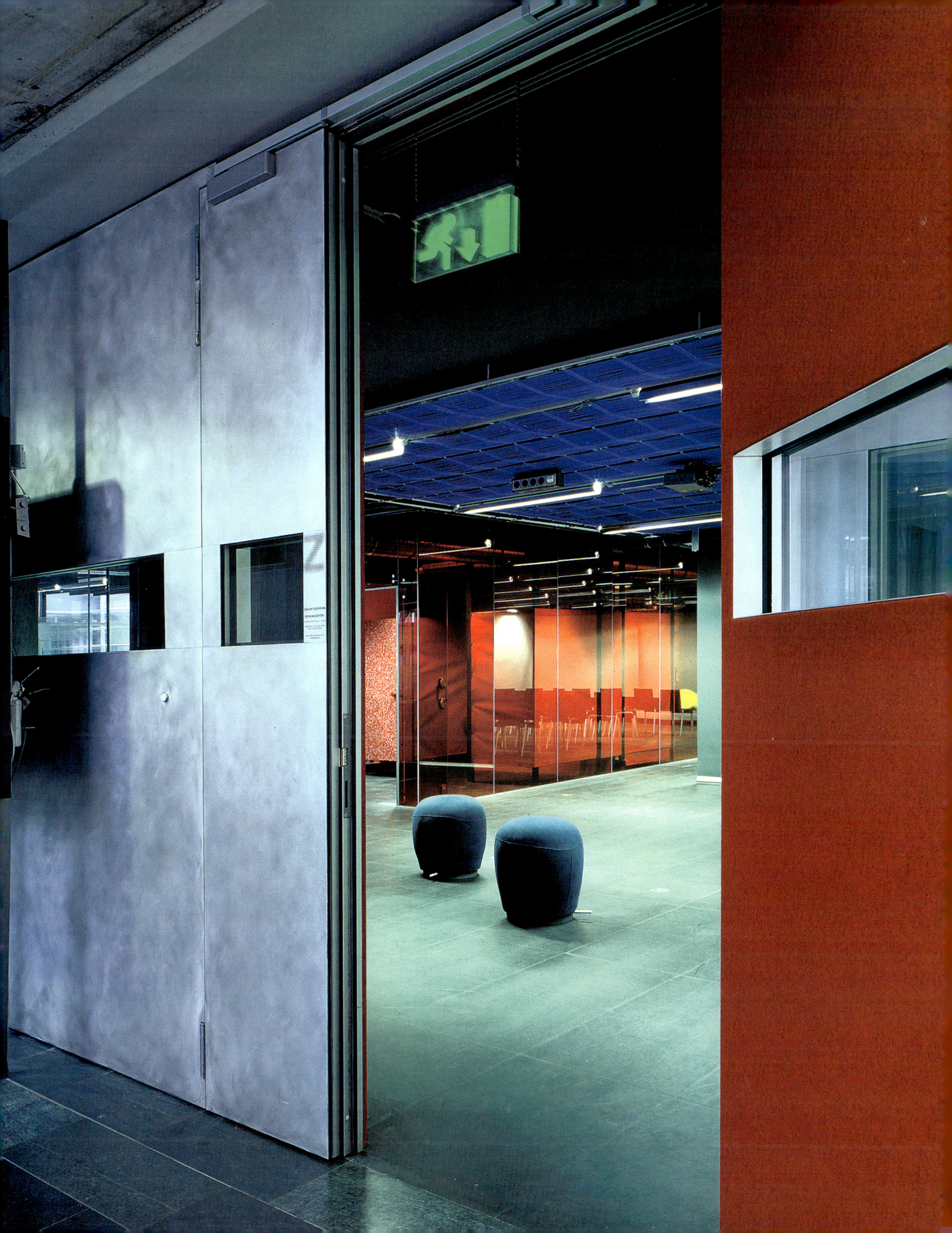

2.4
Momentum
Hørsholm, Denmark
Bosch & Fjord

MOMENTUM is an innovation centre on a Danish science park. It has been conceived as an unorthodox retreat for business people enabling them to step outside the day-to-day pressures of working life for short periods of time in order to help them to think inventive thoughts.

The artist-duo Bosch & Fjord, who transformed a nondescript warehouse to create this provocative environment for creative ideas, believe that 'innovation happens when art and the working process meet'. The project uses art in what they describe as an 'undercover way'. A series of installations creates imaginative spaces that encourage participants to approach their work from a new angle. They include, for example, an 'intimate meeting room' with a deliberately low ceiling that forces you to sit in a sunken pit in the centre of the room. In ways such as this, meetings and decisions at Momentum are bound to vary from the norm.

The steel-ringed tower around a spiral staircase leads up to an open-air meeting space, where a normal meeting with an agenda and business papers is made impossible by the wind and elements. The 'reflection room' is reached via a totally black 'dead-end corridor' and eventually turns out to be a toilet with a special soundtrack playing church bells, the sound of fires crackling and beach parties. The 'screaming room' is covered in reflective panels; here you can confront yourself and let it all out. The 'dynamic space' is for group brainstorming and features a full-length whiteboard wall. The functional kitchen is where everyone is encouraged to eat together.

It is easy to deride all these features as faddish, (there are also a snake-shaped table and an internal lake) but Momentum, which is funded by the SCION/DTU science park, is undeniably a fun workplace for business managers from private and public sector organizations to come together. The scheme does not take itself too seriously, but it is executed with the utmost conviction and its underlying message is an important one: if you want to generate unpredictable ideas, you need to spend time in an unpredictable environment.

Location Hørsholm, Denmark
Client Momentum and SCION/DTU
Completed 2004
Total Floor Space 466 square metres (5,016 square feet)
Accommodates 90

Above Section shows a steel-ringed tower that extrudes from the building, creating an open-air meeting space.
Top A moment of contemplation by the internal lake.
Opposite Inside the 'intimate meeting room' with its deliberately lowered ceiling that changes the dynamic of any business meeting.

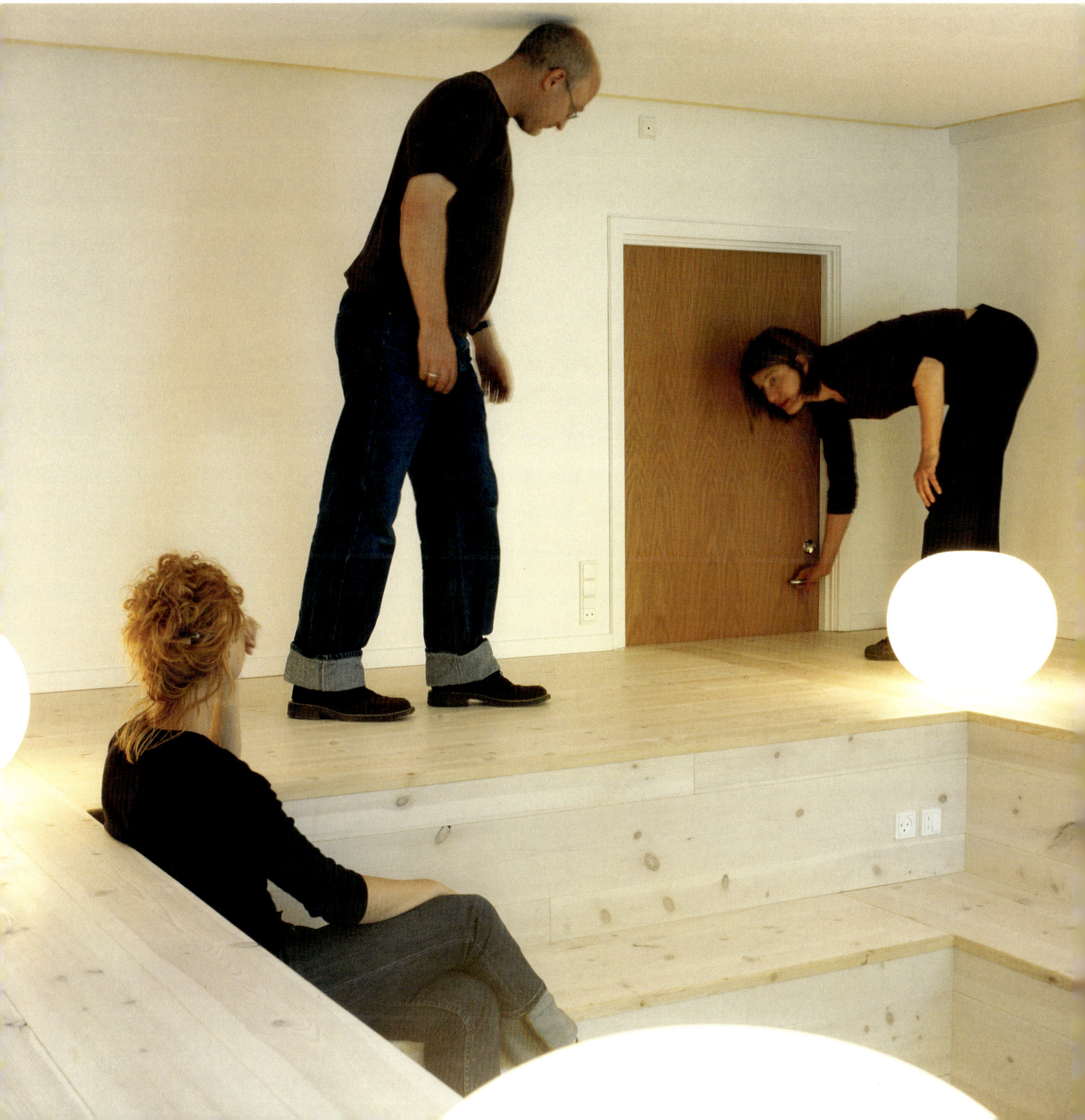

'In Momentum, art has been fused with the aim of the organization, the working processes and the building.'
Helene Øllgaard, Bosch & Fjord

Left to right An unpredictable environment to generate offbeat ideas: snake table; the mirrored 'screaming room'; kitchen diner; and brainstorming area.

Momentum **93**

2.5
Scottish Parliament Building
Edinburgh, Scotland
Enric Miralles Benedetta Tagliabue Embt Arquitectes Associats SL/RMJM

SPANISH architect Enric Miralles' spectacular building for Scotland's new parliament not only creates a landmark for the city of Edinburgh, but also establishes a workplace model that brings together a cluster of working spaces across ten buildings for a group of like-minded people.

The World Heritage Site that sits at the bottom of Edinburgh's Royal Mile, in the shadow of King Arthur's Seat, provided a challenging urban setting for the architects. The new buildings had to be shoehorned into a constrained site on a medieval street plan. The resulting micro-campus nevertheless engages with the city, maintaining an intimacy with its citizens and realizing Miralles' original competition entry, which was based on 'bundles of leaves and sticks representing a gathering of the land'.

The architect's expert play with angles and vistas results in few straight lines or right angles. As a result, everything leaves the visitor with a sense of the new and unexpected, and while externally a sense of intrigue is established, internally the architect has created an excellent Guild environment.

From the members' building with its extruded window pods through to the garden lobby with its roof of 'upturned boats', MPs are led into an almost elliptical debating chamber where adversarial politics have been abandoned, one feels, for a more collegiate, enlightened and inspiring setting.

Throughout, traditional Scottish materials, such as the sycamore joinery and dark Caithness stone, contrast with more contemporary stainless-steel cladding and polished concrete. A mêlée of inspirations ranges from the oriental 'bamboo-like' ornamentation on the windows to the Scandinavian simplicity of the Donald Dewar Library.

As a Guild environment for politicians, it combines this magnificent series of public spaces with well-considered work environments. MPs have discrete, private offices that provide a place for contemplation in the remarkable pods or window seats that hang from the façade of the members' building. These provide a unique quirk in what are otherwise small, functional offices with bespoke furniture and fitted storage that is purpose-designed in oak and sycamore. From these 'monastic cells', MPs can reflect on the issues of the day. The extensive use of glass that maximizes natural daylight is also intended to 'bring the land of Scotland into the building', and the neighbouring Salisbury Crags and Palace of Holyroodhouse certainly provide a dramatic backdrop for this inspiring place to work.

Location Edinburgh, Scotland
Client Scottish Parliament
Completed 2004
Total Floor Space 30,000 square metres (322,900 square feet)
Staff 1,200

Above The Scottish Parliament nestles below King Arthur's Seat at the bottom of Edinburgh's Royal Mile.
Below Site plan of the Parliament showing the cluster of ten buildings.
Opposite View inside an MPs private office, with its bespoke furniture and contemplation seat.
Following pages
Left A typical committee room provides a place for meetings and discussion.
Right External view of the remarkable extruded window pods on the members' building.

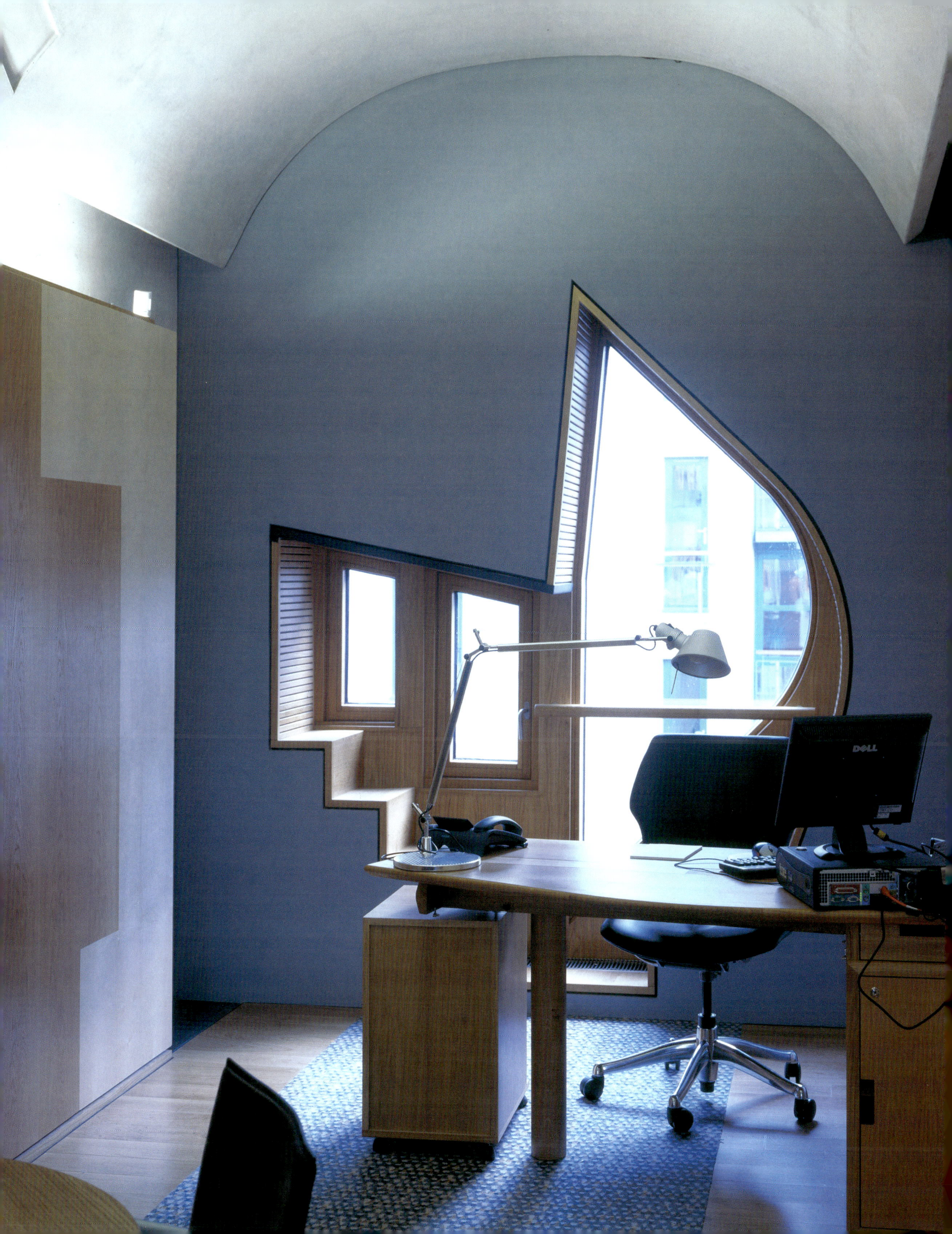

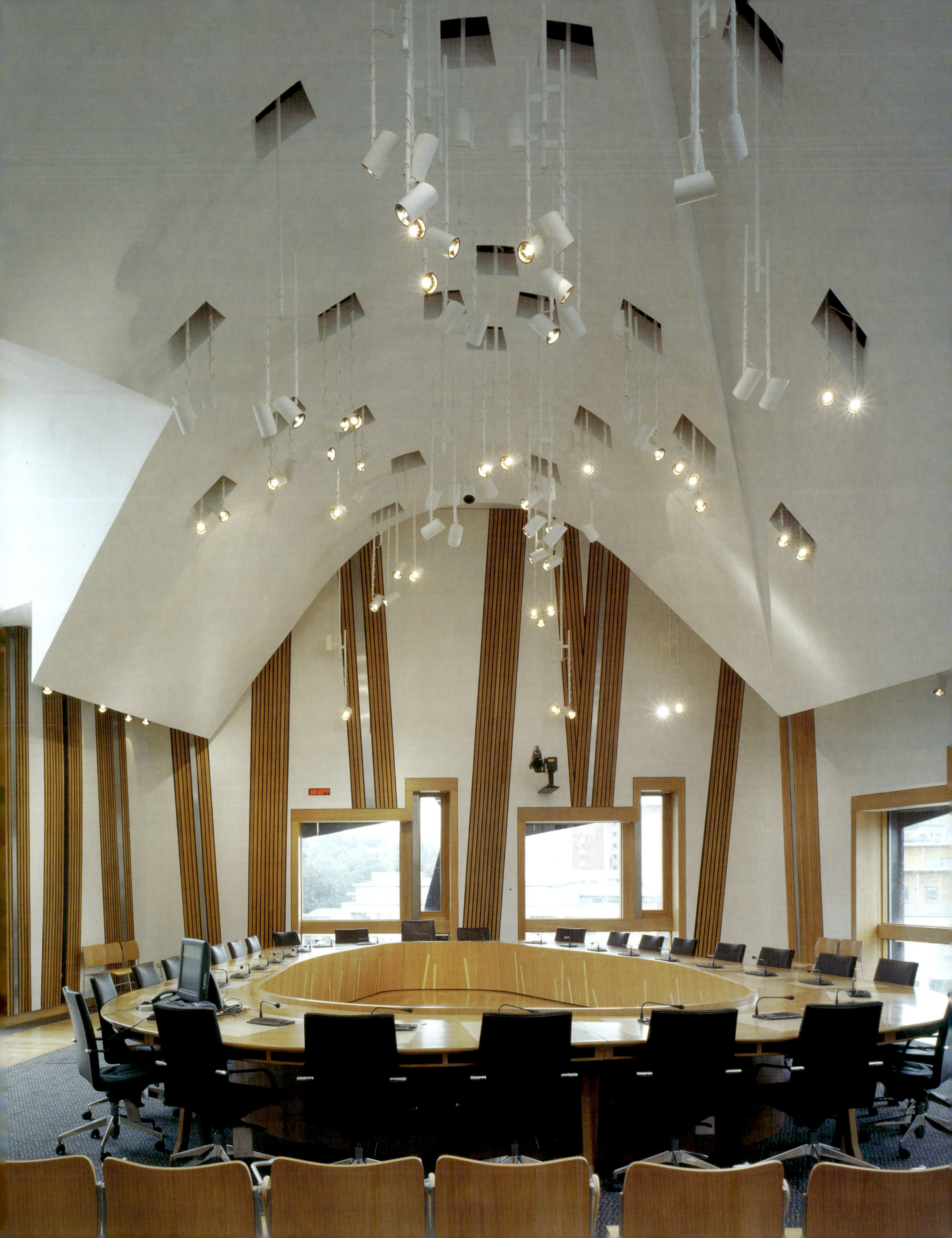

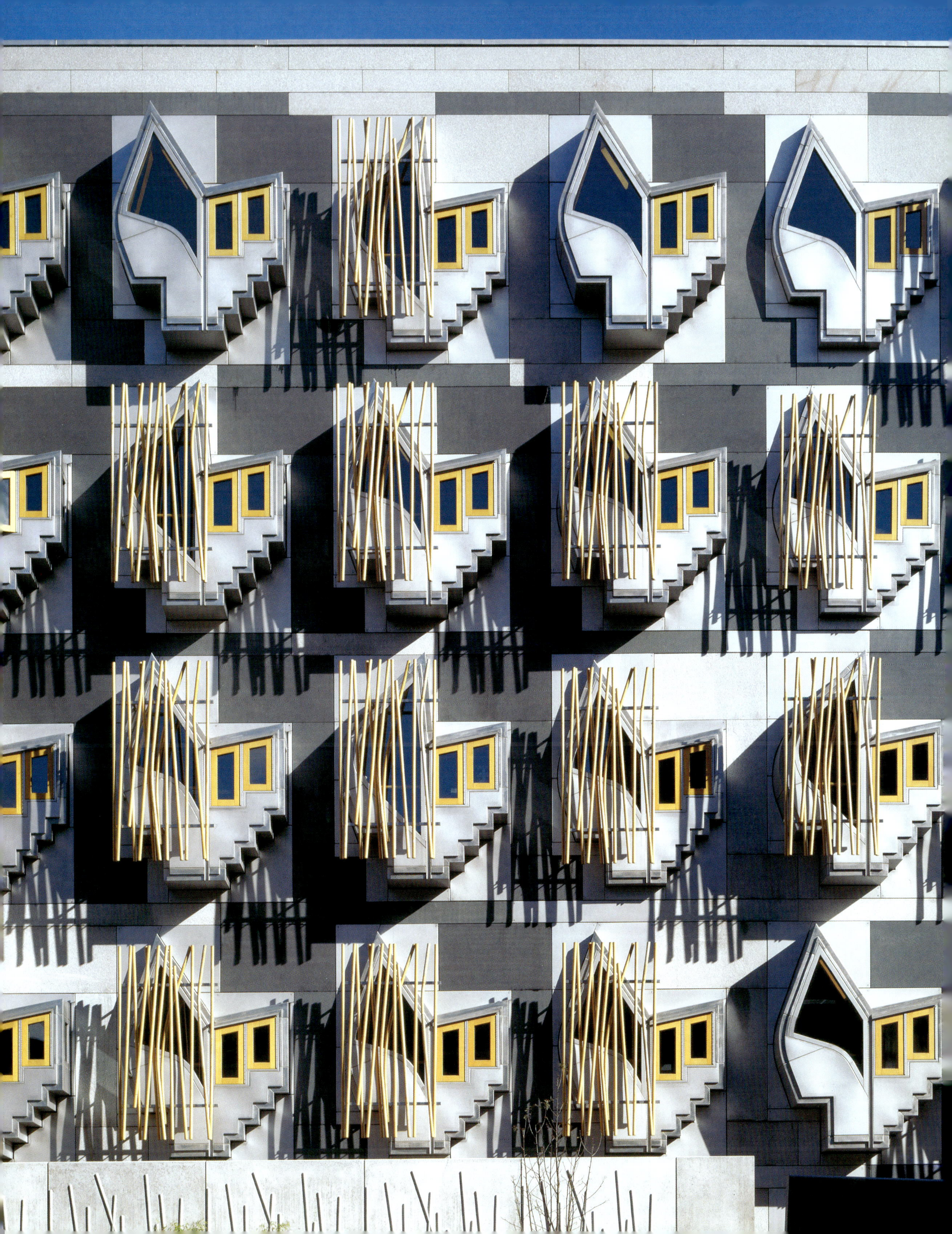

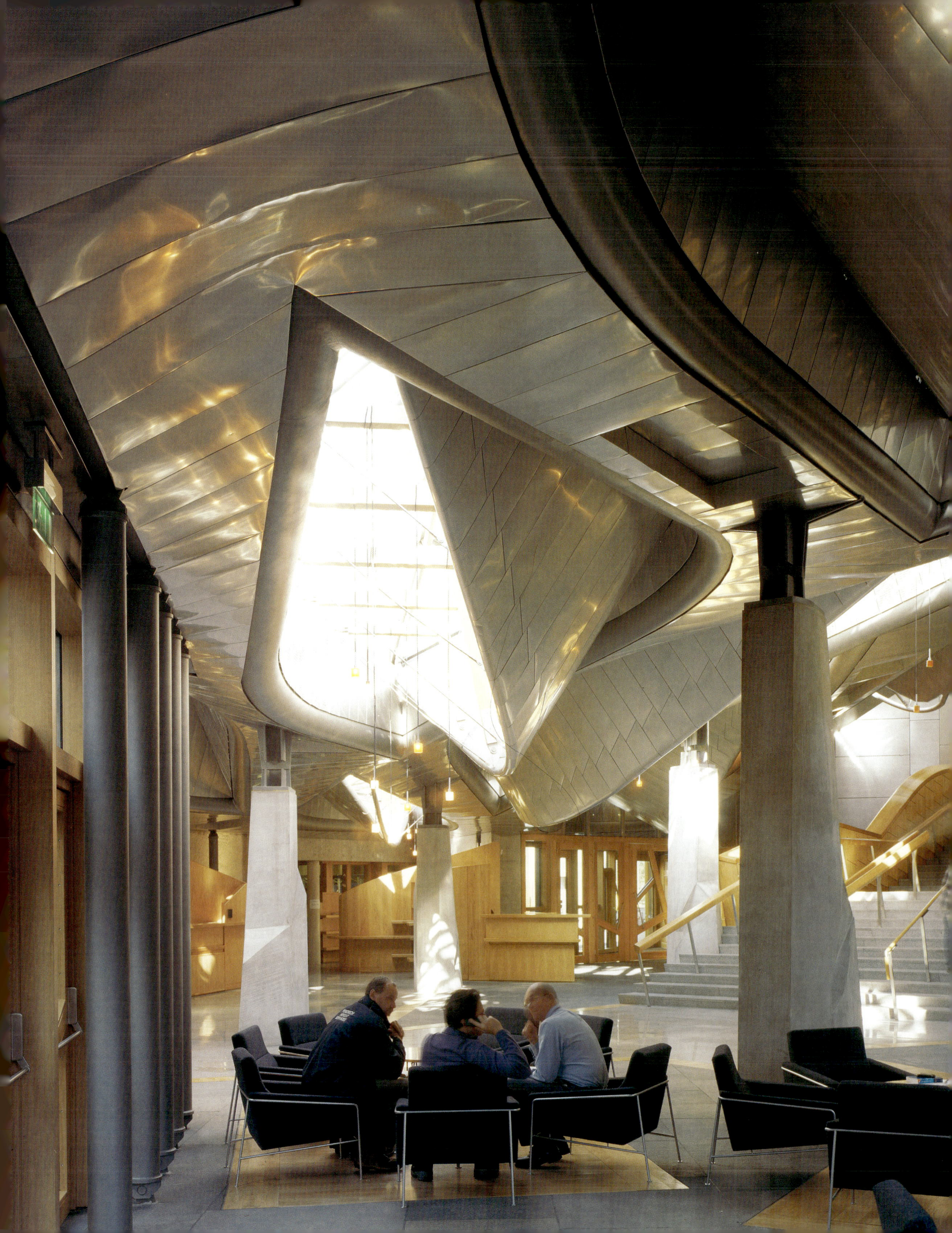

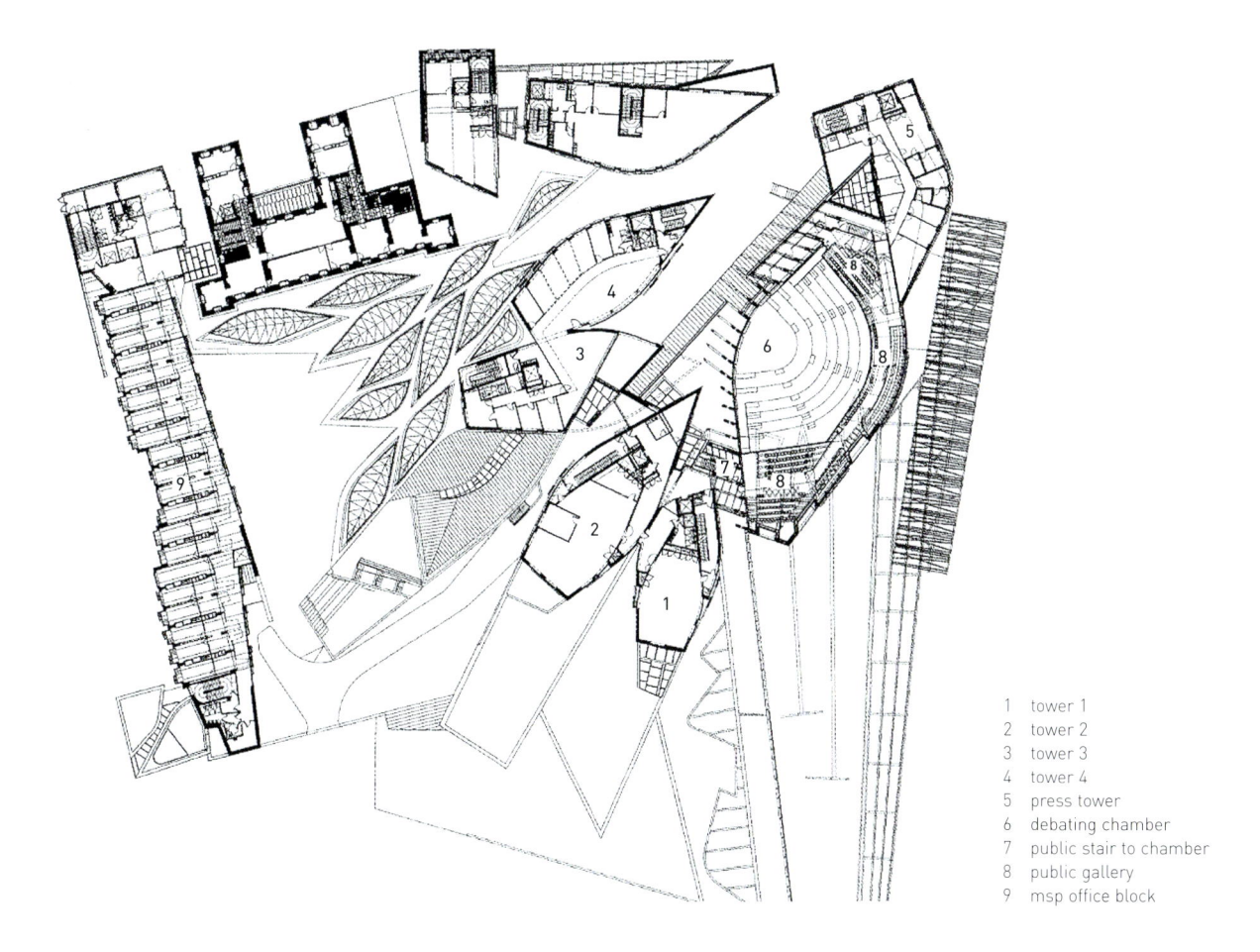

1 tower 1
2 tower 2
3 tower 3
4 tower 4
5 press tower
6 debating chamber
7 public stair to chamber
8 public gallery
9 msp office block

'The Parliament sits on the land. We have the feeling that the building should be land, built out of land. To carve in the land the form of gathering people together.' *Enric Miralles*

Opposite A roof of 'upturned boats' creates a feature in the garden lobby.
Top Miralles' original competition entry for the building described 'bundles of leaves and sticks'.
Above Materials such as sycamore have been used to give spaces such as the Donald Dewar Library a Scandinavian simplicity.

Scottish Parliament Building **99**

2.6
ESO Hotel
Cerro Paranal, Chile
Auer+Weber+Architekten

BUFFETED by uncontrollable winds, exposed to blazing sun by day and extreme cold by night, lacking water and vegetation, and with every chance of an earthquake, the ESO Hotel can hardly be described as the perfect site for tourism. For professional astronomers, however, its hostile location, on the top of a small mountain in northern Chile's Atacama Desert at the coastal location of Cerro Paranal, makes it an ideal workplace.

It is here that the European Southern Observatory (ESO) has sited a large telescope for use by its astronomy researchers. The ESO Hotel is where the researchers stay and work. Partly buried in a desert hollow at the foot of the mountain, this 'trade-only' hotel has been designed by the Munich-based firm Auer+Weber+Architekten on the principle of 'earth architecture as land art'. Accordingly, their austere-looking building has an almost art installation quality, owing to its desert location and the way local materials have been used to match the earthy, reddish colours of its surroundings.

Contemplation for the visiting specialists and protection from the elements are the keynotes of this scheme. Its 108 bedrooms, offering infinite views over the desert, are arranged in linear rows with light penetrating them horizontally. The public spaces are protected from the sun by being grouped in the centre of the building and lit only from above through translucent polycarbonate slabs. These spaces, described by the architects as 'sunken courts serving as climatic wells', include a circular courtyard of cactuses and palm trees, and a swimming pool under a geodesic dome.

This is very much a one-off project in terms of topology and function. In creating a Guild-like space for astronomers to live together and share their views, it demonstrates a creative and practical achievement amid an extremely hostile natural environment.

Location Cerro Paranal, Chile
Client European Southern Observatory
Completed 2002
Total Floor Space 12,450 square metres (134,000 square feet)
Accommodates 120

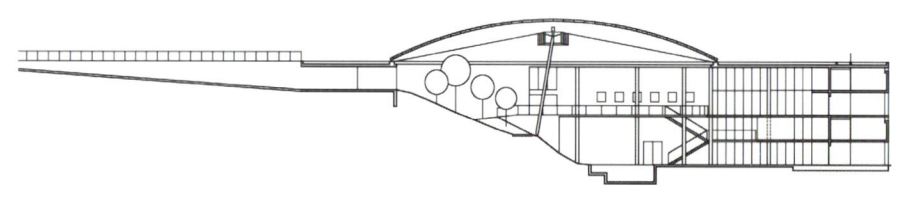

Above and below Sections show how this professional base for astronomers is built into the landscape.
Left and opposite Interior views reflect the themes of protection from the elements and contemplation.

'There is a stimulating correlation for the mind and the senses between "sky" and "earth".'
Auer+Weber+Architekten

100 Guild

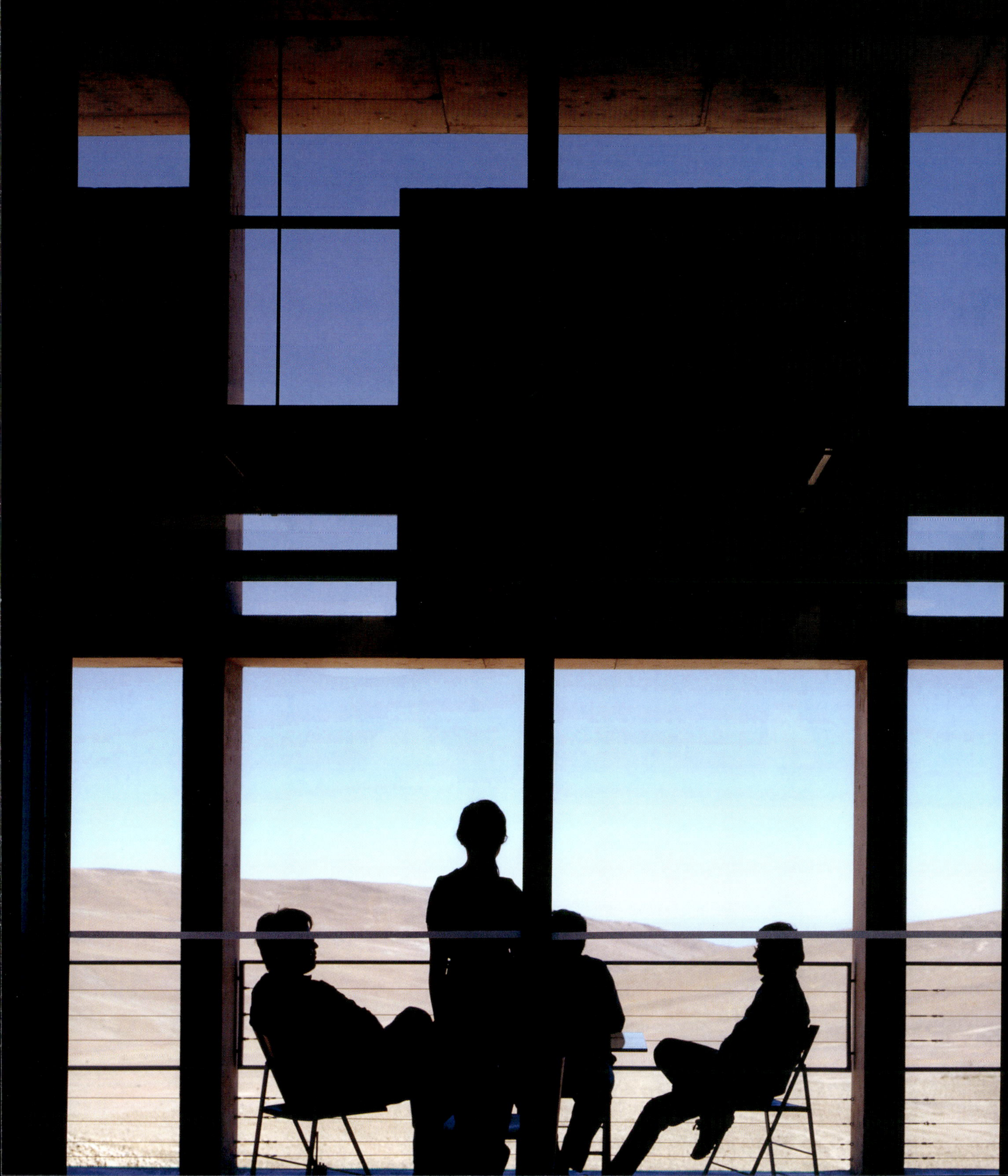

2.7
The Royal Society
London, UK
Burrell Foley Fischer LLP

THE Royal Society in London is one of the world's greatest scientific institutions. Its grand home, in a Grade 1 listed Nash building in London's Carlton House Terrace, reflects its historic status as a place where the finest minds congregate. This sense of tradition, however, was not considered sufficient to marry its rich research heritage to a more modern and progressive image, so in 1999 the Royal Society decided to completely reorganize and refurbish its headquarters in the four connected houses it had occupied since the 1960s.

The brief to the architects specified a scheme that reflects the Royal Society's position at the forefront of science, but also provides a flexible and efficient working environment. Better use of space, clear zoning of areas for access by visitors, Fellows and staff, and suitable facilities for the ceremonial and social functions of the Royal Society were also included in the brief.

The resulting scheme, cleverly phased in over four years so that the organization did not have to move out, creates a contemporary Guild space that enhances the environment of this scientific community in a spectacular and timeless fashion. The redevelopment also provides additional facilities for exhibitions, scientific meetings, seminars, media events and video conferencing, with a new sequence of spaces opened up in the basement. It pays close attention to improved public circulation, provides a new entrance and creates a top-lit glazed atrium in a former light well on the upper levels as a focus for the new offices. These offices optimize the use of space within the envelope of the terrace, providing 30 per cent more desk space through a linked series of work areas.

The overall effect is one of an august organization, resplendent in coordinated new interiors that give a sense of calm and understated authority. Given the architectural provenance of the building – as the German Embassy in the 1930s it underwent a refurbishment variously attributed to Speer and Ribbentropp – this was a high-profile project, but the interventions have been skilfully planned and detailed, creating a space where scientific leaders can learn from each other.

Location London, UK
Client The Royal Society
Completed 2003
Total Floor Space 6,040 square metres (65,000 square feet)
Staff 129

Above Sectional perspective shows new entrance, waiting and exhibition areas, main staircase and upper-level atrium.
Left A new front door completes the scheme.
Opposite View of atrium.

$$\frac{d\sigma}{d\Omega} = \left(\frac{Ze^2}{4\pi\varepsilon_0 m v^2}\right)$$

$$i\hbar \frac{\partial \psi}{\partial t} = (\alpha \cdot cp + \beta m_0 c^2)\psi$$

DIRAC

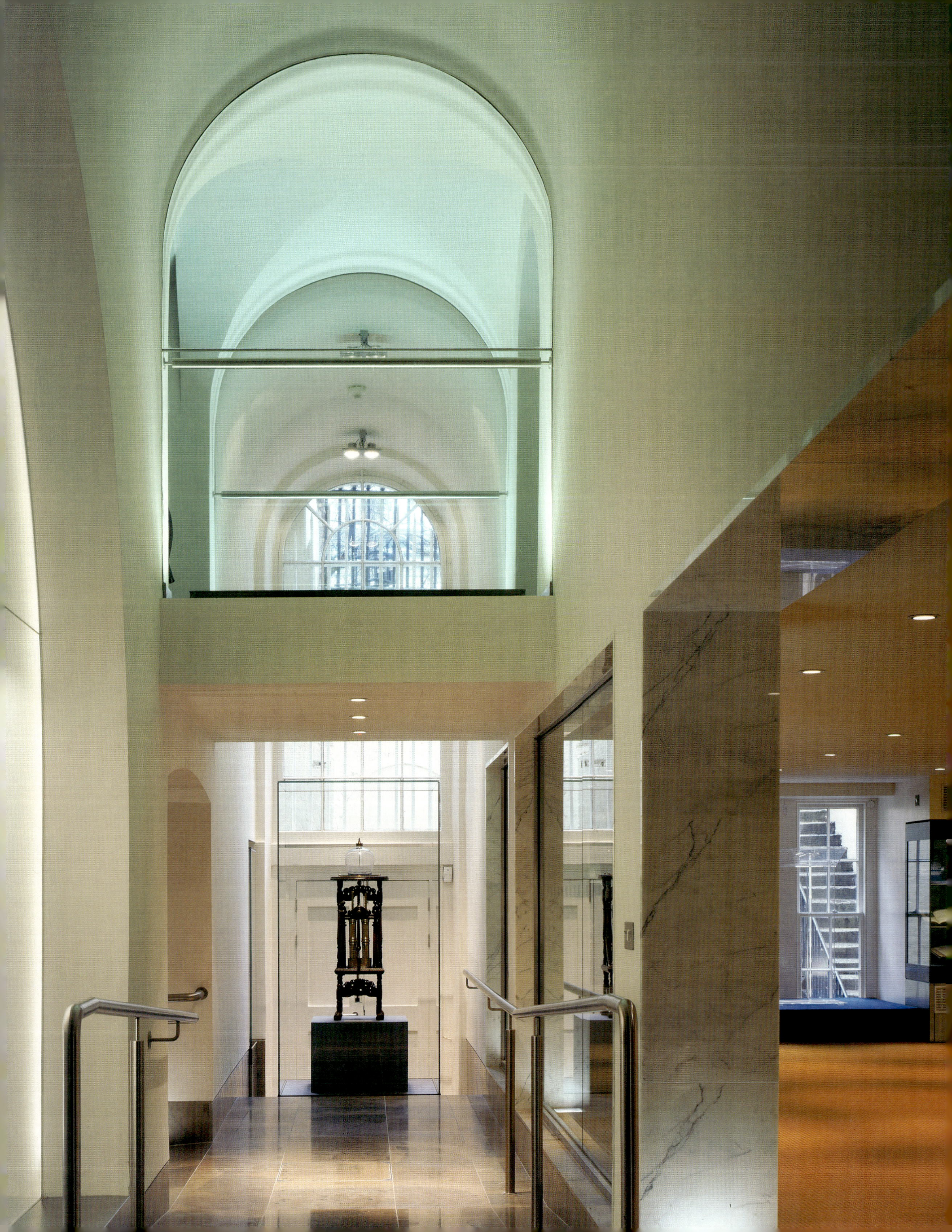

'The project celebrates the individual histories of four houses, while achieving coherent organization and presentation of the Royal Society's facilities and values.'
Stefanie Fischer, Burrell Foley Fischer

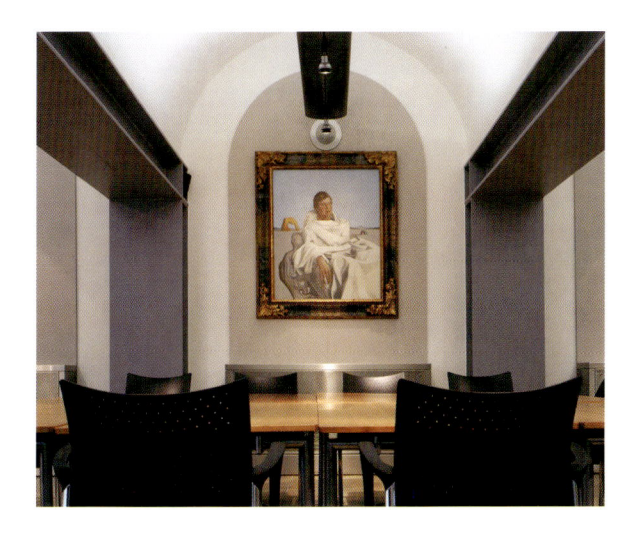

Opposite Ramped access to Brian Mercer Suite with view of bridge to library stacks.
Top left Vaulted meeting space in Brian Mercer Suite.
Top right New reception space.
Above Archive room with dining room beyond.

2.8
Pixar Animation Studios
Emeryville, USA
Bohlin Cywinski Jackson

PIXAR is the award-winning computer animation studio responsible for such popular movie hits as *Toy Story*, *A Bug's Life*, *Monsters, Inc.*, *Finding Nemo* and *The Incredibles*. Creatively led by former Disney animator John Lasseter, the company has built a reputation for combining artistic originality and humour with ground-breaking technical expertise. Indeed Pixar's CEO is Steve Jobs, founder and chief of Apple Computer.

The key to Pixar's success lies in uniting all the crafts required to make a feature-length animation within one dynamic creative process. The onus is therefore on maintaining a culture and environment in which some of the world's best writers, artists, animators and computer engineers can come together to collaborate effectively.

Pixar started as a small independent studio in 1996 with just 44 staff. But as its fame grew so did the organization and the requirement for a larger base. A new corporate headquarters and animation studio was planned for a 6-hectare (15-acre) rural campus at Emeryville, a small town just 20 minutes drive from San Francisco across the Bay Bridge. Not surprisingly, communication between professional peers and cross-pollination of ideas lay at the heart of the design challenge to architects Bohlin Cywinski Jackson.

The resulting industrial-looking facility is vast, but also carefully crafted to be human in scale. There are only two floors, so staff can go anywhere without taking an elevator. A communal fleet of kick scooters also helps to shrink distances. The main building is set in verdant landscaped grounds with room for expansion.

A simple, exposed architectural language is described by a rigorously limited palette of materials – brick, glass, wood decking, sandblasted structural steel and stainless steel – in an unconscious metaphor for the way that Pixar lays itself bare as an incubator of ideas within the space.

The creative and technical sections at the east and west ends of the building are linked by a large central atrium, measuring 18 metres (60 feet) across, which acts as the 'town square' of the scheme. Incorporating a 25-seat theatre, café, conference rooms and lounges, this internal piazza is spanned by 15 triangular trusses and two pedestrian bridges suspended by cables from the roof trusses. It provides a sense of social animation right at the heart of a Guild environment dedicated to attracting and retaining the top talent in the field.

Location Emeryville, USA
Client Pixar Animation Studios
Completed 2000
Total Floor Space 18,580 square metres (200,000 square feet)
Staff 500

Above The façade of the Pixar main building at night exposes the workings within.
Opposite View of the main steel-framed central atrium with social spaces to promote chance encounters between animation professionals.

Pixar Animation Studios **107**

'The integration of light, volume and technology facilitates a sophisticated, humane and interactive workplace.' *Bohlin Cywinski Jackson*

Above View of the café area within the main 'town square'. The industrial aesthetic of elegant, robust design is carried through to other shared spaces **(opposite)** within the main building.

2.9
Max Planck Institute of Molecular Cell Biology and Genetics
Dresden, Germany
Heikkinen-Komonen Architects

ON a landmark site just a few kilometres from the historic centre of Dresden, on the edge of a university campus and adjacent to the River Elbe, is the Max Planck Institute of Molecular Cell Biology and Genetics, a working community for scientists that is designed to promote, above all else, their interaction with each other.

The Institute's Finnish director, Kai Simons, believes that 'the key to science is communication'. He wanted to make sure that his researchers talked to each other every day, so he appointed Finnish architects Mikko Heikkinen and Markku Komonen to create an environment in which a problem shared is a problem solved. Right from the start, the government-funded project set out to encourage scientists not to hide away in their labs, but to mingle constantly with their professional peers and colleagues.

The institute is planned in linear form around six laboratories, each of which is 1,100 square metres (11,840 square feet) in size. These connect to a large central hall that has an espresso bar and restaurant on the ground floor and a library, auditorium and office facilities nearby. A cluster of access towers in the centre of the hall links this communication centre to the rest of the building, which has a foyer and meeting space on each floor.

Externally, a green, mesh-like aluminium grill regulates the flow of natural light into the building. This fronts the blue-coloured aluminium panelling and clear and opaque glass of the façade and acts as a filter to create a more atmospheric light. This lightness of exterior treatment also contrasts with the more solid, earthy interior tones, which feature a ground floor laid with German sandstone and lift towers and bridges of concrete. Built into the façade are two wooden pavilions, one at each end, designed for social use in the summer and affording excellent river views. These form part of a meticulous and surprisingly elegant architectural strategy to create a Guild-like workplace for molecular scientists to contribute to the economic revival of the former East Germany.

Location Dresden, Germany
Client Max Planck Institute of Molecular Cell Biology and Genetics
Completed 2001
Total Floor Space 22,070 square metres (237,600 square feet)
Staff 280

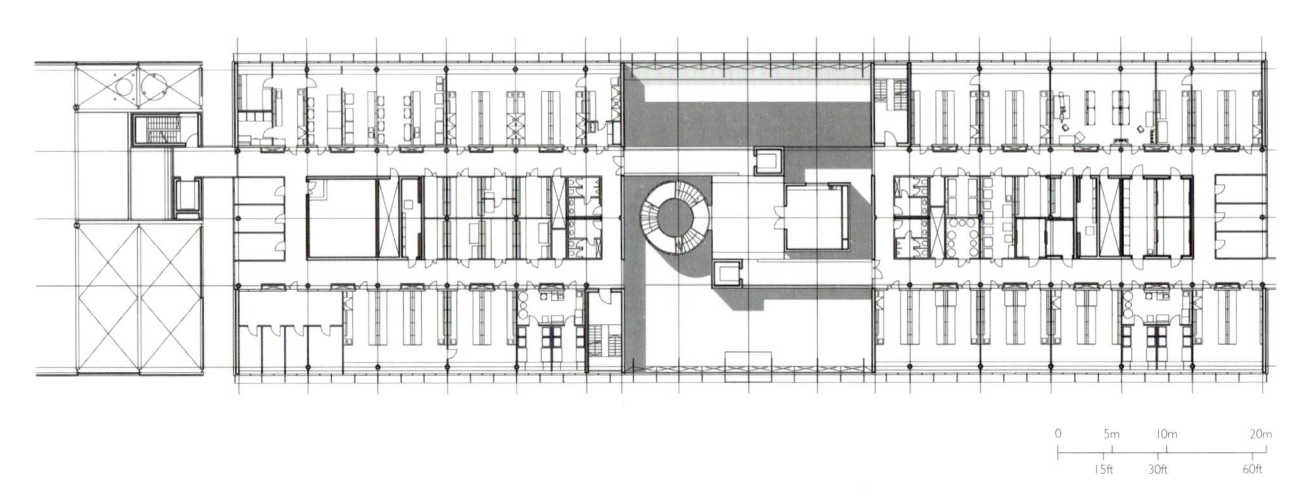

Above Second-floor plan, with patio and meeting space at the centre for social interaction.
Top Wooden pavilion incorporated into the building façade.
Opposite View of the ground-floor study lounge which sits next to an auditorium.

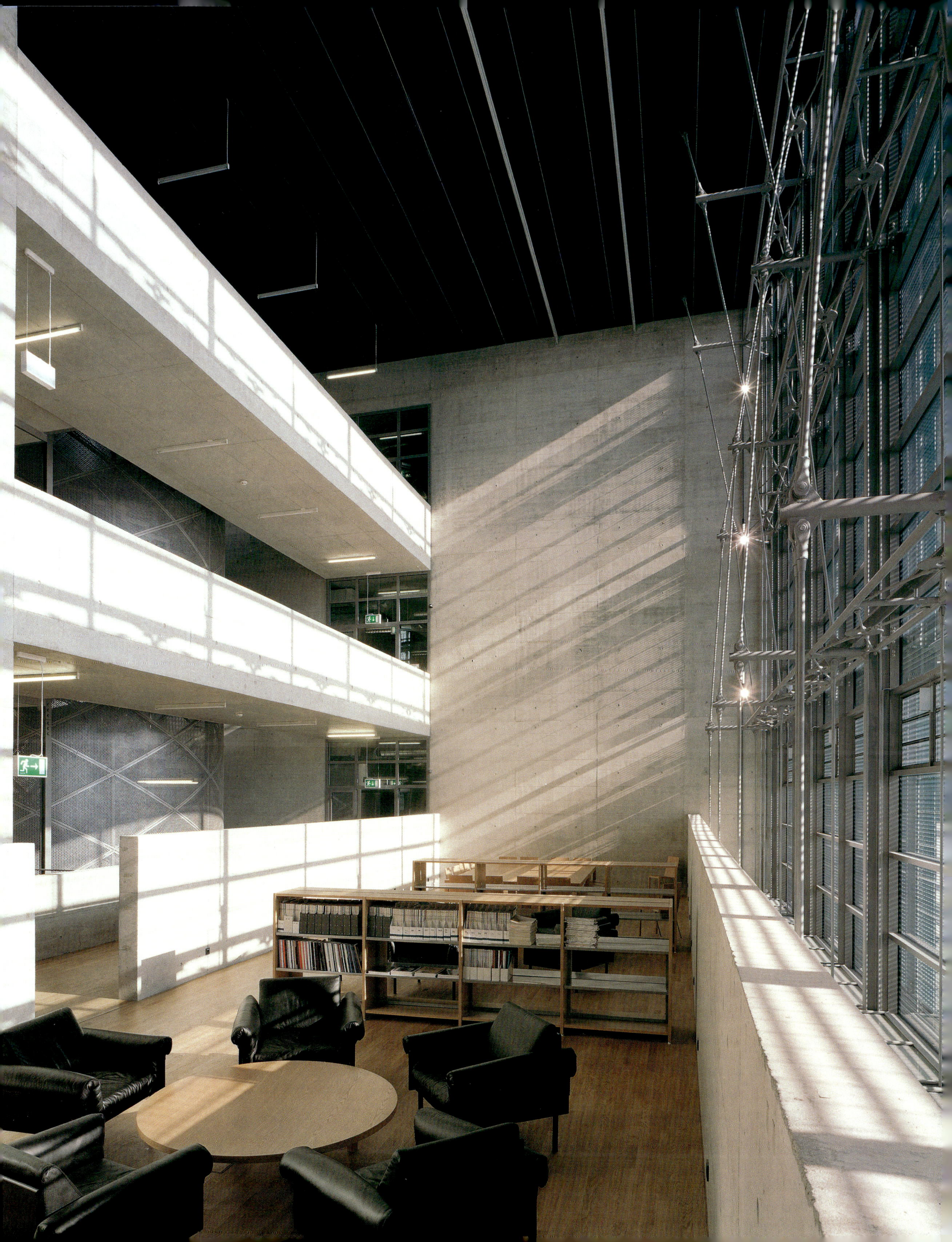

Above View of work area.
Right Ground floor café area with aluminium window grille that regulates light flow into the building.
Far right Architect's concept sketches reveal emphasis on communication and exchange of knowledge in a marketplace-style environment.

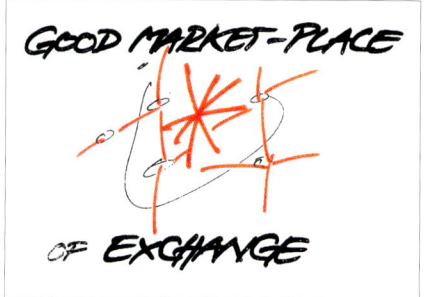

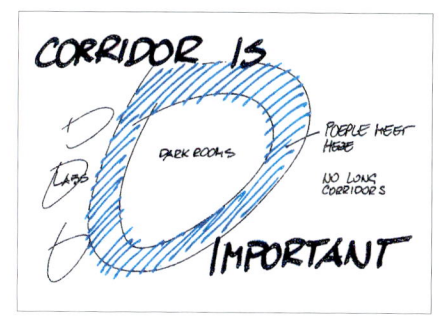

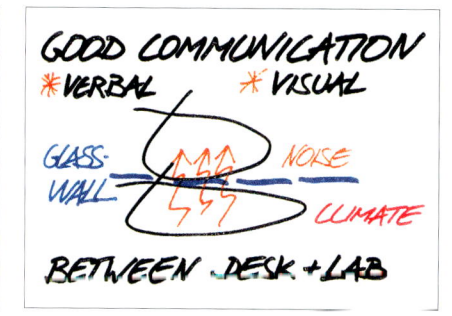

'The idea was to try to force the scientists to come together to create the critical mass necessary for new discoveries.'
Kai Simons, Institute Director, Max Planck Institute of Molecular Cell Biology and Genetics

Max Planck Institute

3 Agora
the public workplace

Aloof and segregated, offices were once hidden away, enjoying little connection with the cities and communities in which they were based. Companies would place the emphasis on security rather than society, and behind closed doors, organizations created their own insular worlds. Today, a new workplace wave is blurring the boundaries between the private and the public, connecting office life to the wider world of culture, leisure and transport.

'Agora', a Greek word meaning an open space in a town (originally the commercial, administrative and social heart of ancient Athens), is the term that has been chosen to describe this new approach to the workplace. Office buildings taking the Agora style have a public face, enabling companies to achieve a higher visibility. Public buildings begin to accommodate workplaces, allowing people to do their job permeably across the city, right in the marketplace and closer to customers.

The interiors in this section express the concept of the Agora in different ways. Some projects use the tactics of landmark art and architecture, while others breathe working life into public buildings or reflect the move towards mixed-use developments.

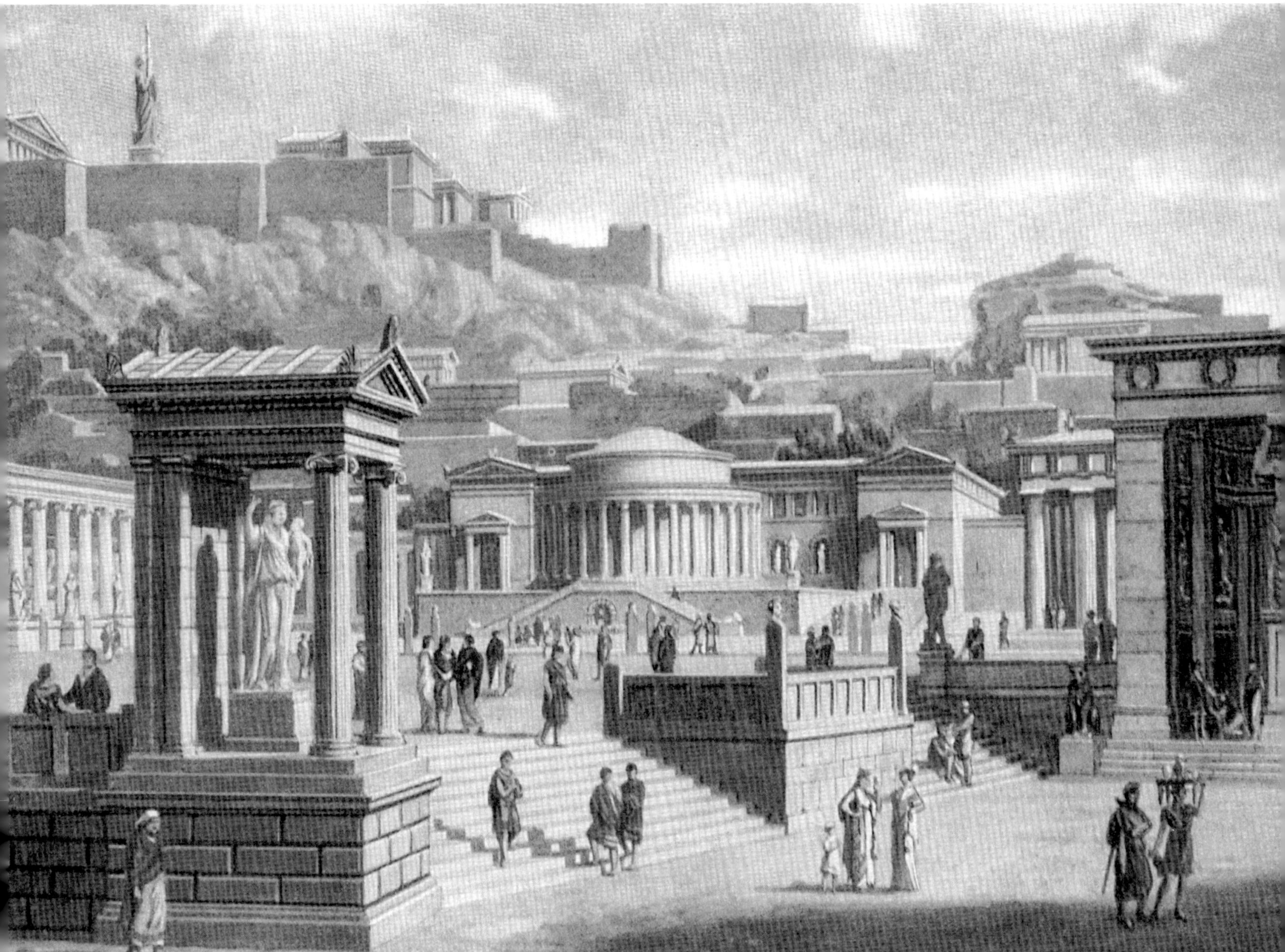

3.1
Coblentz, Patch, Duffy & Bass LLP
San Francisco, USA
Aston Pereira & Associates

WHEN the long-established San Francisco law firm Coblentz, Patch, Duffy & Bass LLP decided to move to new premises, in order to attract new staff and broaden its client base it chose one of the city's most recognizable public landmarks for its new home. Originally built in 1898, the San Francisco Ferry Building was a notable survivor of the 1906 earthquake, and the city's main transport hub for half a century before falling into disrepair. Now it has been completely refurbished and revitalized in a spectacular scheme by architects SMWM that creates a major new gathering space for the city.

Externally, a new promenade has been built to connect the project to the San Francisco Bay, giving visitors direct access to the water. Internally, an amazing public market hall runs the entire 201-metre (660-foot) length of the building and features various food and restaurant enterprises. Exposed beams and natural light create an exceptional space within which two anchor tenants were given the opportunity to construct Agora-style workplaces.

Coblentz, Patch, Duffy & Bass LLP, which has been in existence almost as long as the Ferry Building itself, jumped at the chance to be part of the rebirth of a San Francisco legend. Architects Aston Pereira & Associates overcame the problems associated with the unevenness of an old structure, inevitable in a refurbishment of this type, stacking the firm on two floors and retaining open views of the historic trusses and extended spaces.

The scheme is organized in three zones. There is an outer business zone for attorneys, paralegals and secretaries that is designed as a quiet space away from the buzz of the main area, and a middle zone that provides space for the firm's support functions, such as library, records, accounting and document reproduction. A social zone in the central nave connects visually to the building's vast atrium and houses a variety of spaces for receiving visitors, meetings, events and staff interaction.

The plan creates a large, elegant, expansive workplace that is legible and easy to navigate. To meet the stringent challenges of an historic building, offices are fronted with glass, and movable glass and fabric walls fold back when certain rooms are not in use. As a result, the lawyers are given the best of both worlds: a modern, progressive image within a city landmark of great public significance.

Top and above Views of the refurbished San Francisco Ferry Building of 1898, with new external promenade and public market hall.
Opposite The historic structure creates an elegant new office for Coblentz, Patch, Duffy & Bass.

Location San Francisco, USA
Client Coblentz, Patch, Duffy & Bass LLP
Completed 2003
Total Floor Space 6,410 square metres (69,000 square feet)
Staff 100

116 Agora

Coblentz, Patch, Duffy & Bass LLP 117

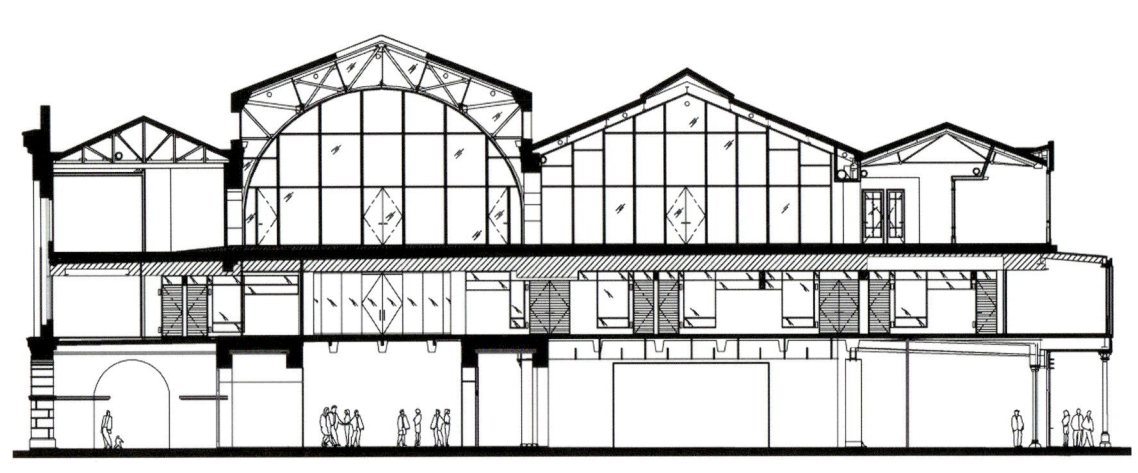

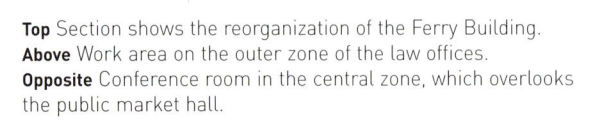

Top Section shows the reorganization of the Ferry Building.
Above Work area on the outer zone of the law offices.
Opposite Conference room in the central zone, which overlooks the public market hall.

118 Agora

'We were believers with our client from day one. We knew we had an interior with the potential to bring the best talent in their field to their door.' *Aston Pereira*

3.2
Less Limited
Hong Kong, China
Dou Design/Bill Price

IN high-density Hong Kong, finding and affording the right office space can be a nightmare for small firms. One enterprising company, however, has commissioned an unorthodox answer to a pressing problem: an office space in the St George's Building on Ice House Street that doubles at night as a dance/yoga studio.

Less Limited has just four staff and promotes ecological awareness in the investment sector – consequently, it wanted to find a sustainable solution to the shortage of available office space. Their brief to interior designers Dou Design was to create a flexible, dual-function space, and right from the start the accent of the project was on an ecological choice of materials.

The scheme was conceived as a flowing continuum – a single-layered surface of Portuguese cork, a material with green credentials, running along the north-south axis of the plan. Office functions are revealed through the act of 'peeling'. In the conference area, for example, the layer of natural cork appears to peel up and back to create the table and benches. It also reveals a contrasting under-layer of black cork. Similarly, a 'phone alley' for making private calls was created through the peeling-up of a curvilinear wall, an innovation requested by the client to offset the lack of privacy in the open-plan space.

A wireless network within the office enables staff to work, without cabling, at mobile work terminals, and an existing staff toilet has been converted into an ingenious shower/changing pod, complete with water-sealed locker. These features, plus the illuminated artworks that hang on the wall, help the space to transform easily from an office workspace to a dance/yoga studio at night.

This is a sensual project in which the flexible, sinuous lines of the design hint at the alternative use of the space, and make it easy to transform from a serious office environment during the day to a more relaxed leisure-time space at night. It is a neat way of solving a shortage of space in an overcrowded city, and enabling a small company to afford its own office space by sharing the cost with a companion activity.

Location Hong Kong, China
Client Less Limited
Completed 2002
Total floor space 90 square metres (969 square feet)
Staff 4

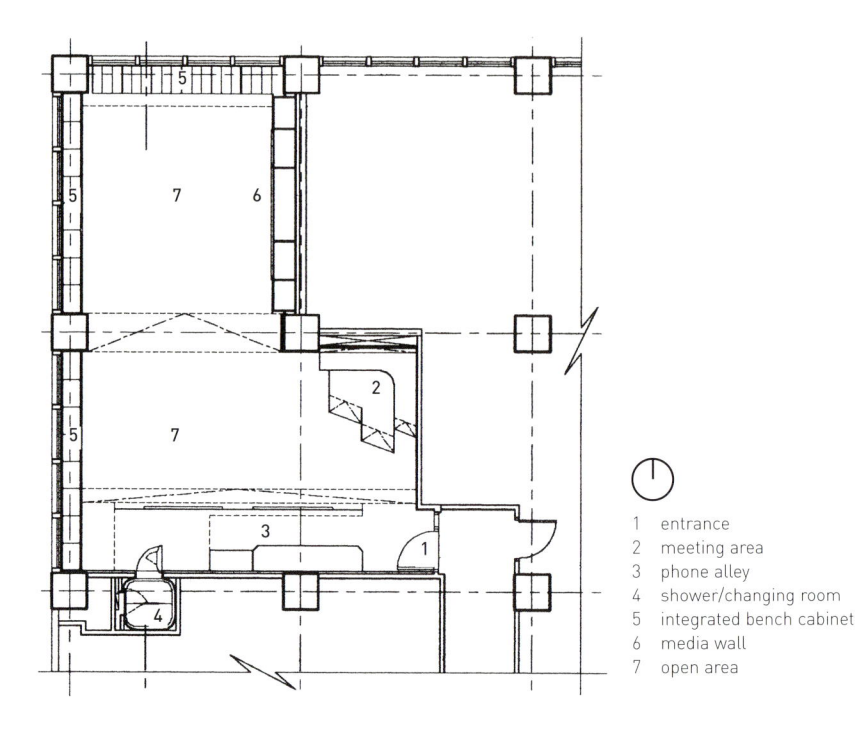

1 entrance
2 meeting area
3 phone alley
4 shower/changing room
5 integrated bench cabinet
6 media wall
7 open area

'The notion of stripping or peeling served as a conceptual departure for the office design.'
Lambert Ma, Dou Design

120 Agora

Above A lounge setting for relaxed work.
Below Cork layers are peeled upwards to create furniture (**right**) and a partition wall (**left**).
Opposite Plan of office and view of changing pod/shower.

Less Limited **121**

3.3
Porta22
Barcelona, Spain
Interiors Disseny

PORTA22 is a public space that has been designed for the exchange of knowledge. It is a place for information, guidance and training for people who are hoping to change careers or develop their skills. Its mission is to create awareness among the citizens of Barcelona about the new employment opportunities that are emerging in the knowledge economy.

Externally, the designers have created a green-coloured container, within which Porta22's career information resources are housed. With most of the technology hidden away, the interior is much more personal, and reflects the need to make the space inviting and human for a broad, and often technologically illiterate, audience. To achieve this, the interior was designed to be more domestic in feel and personal in scale – providing set spaces for different tasks. A 1:1000 scale drawing of the street plan of Barcelona has been cast into both the floor and desk surfaces, giving a familiarity to the space that also defines Porta22's geographical sphere of influence.

This Agora workplace is designed to present future occupations in an environment that has few barriers. New technology can often be perceived as overbearing and intimidating, so the designers have attempted to create a friendly space where the necessary ubiquitous technology does not alienate the visitor. The space itself is open, uncluttered, inviting and easy to use, with clear identifiers that point to the various elements of Porta22's services.

People are encouraged to search for knowledge themselves, although a personalized service is also provided. From an interesting audio-visual technology arena to a space for temporary exhibitions, ideas are disseminated through different media and formats. This public facility sets out to promote the 'democratization' of new technology, presenting a high-tech resource to an audience that is unfamiliar with what can be achieved. The space succeeds by being unpretentious and unassuming, providing an effective environment for members of the public to explore new work styles, careers and skills for the future.

Location Barcelona, Spain
Client Barcelona Activa
Completed 2003
Total floor space 2,000 square metres (21,530 square feet)
Staff 22

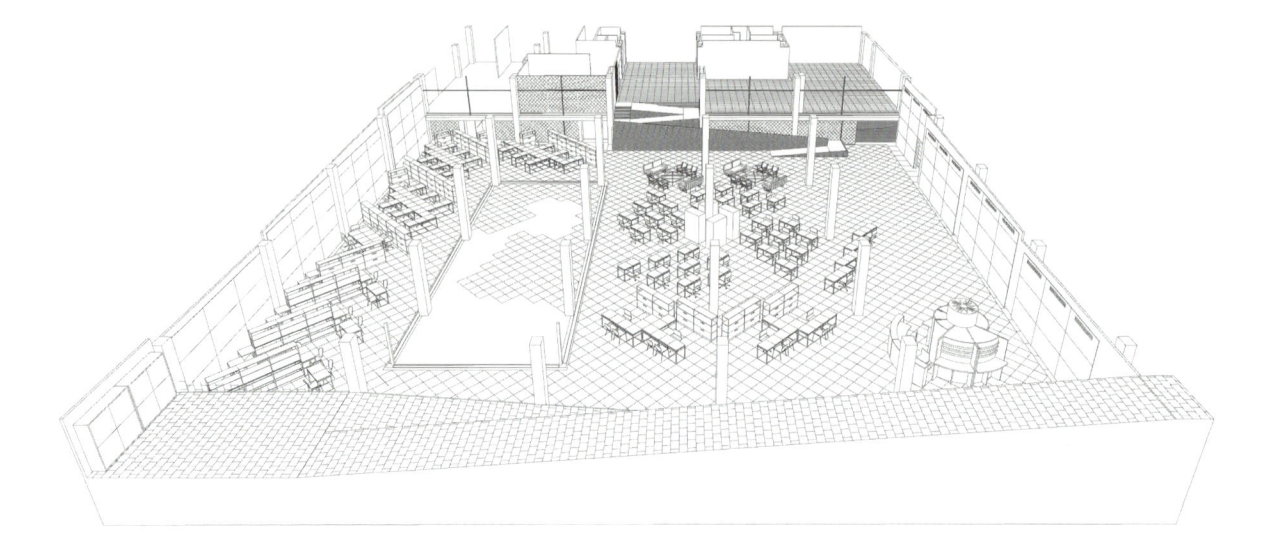

'Porta22 is a space for exchange through highly diverse services and tools that coexist in the same environment.' *Interiors Disseny*

Opposite top As a place for members of the public to engage with new technology, the design is welcoming and does not intimidate the visitor.
Opposite bottom Axonometric of the space showing the different zones.
Above View across the main environment illustrating the scale map of Barcelona that has been etched onto desks and the floor.

3.4
30 St Mary Axe
London, UK
Foster and Partners

FOSTER and Partners' landmark tower, 30 St Mary Axe in the City of London, takes thinking outside the box to a new level. Not only does this spectacular building, owned by insurance company Swiss Re, rethink the traditional box-like office building, with its dynamically curved form achieved with the aid of parametric computer modelling, but it also renegotiates the relationship between the skyscraper and the city.

Set in a generous public plaza with a cluster of shops, cafés and restaurants around its tapered base – the project creates a powerful presence within the dense urban landscape. The thinking behind its iconic design was, allegedly, that anyone should be able to jump in a cab at Heathrow Airport and instruct the taxi driver to take them to the Swiss Re building without having to give the address.

Nobody can deny that the 40-storey tower, clad in triangular and diamond-shaped glass panels and popularly known as 'The Gherkin', has made its visual mark on London. On top of this, it is also one of the world's most progressive office buildings in environmental terms, requiring half as much energy to run as a normal structure of its type. Spiralling light wells draw fresh air and natural light upwards through a high-tech scheme that features a series of overhanging balconies next to each light well. These fan out as the building rises, to achieve a sense of connection from floor to floor.

Giant aluminium panels flow from the public plaza into the heart of an imposing double-height entrance lobby in one continuous sweep, setting the tone for the complex fluid geometries that characterize the project. The Foster team were also responsible for the interiors at the top of the tower: the private dining rooms on the 38th floor, a restaurant on the 39th floor and the bar situated above that – the highest occupied vantage point in the City of London. These spaces offer unrivalled panoramic views of the capital within an ambience of almost monolithic modern design.

The space planning of the Swiss Re-occupied areas between floors one and 15 is the work of London based Bennett Interior Design, brought in to make Foster's template fit the more orthodox demands of commercial letting. Here there is a tension between achieving efficient tenant spaces while respecting the uniqueness of the tower's circular plan, whose resolution remains to be seen. Notwithstanding this, 30 St Mary Axe occupies a special place in any discussion of the evolving relationship between workspace and the city. It reaches out to its surroundings in a captivating way, and it has certainly put Swiss Re on the map.

Location London, UK
Client Swiss Re
Completed 2003
Total floor space 46,000 square metres (500,000 square feet)
Staff 3,500

Above Architect's sketch shows the four-storey increment of each 'diamond'.
Right The entrance lit dramatically at night.

Above and left The architect's sketch triumphantly realized on the London skyline, offering spectacular views of the city from upper-level balconies.

Above Section reveals the dynamic form of the building.
Opposite Bar area at the highest point in the City of London.

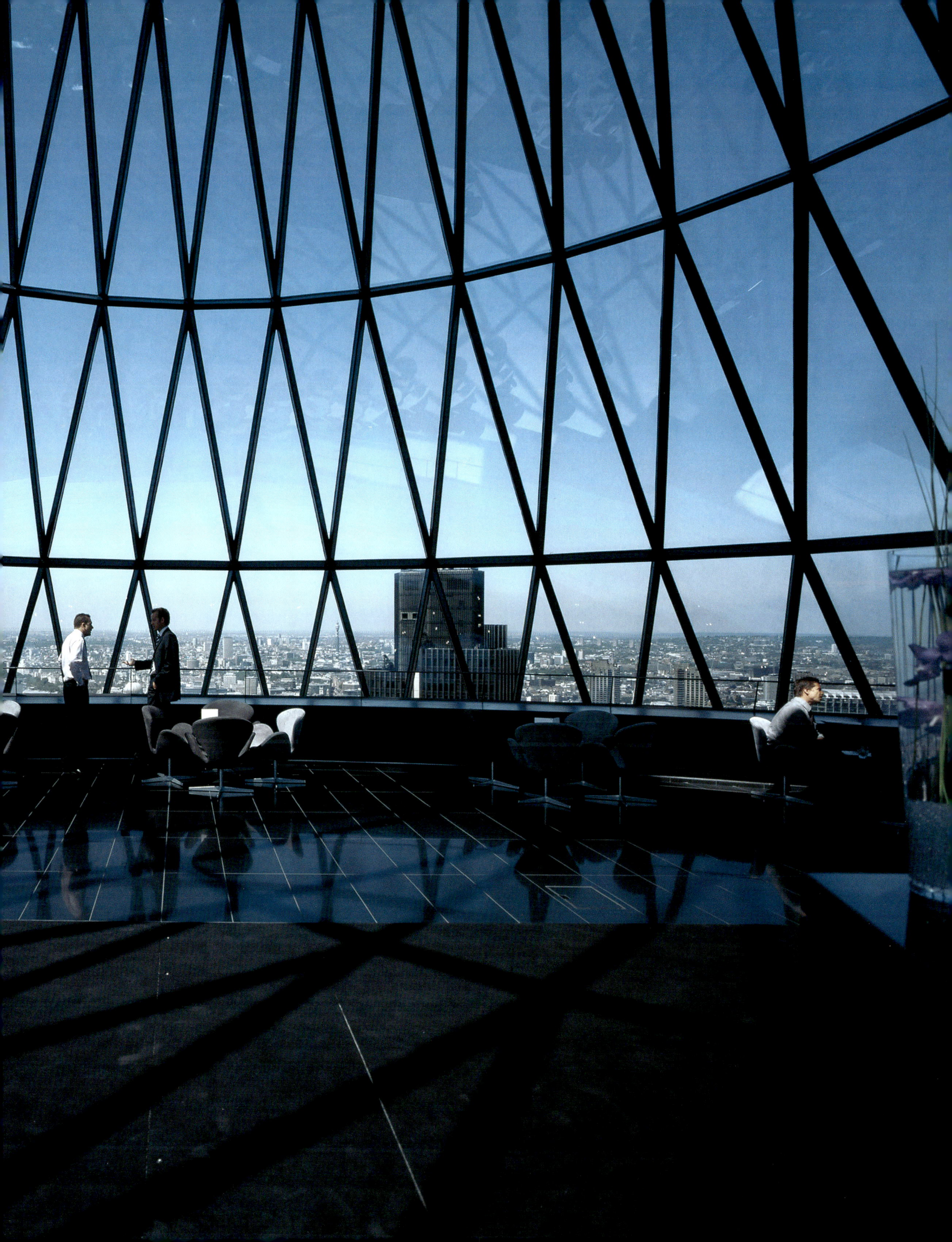

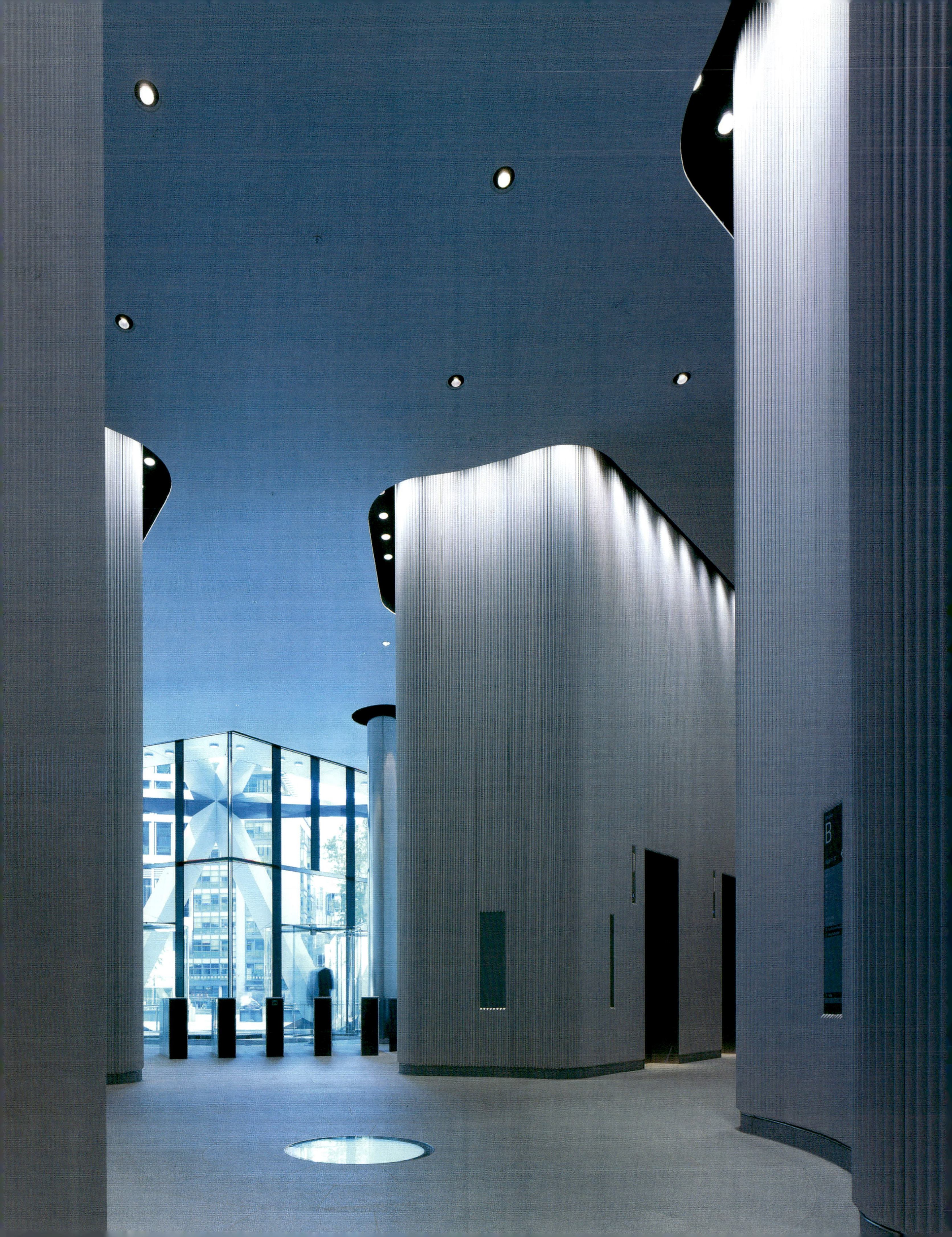

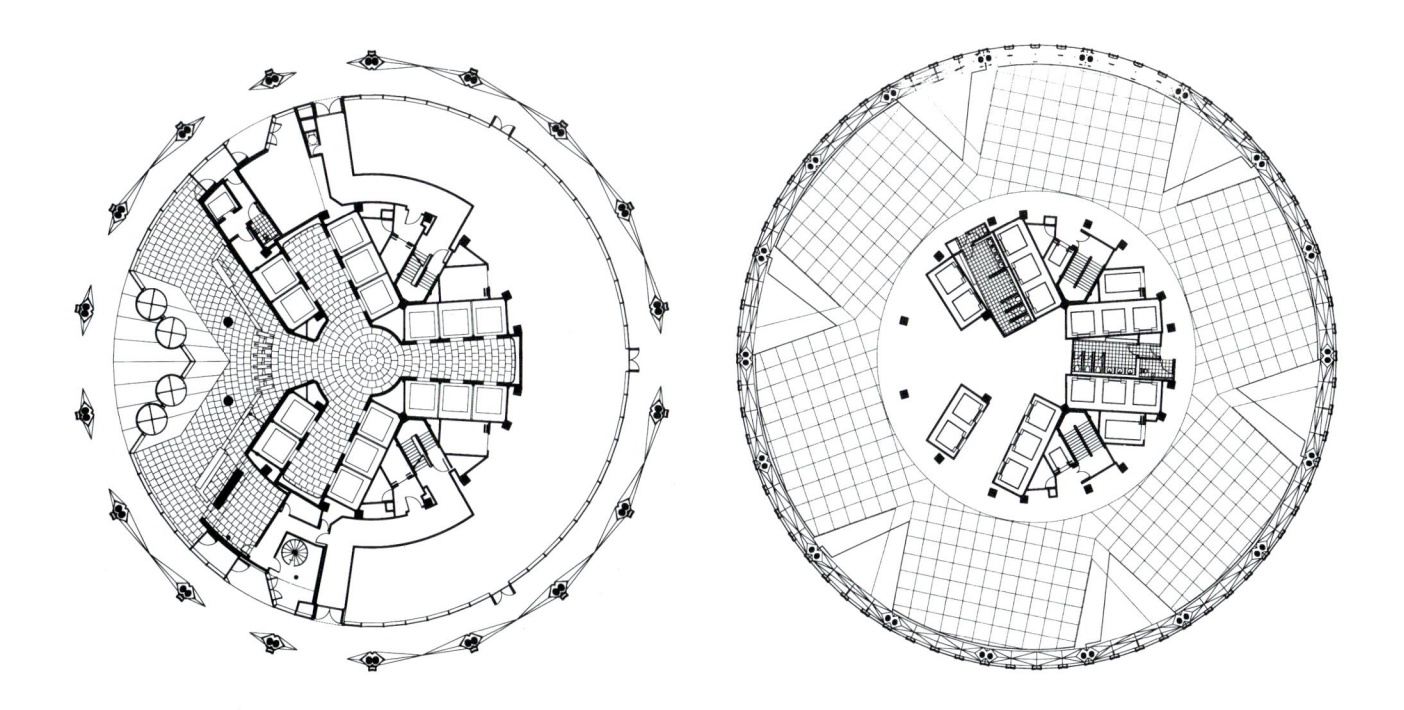

'This is an exceptional project, which demanded an exceptional design response.'
Sara Fox, New Building Project Director, Swiss Re

Opposite Lift lobby area at ground-floor level.
Above Classic furniture at the entrance to each office floor.
Top Floor plans within the circular template.

3.5
Madrid Regional Documentary Centre
Madrid, Spain
Mansilla + Tuñón

IN building a government archive and library on the site of Madrid's historic El Aguila brewery, this scheme has not only created an outstanding public workspace, but it has also done it while meeting the stringent requirements of cultural heritage.

The roots of the project go back more than a decade, to an architectural competition in 1994. First-prize winners Luis Mansilla and Emilio Tuñón were charged with extending the Madrid's Paseo del Prado cultural axis and opening the city up to the south. Faced with such a sensitive brief, they chose as their main strategy to utilize the spaces between the old brewery buildings, colonizing the voids, interfaces and expansions of surface areas for different activities.

The result is a project of power, scale and uncompromising quality in which old and new co-exist. At the heart of the scheme are 30,000 square metres (322,900 square feet) of regional archives, organized into three modules: contributions, storage and public access.

The storage building contains 100 kilometres (62 miles) of shelving across six floors, and is surrounded by a thermal quilt in the form of an ambiguously translucent double façade. As if this is not enough, it is in the public library that the idea of the Agora, the public workplace blurring the boundaries of the personal and the professional, truly comes alive. Here, the 10,000-square-metre (107,600-square-feet) multimedia library renovates industrial space for the knowledge era, creating calm and intelligent browsing and study areas in spaces that were once witness to the brewer's art.

If there is something symbolic about silos that used to hold barley now holding every book published in the Madrid region, the architects have not overdone the metaphor. This is a project that is understated and elegant in its use of space and materials, and in its provision of modern working conditions for an important seat of regional government.

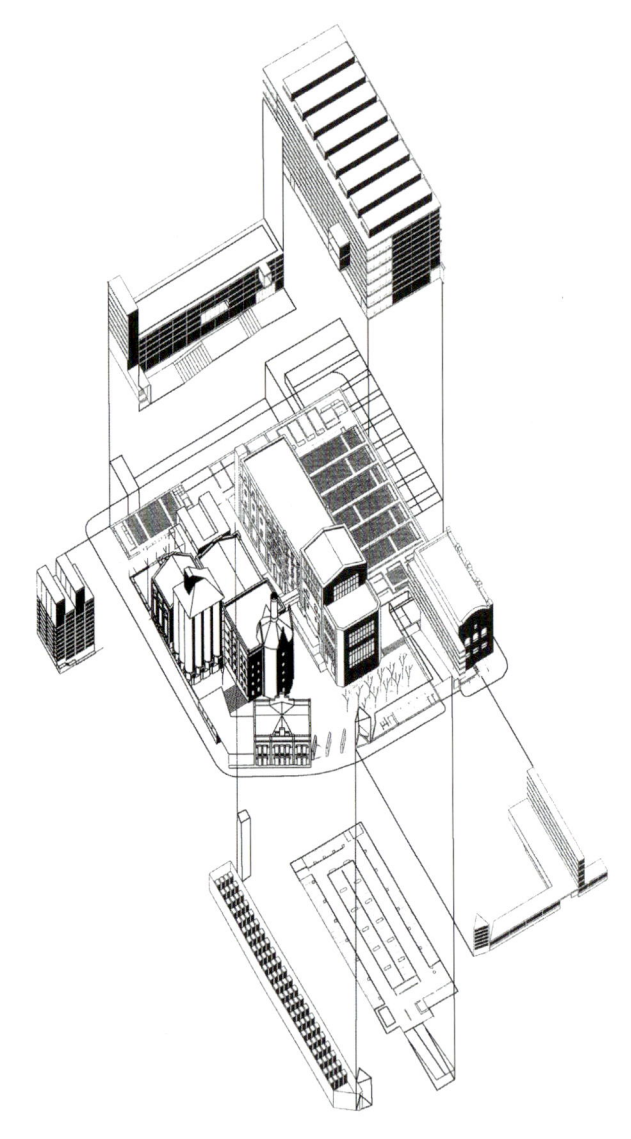

Above Axonometric shows the sequencing of the main building elements on the old brewery site.
Right Modern work areas coexist with giant relics of Madrid's industrial past.

Location Madrid, Spain
Client Madrid Regional Government
Completed 2002
Total floor space 40,000 square metres (430,600 square feet)
Staff 230

'This is a symbol of the desirable future convergence between environment and architecture.' *Mansilla + Tuñón*

Madrid Regional Documentary Centre 131

3.6
Kennispoort
Eindhoven, Holland
Koen van Velsen

LOCATED in a park between the university and downtown Eindhoven, this spectacular multi-use building carves out a new format for public space. The building contains not just office space, but also a restaurant, information centre, conference rooms and the local chamber of commerce.

Externally, the building features a striking metallic silver cladding, which contrasts beautifully with the interior. Here warm iroko wood panelling has been used extensively in the public areas for floors, walls, ceilings and stairs. The trees surrounding Kennispoort also create an interesting contrast with the silver façade and its elliptical form, cut away in a series of incisions that change the orientation and shape of the building. This creates an interesting and unconventional floor plate which in turn challenges the configuration of the workplace.

Internally, a series of atrium spaces links the floors together in a collage of interior environments; these encourage collaboration between people as they move through the different areas of the building. Overall, the height of the building had to be minimized in order to maintain sight lines, and an underground car park has been used to hide away services and delivery areas. At the centre of the building is an interactive area, or 'centre hall', that provides a focal point and meeting place.

While the exterior side facing the city has been kept intact, the elevation facing the university has had a swathe cut from the side of the ellipse to form a large patio area. This extends into the public environment and links the internal spaces with public landscaped grounds. In ways such as this, Kennispoort meets the needs of a diverse range of audiences. The different incisions create shapes that play on the uniqueness of the form, and present a building whose scale cannot easily be determined. The result is a public workspace full of surprise and mischief.

Above Silver façade of the elliptical building, scarred with several 'incisions'.
Right Extensive use of iroko wood creates a warm environment that contrasts with the metallic exterior.

Location Eindhoven, Holland
Client Eindhoven University of Technology
Completed 2002
Total floor space 9,700 square metres (104,400 square feet)
Staff not available

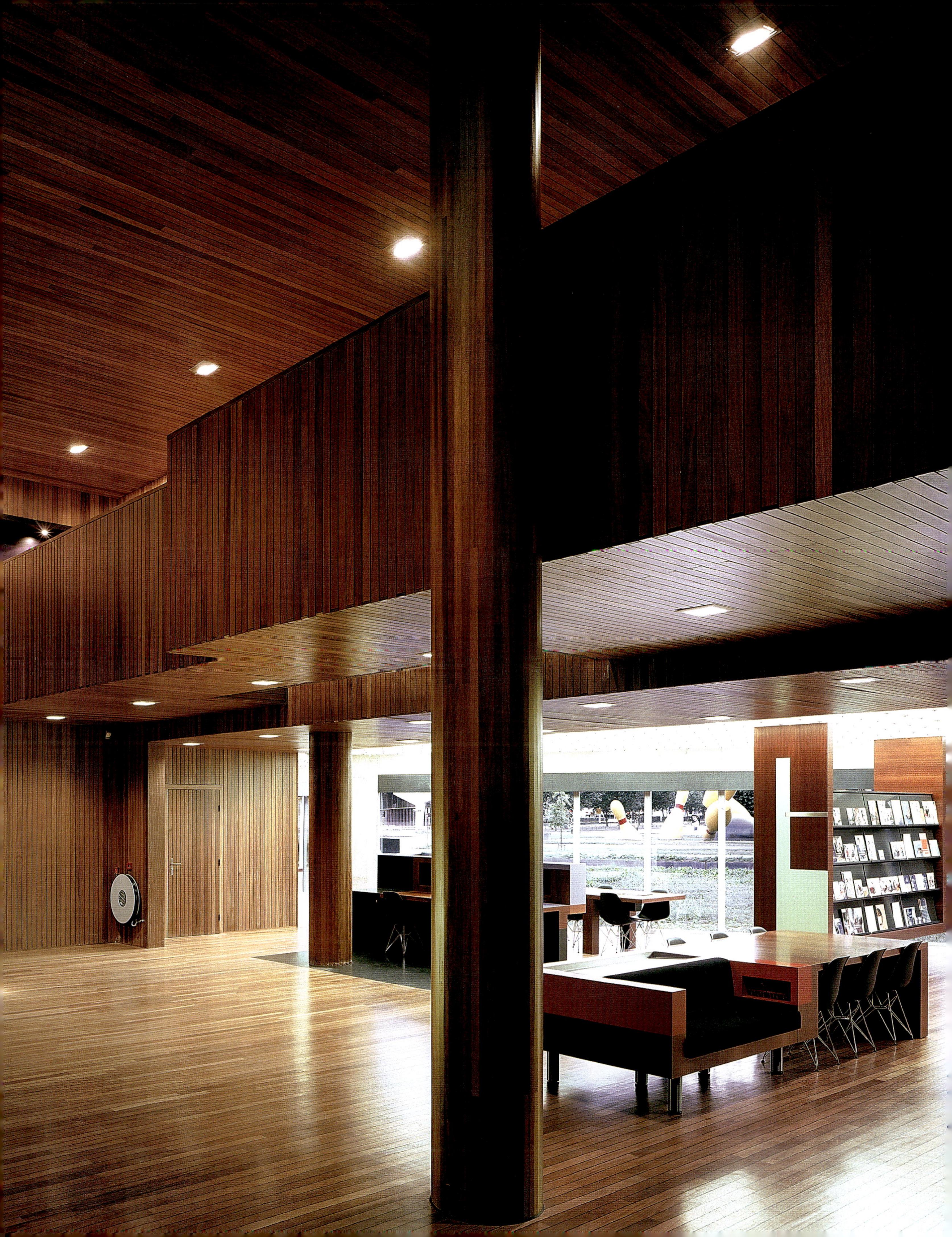

'The building's floor plans reflect the architectural interplay of the elliptical shape and the incisions; the office function finds its niche there.' *Koen van Velsen*

Top The restaurant has been designed as a central public space, linking with the external patio that has been created by a swathe cut from the side of the ellipse.
Above The building provides information resources, as well as housing the local chamber of commerce.
Opposite Good communications have been maintained throughout, with open staircases that link the floors and the creation of clear vistas and sight lines.

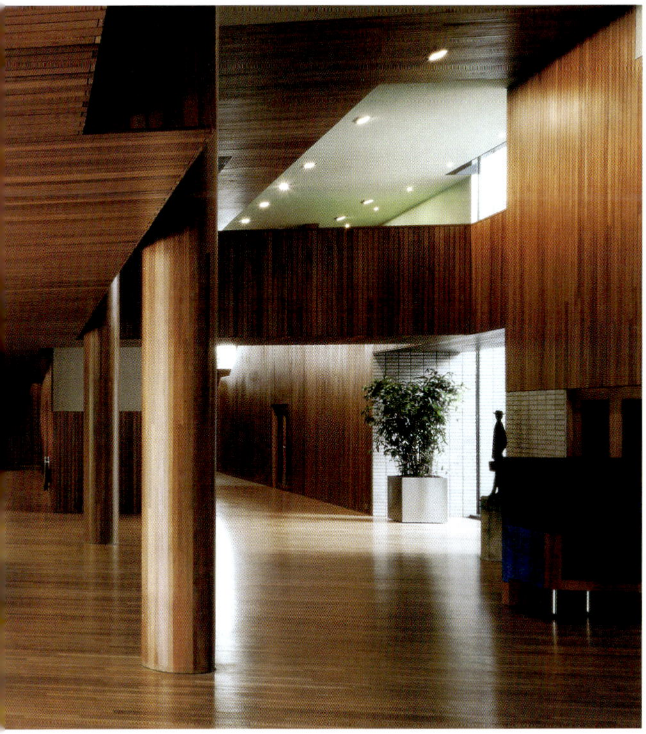

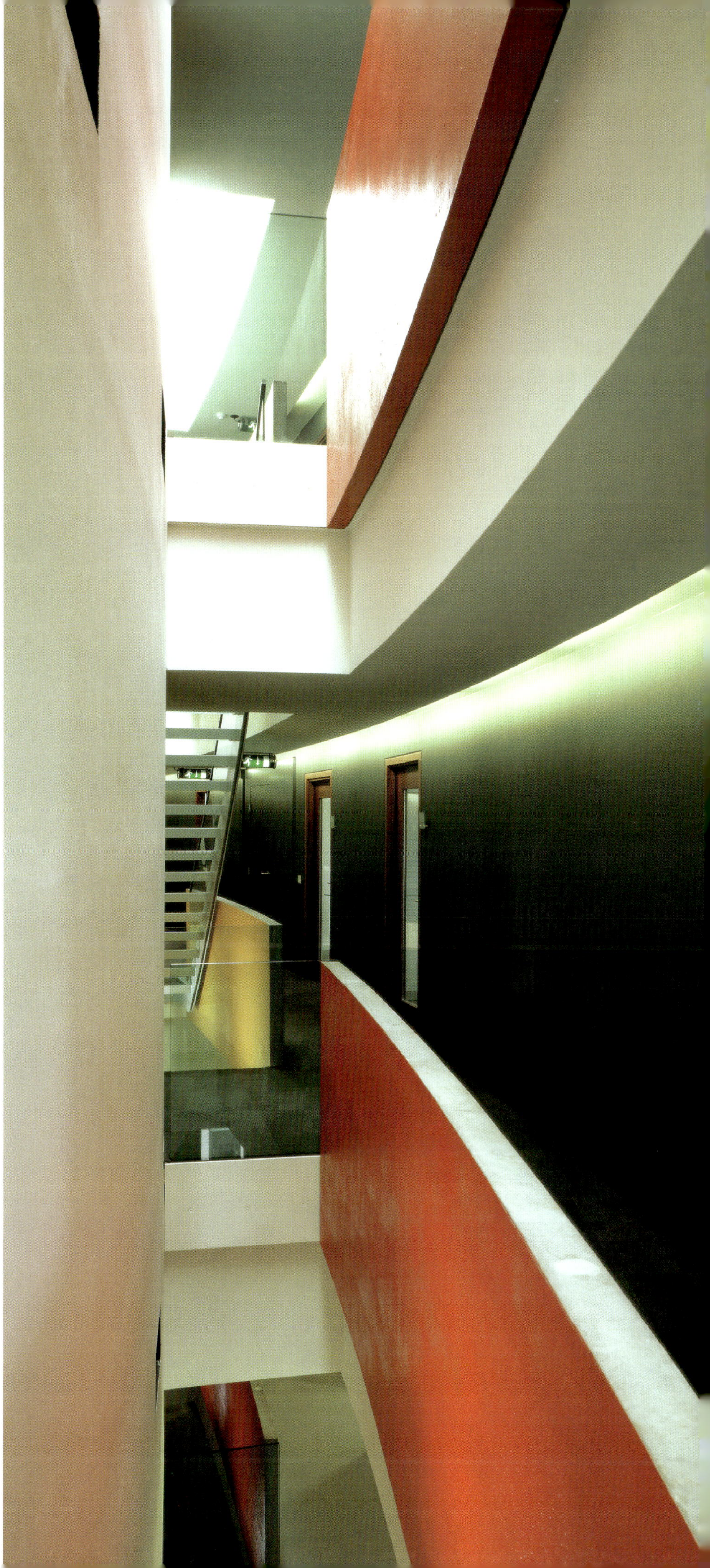

3.7
One Omotesando
Tokyo, Japan
Kengo Kuma & Associates

FASHION companies need to be more approachable and open to their customers than most other businesses. They cannot afford to hide their corporate functions away from the high street, and need to connect directly to the world that they are helping to shape. Such thinking helped to define the architectural strategy behind Kengo Kuma's sensitive headquarters building for fashion group LVMH in Tokyo.

LVMH is based at One Omotesando, a tree-lined avenue that leads to Tokyo's largest Shinto shrine, Meiji Shrine. The street has often been described as the most beautiful avenue in the city – unlike elsewhere in Tokyo the façades are continuous and the rooflines maintained at a constant level. It is also surprisingly green, given the urban location. The architects responded to this natural setting by presenting the façade of the building as a series of 84 vertical wooden louvres, each 100 millimetres (4 inches) wide and 21 metres (69 feet) in length, spaced at intervals of 600 millimetres (24 inches). A façade with a total length of around 50 metres (164 feet) was created to harmonize with the large trees that line both sides of the street.

Internally, the delicate play of natural light that is achieved by the wooden louvres creates a public lobby and work environments that are bathed in soft light and shadow. Long lines extend through the space as the day progresses, according to the height of the sun. Illuminated furniture elements add to the softness of the textures and sense of radiance within the space.

Kengo Kuma describes this approach as 'an attempt to liberate architecture from its conventional role as object'. The building programme was based, he explains, on breaking things down to their constituent elements (or 'particles'). The result is an office scheme that reaches out to this particularly verdant corner of the city, and is in turn influenced by the patterns of the external environment.

Location Tokyo, Japan
Client Riso Kagaku Corporation
Completed 2003
Total Floor Space 7,690 square metres (82,770 square feet)
Staff 300

Above Exterior view of the building's distinctive wooden louvres.
Below Plan shows the project set within its urban environment; the offices are on the third floor, above the retail space.
Opposite Interior view of the public lobby extends the preoccupation with light and shadow.

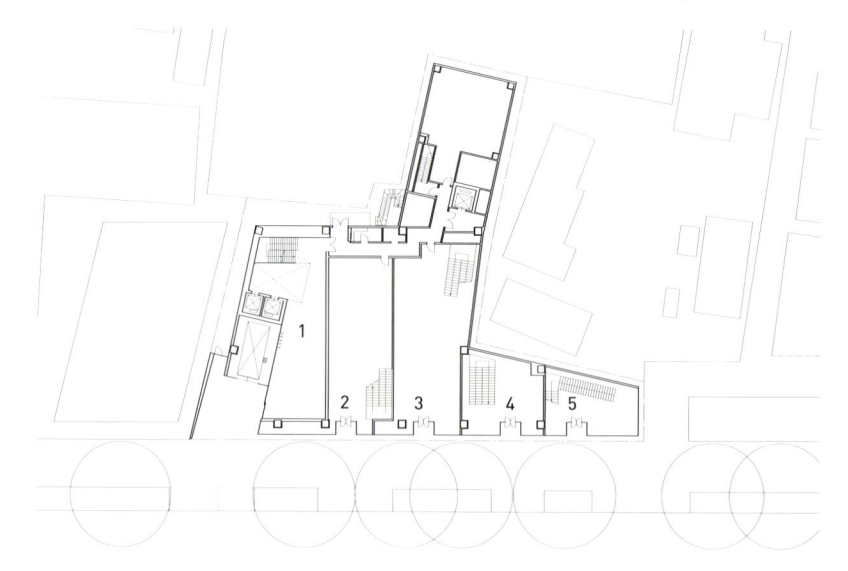

1 entrance hall
2 retail
3 retail
4 retail
5 retail

'Instead of developing ideas based on form or silhouette, I began to think about architecture from the level of the particle, and then from the point of view of light and shadow.' *Kengo Kuma*

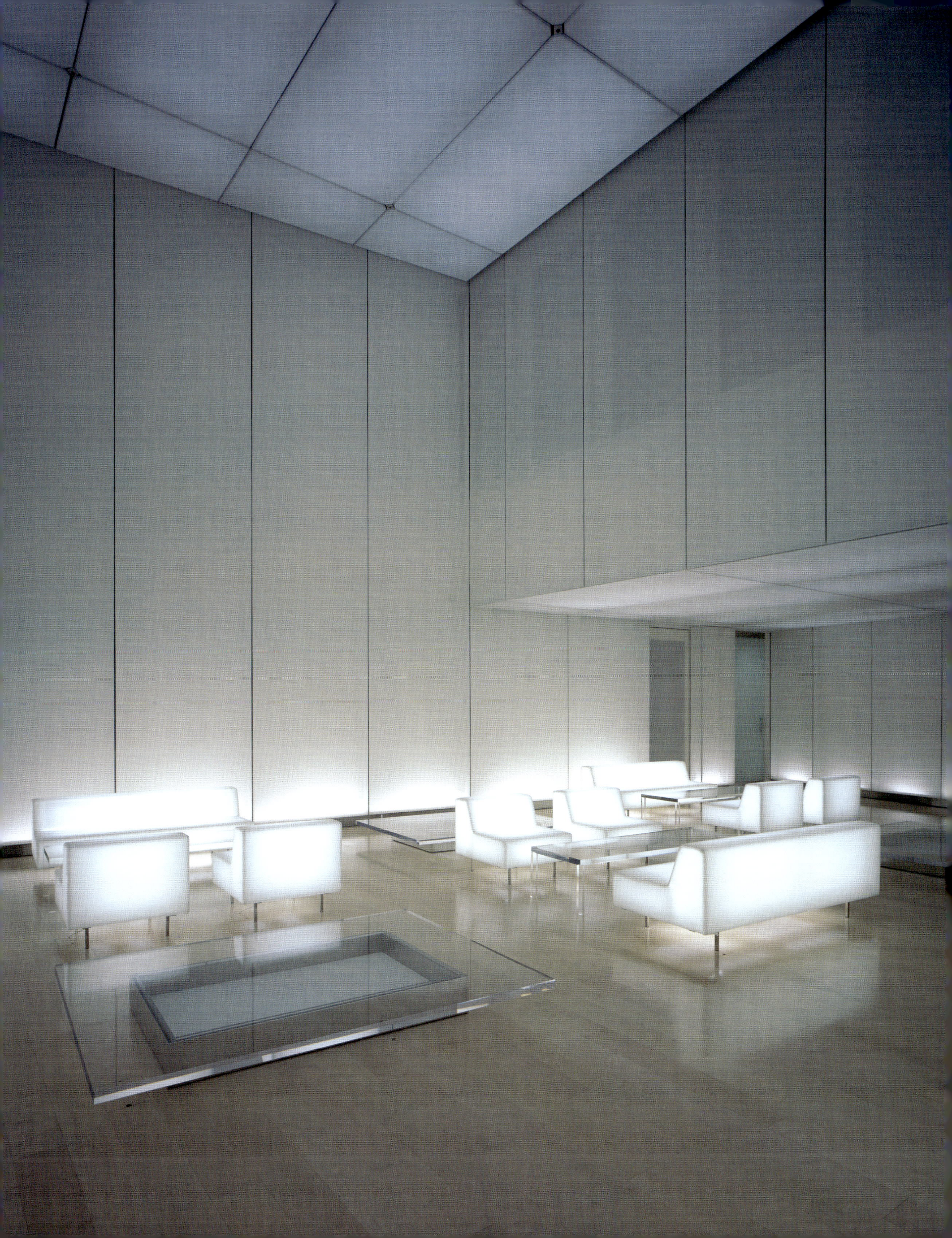

3.8
Maison de l'Architecture
Paris, France
Chartier-Corbasson Architectes

WHEN architects design their own workspace the results can often be rather out of the ordinary, but when the scheme is also for the regional Ordre des Architectes d'Ile-de-France (Office of the Order of Architects), you can expect something really special. This scheme, by architects Chartier-Corbasson, occupies a seventeenth-century building that was originally used by Capuchin monks of the order of St Francis. The stunning vaulted chapel has become the centre of this multi-functional public space.

Dominating the chapel is the grand staircase, a remarkable piece of engineering that can be raised or lowered to turn the floor into either a podium or a raked seating area, thus giving the space an element of flexibility. Metal plates, made of corten, are used on the concrete floor to give the space a series of 'patches', On the walls the plates are used as scenic shutters. The functionality of the different finishes contrasts dramatically with the architectural beauty of the space.

On the first floor, at one end of the building, are the office areas, occupying a double-height space with high arched windows that flood the workplace with daylight. Clean, modern furniture from Ahrend and Wilkhahn provides a contrast to the building's raw, exposed structures. A polyurethane floor covering lends a neutrality to the environment and helps to emphasize the architectural elements as a backdrop for work.

This cultural and artistic centre provides not just a place for work, but also a serious public space that can be transformed with ease. The dramatic, innovative and dominant grand staircase provides a sense of theatre and offers a slightly surreal experience as the ancient interior provides the backdrop to a modern, functional meeting and event space.

Location Paris, France
Client Conseil Régional de l'Ordre des Architectes d'Ile-de-France
Completed 2004
Total floor space 1,200 square metres (12,920 square feet)
Staff 15

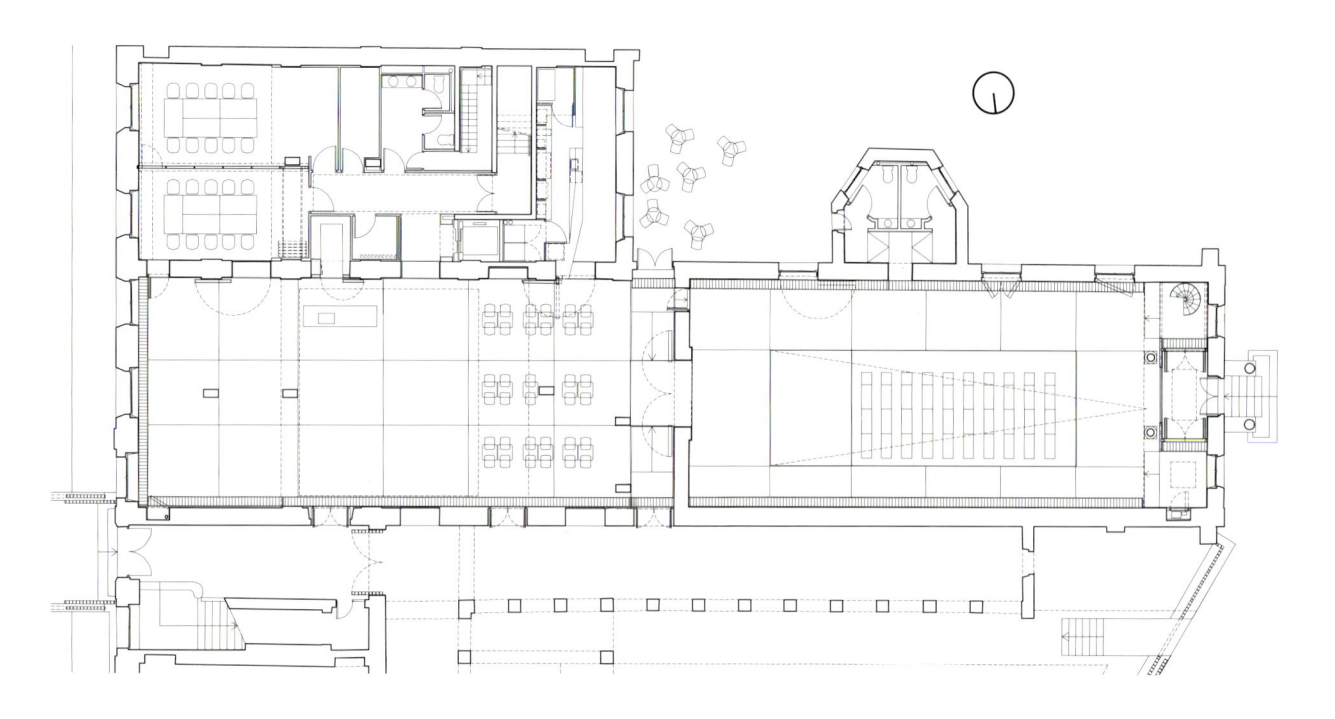

Above Floor plan of the seventeenth-century building.
Opposite The vaulted ceiling of the former chapel now houses a multi-functional meeting space with the grand staircase as its versatile centrepiece.

Maison de l'Architecture **139**

Above The grand staircase can be raised or lowered to create either a podium or a raked seating area.
Right Original detail and art from the period when the building was used by Capuchin monks.
Opposite The office areas occupy a double-height space that provides a contrast between original architectural elements and a clean modern workspace.

'The building had, before our project, the appearance of successive layers of time and space. Our intention was to take part in this process.' *Karine Chartier and Thomas Corbasson*

3.9
Rotterdam Chamber of Commerce
Rotterdam, Holland
Veldhoen + Company

THIS 200-year-old Chamber of Commerce decided on a traditional route to new office accommodation, but changed course during the project. It ended up creating an innovative public space that meets the needs of its customers while at the same time transforming the work styles of its employees.

At the heart of the building is a large hall that unifies the space and provides a 'courtyard' for the adjoining offices. The space is very open and egalitarian, with few barriers and walls, and everything has been designed to revolve around visitors as they stand in the atrium. With this new building, the culture of the Chamber switched from a 'receive' to a 'retrieve' mentality. People are now encouraged to feel at ease and to access information as they need it.

The building is planned by 'territories'. At ground-floor level, the customer area or public space forms the focal point of the building. Working areas are located on the second and third floors and a visitor area, with meeting rooms, occupies the first floor. Before the move, the Chamber was scattered over several floors of the World Trade Centre across the street, and all of the employees were allocated their own desk or office. Now, in what was termed the 'CoC@work' project, they have no fixed workstation and have become free to work anywhere within the building.

A wireless network has been installed so that everybody can effectively work from anywhere. To get the ergonomics of shared furniture right, people carry a key-ring chip that automatically adjusts movable furniture to their pre-programmed settings. The Chamber has also moved towards a paperless environment to encourage this kind of flexibility in the workplace.

As an organization, the Chamber of Commerce owes its origins to the *chambre*, or room, in which business people gathered to discuss common issues. Originally conceived as a place to meet and talk, the project's strapline became a 'room for business'. Herman Kraaijvanger, who designed the original building, was a proponent of 'total city architecture', where the boundaries between working and private lives were blurred. This Agora space is a perfect example of an environment that reverses the traditional separation between public and private, and achieves a space in which people can access knowledge, work, and interact without the constrains of a traditional work environment.

Above The new Chamber provides a visionary workstyle concept called CoC@work and a great public space for business.
Top right A large central 'courtyard' unifies this public space and provides a focal point for the building.
Bottom right Visitors are encouraged to retrieve information in an environment that puts them at the centre of the space.

Location Rotterdam, Holland
Client Rotterdam Chamber of Commerce
Completed 2001
Total Floor Space 3,500 square metres (37,673 square feet)
Staff 220

'The unusual design of the offices and public areas and the new working methods are the visible manifestations of the organization's efforts to be accessible.' *Wim Kok, Dutch Prime Minister*

3.10
Virgin Atlantic Clubhouse
Johannesburg, South Africa
W1 Studio

WHEN Virgin Atlantic creates a space for people on the move, the airline generally does it well. This project has all the hallmarks of a cleverly considered, multi-use environment in what is one of the most dynamic public places for work – the transportation hub. This lounge is an exclusive enclave for Virgin's elite Upper Class passengers and, as one would expect, nothing is left to chance. Opulence and individuality provide these special customers with a place to work, relax and be entertained.

W1 Studio have provided highly effective 'touchdown desks' for work, in a space that is designed to reflect the traditions of South Africa and evoke its dramatic sunsets through tones of gold and red. Shapes and patterns echo the local traditions, with materials such as slate and carved wood being used extensively. This contrasts effectively with the modern Italian furniture and fittings.

Passengers are provided with every amenity, from hotel-quality bathrooms and showers (complete with built-in television) to seating areas with games consoles, in a space where the mood is carefully acoustically controlled through zoned speakers. A chef is on hand to prepare meals in the open kitchen, which provides a sense of theatre. The designers have deliberately kept the 372-square-metre (4,000-square-foot) scheme open by locating the toilet and kitchen blocks in the centre of the space using glazed partitions.

The designers set out to create a 'high touch' environment, partly through the specification of an interesting array of materials and finishes. Leather floors, velvet upholstery, hand-blown glass and pebble columns present a sense of the unexpected in an airport setting that is usually synonymous with highly technical finishes. Visually it is a treat, demonstrating that a public place designed for work need not be predictable.

The airport business lounge is perhaps the ultimate challenge for understanding and catering for the needs of an increasingly global, nomadic and demanding 'knowledge worker'. Creating a stimulating space, and achieving the right mix between work, relaxation and entertainment, as we see here, is the key to a successful Agora workplace.

Location Johannesburg, South Africa
Client Virgin Atlantic Airways
Completed 2002
Total floor space 372 square metres (4,000 square feet)
Staff 85

Above and opposite Rather than the usual monotonous, bland environment, this business lounge provides a variety of interesting spaces designed for both work and leisure. The range of different settings reflects the need for choice, based on the tasks and mood of an increasingly nomadic workforce that has to 'work on the pause'.

'We were lucky to start with one open space. This gave us the option not to build full-height walls with dead-end spaces.' *Patrick Hegarty, Director, W1 Studio*

Virgin Atlantic Clubhouse 145

3.11
Munich Re
Munich, Germany
Baumschlager & Eberle

WHEN Austrian architects Carlo Baumschlager and Dietmar Eberle won an international competition to renovate a 1970s office building for the German insurance company the Munich Re Group, they certainly didn't choose the safe option.

The designers were faced with a rather severe-looking five-storey concrete structure, built in 1973 and totally at odds with the other buildings in the neighbourhood which consisted mainly of old houses with landscaped courtyards. Rather than knocking down this ugly duckling and starting again, they decided to reshape the building entirely to fit its urban context, and commissioned a series of artists to redefine its relationship with the city. The result is a project of great verve within the rigorous geometry of the site.

The key to the design strategy was the decision to build a fourth module to complement the three existing modules of the steel-framed structure. This had the effect of opening up the dark interior and adding extra office space. A new main entrance and garden side-entrance were then inserted to consolidate the new S-shaped configuration. A large, two-storey reception and event space, clad in Canadian maple and naturally lit by skylights, was cut deep into the building, bringing light and views to the entire project.

The architects have retained the original building's grid of small individual offices, which are just 1.87 metres (6.14 feet) wide, but has compensated for this by upgrading the public circulation areas, which are now a series of inter-connecting galleries. The client is a well-known patron of modern art, so the work of artists such as Keith Sonnier, with his *RedBlueYellow* underground passageway of ceiling-mounted neon tubes, and Peter Kogler, with his stairwell of computer-generated biomorphic imagery, are entirely in keeping with the spirit of the interior.

Munich Re extends a modern, artistic face to its mainly nineteenth-century neighbours, and this seems to work exceptionally well. Swiss landscape architect Günther Vogt was commissioned not only to design the inner courtyard around which the new office block is organized, but also to create green environments externally. These are echoed by artist Olafur Eliasson's wall of artificial evergreen moss above the main entrance. Eliasson also created a light installation for the exterior that transforms the horizontal banding of the building by day into vertical lines at night. The overall effect creates a new relationship with the city through art and lighting, making Munich Re a high-profile Agora workspace in a setting of previously low expectations.

Above Exterior façade at night with light installation by artist Olafur Eliasson.
Below Plan shows new addition to the building.
Right Keith Sonnier's neon artwork in the underground passageway linking the new building with the existing one.

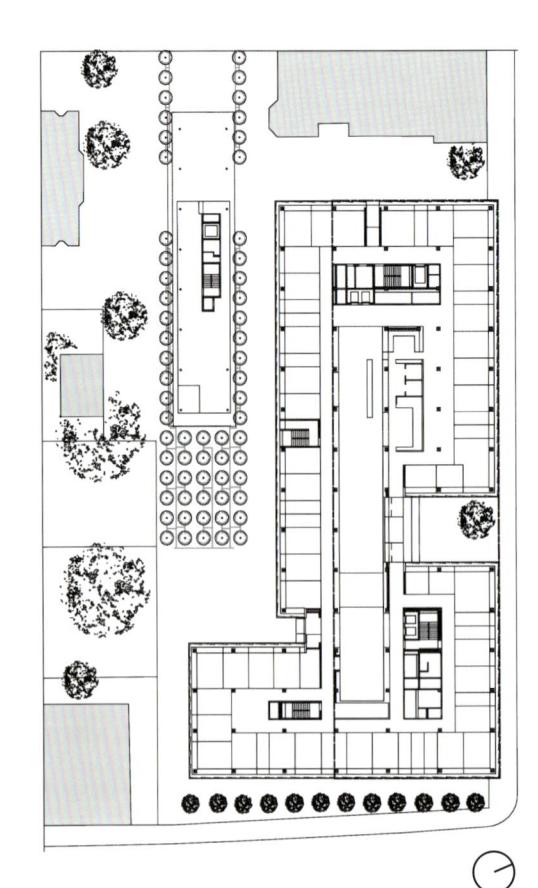

Location Munich, Germany
Client Munich Re Group
Completed 2001
Total Floor Space 2,718 square metres (29,256 square feet)
Staff not available

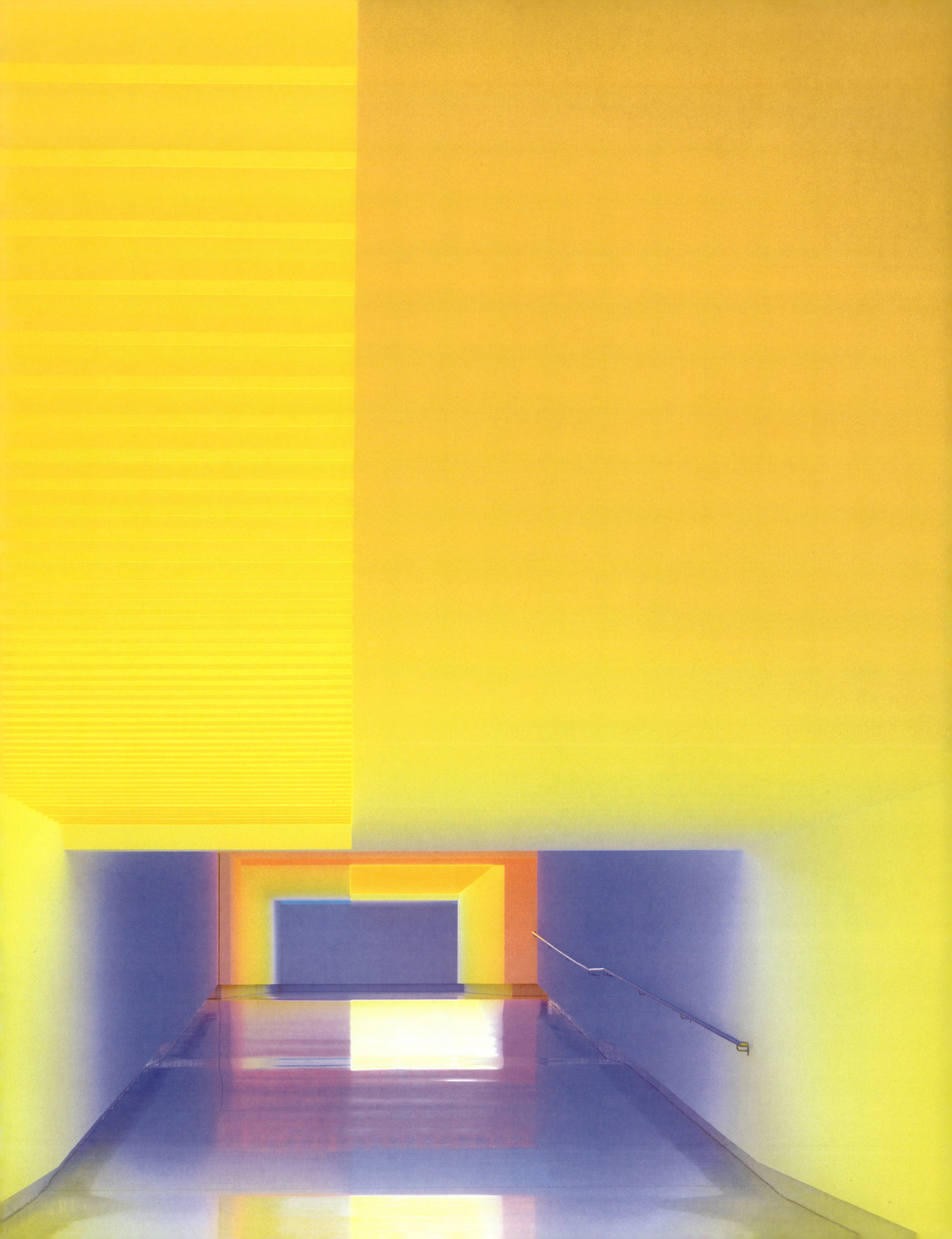

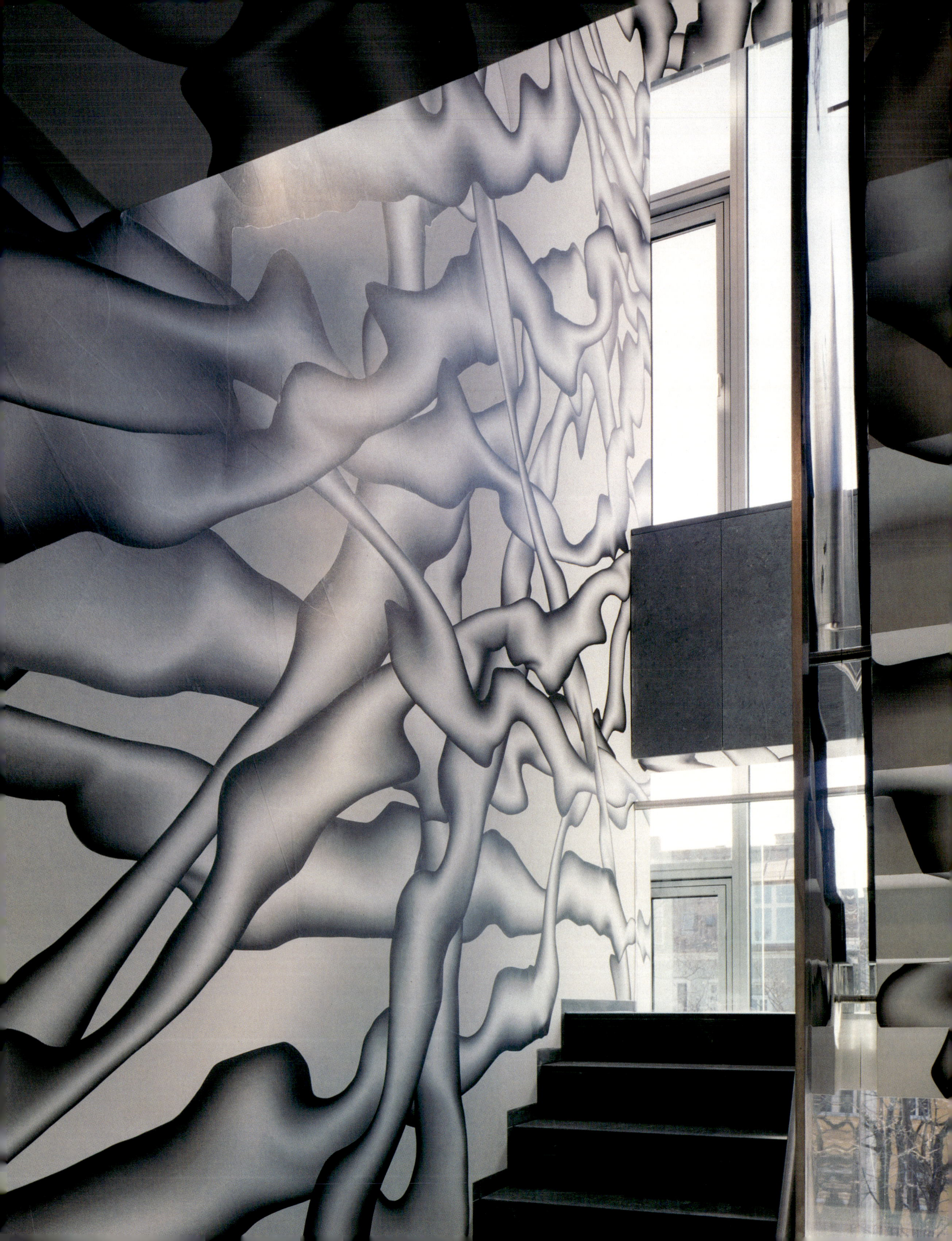

'We compensated for the lack of office space by creating traffic areas with the ultimate in experiential quality.'
Carlo Baumschlager

Opposite Stairwell murals by Peter Kogler.
Above Aribert von Ostrowski murals.
Right Murals by Felice Varini.
Overleaf Views of the main reception hall, clad in Canadian maple. German art duo M+M have created an artwork in which a 90-cm (35-inch) panel in the wall opens every hour to reveal a plasma screen showing an artificial landscape.

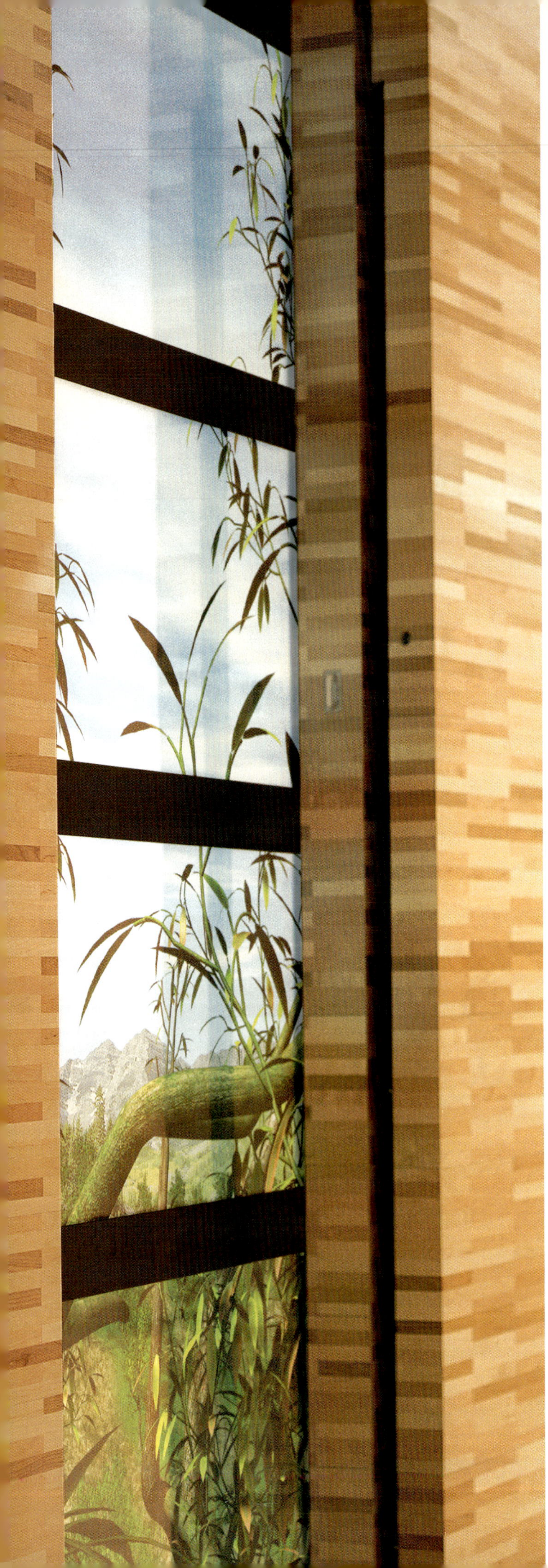
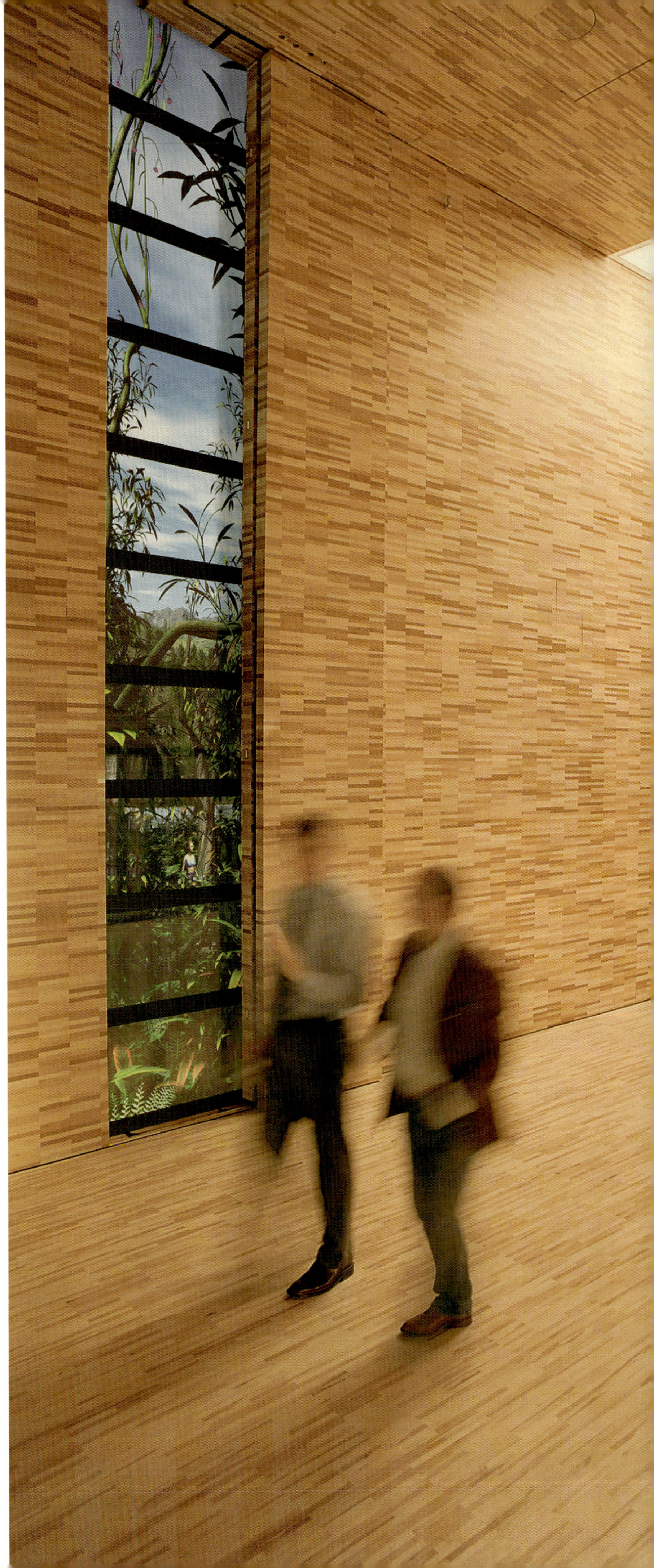

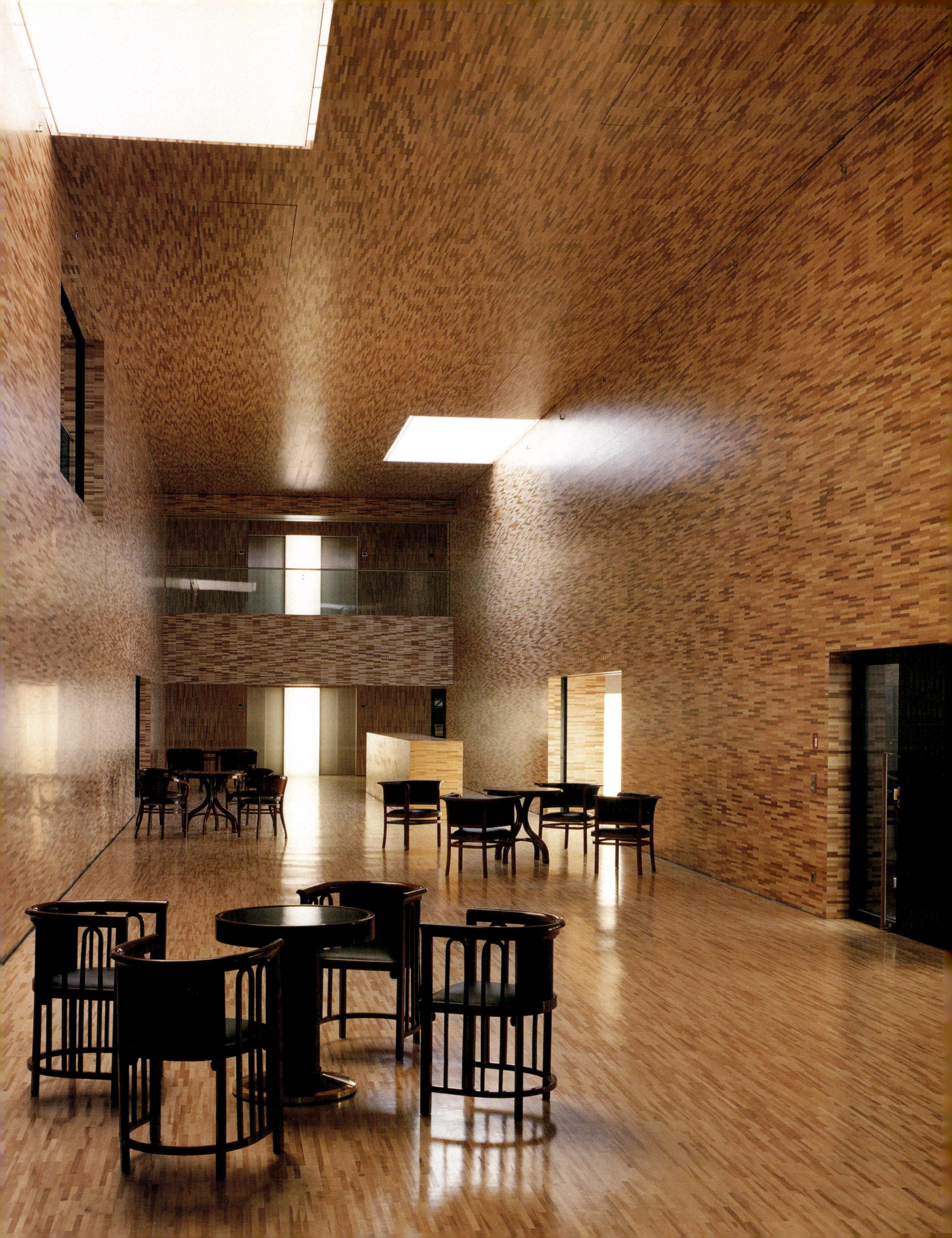

3.12
Academyhills Roppongi Library
Tokyo, Japan
Kengo Kuma & Associates

MODERN Tokyo is a pioneer in blending commerce and culture, its latest wave of new buildings integrating the activities of the corporation with other aspects of city life. No project symbolizes this direction more clearly than the Mori Tower in Tokyo's Roppongi Hills district, which sits in a vast new landscaped complex dedicated to uniting industry, academia and art.

The tower itself contains many different elements, including a museum, an arts centre and an exclusive members' club. But the facility that most strongly expresses the idea of Agora-style 21st-century working is the Academyhills Roppongi Library, a purpose-designed hub for creativity, learning and intellectual exchange on floors 49 and 50 of the skyscraper.

The scheme, designed by architect Kengo Kuma, has four main functions. Within the space are a school, a forum, a research network and a 24-hour membership library. The plan is based on the classic Japanese concept of *Engawa*, the linear space between the veranda-like porch and the inner rooms of a traditional Japanese house. This scheme is flexible in function and it creates a space off which the architect has laid out an auditorium, sky studio, library café, work areas, book stack and adjoining areas.

Academyhills is a global knowledge network, led by senior Japanese academics and dedicated to working with business and technology. The Academyhills Roppongi Library is a key platform for its work: an urban destination that acts as a magnet for knowledge workers to come and browse through books, speak at events and share ideas.

Different parts of the project are not tightly delineated; instead there is a boundary-free aspect to this spacious, elegant and relaxed-looking interior that reflects working without boundaries. Each space flows into the next; indeed the library itself sits neatly within the bigger frame of what the Mori Tower at Roppongi Hills is seeking to achieve – an integration of industry, learning and creativity.

Location Tokyo, Japan
Client Academyhills
Completed 2003
Total Floor Space not available
Accommodates not available

Above Individual workspace offering a spectacular view of Tokyo.
Opposite View inside the library stacks.

Academyhills Roppongi Library

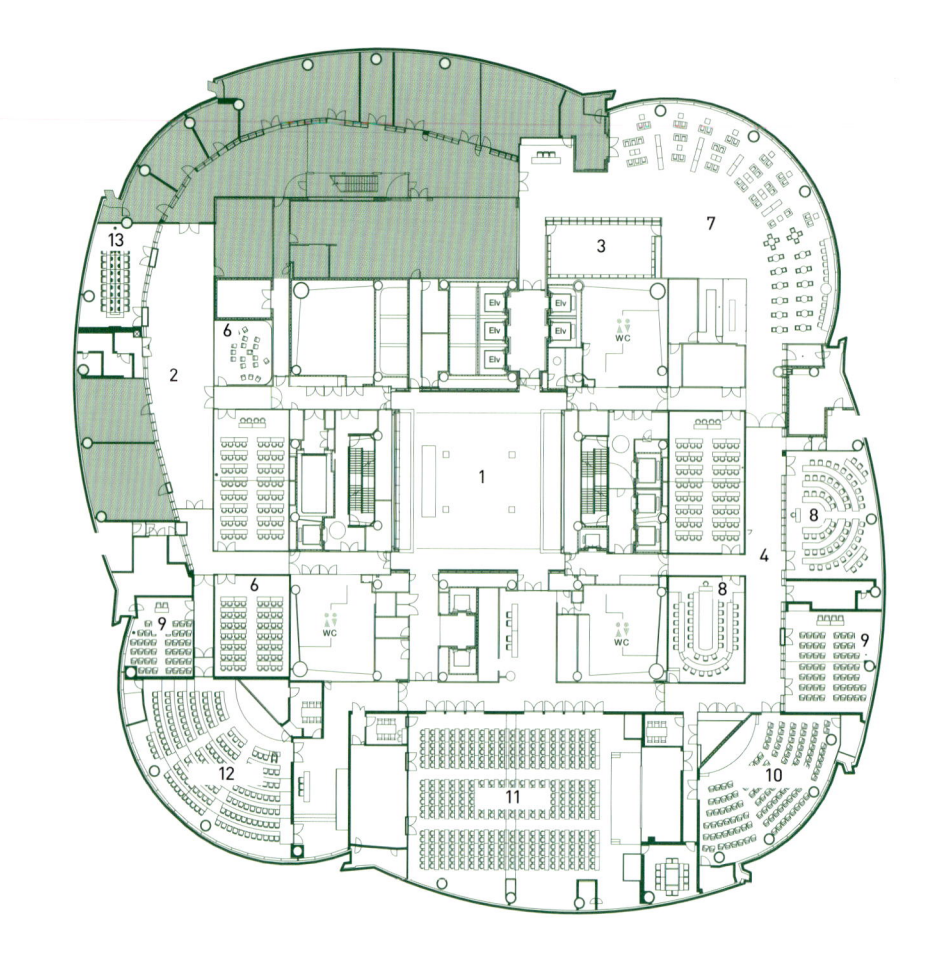

1 reception area
2 my library
3 great books library
4 library book store
5 conference room
6 brainstorming room
7 library café
8 step room
9 collaboration room
10 sky studio
11 tower hall
12 auditorium
13 salon

154 Agora

'I planned the Library as a contemporary *Engawa*: everything is feasible due to this ambiguous passageway space.' *Kengo Kuma*

Top View of the connecting corridor.
Above Work area.
Opposite above Floor plan shows the different facilities of the knowledge exchange, connected by a continuous looping passageway.
Opposite below Café area.

Academyhills Roppongi Library 155

4 Lodge
the live-work setting

Offices once represented the polar opposite of home. Living and working were two separate activities, and this was reflected in the evolution of entirely different building typologies. Today, with advances in technology and growing concern about work-life balance, a new paradigm is emerging: space that is designed to fuse living and working in one environment.

'Lodge' is the term chosen here to describe a growing property trend that re-integrates the office into the domestic sphere. In some cases, homes are adapted for work – increasingly a new hybrid is being developed to combine the two functions in the dedicated live-work unit. These are spaces that contain work in the antithesis of a corporate setting, redefining the rhythm of working life in the context of family and friends.

The following selection of schemes expresses the concept of the Lodge in its embryonic form – from urban lofts and media community centres to a charming garden workspace.

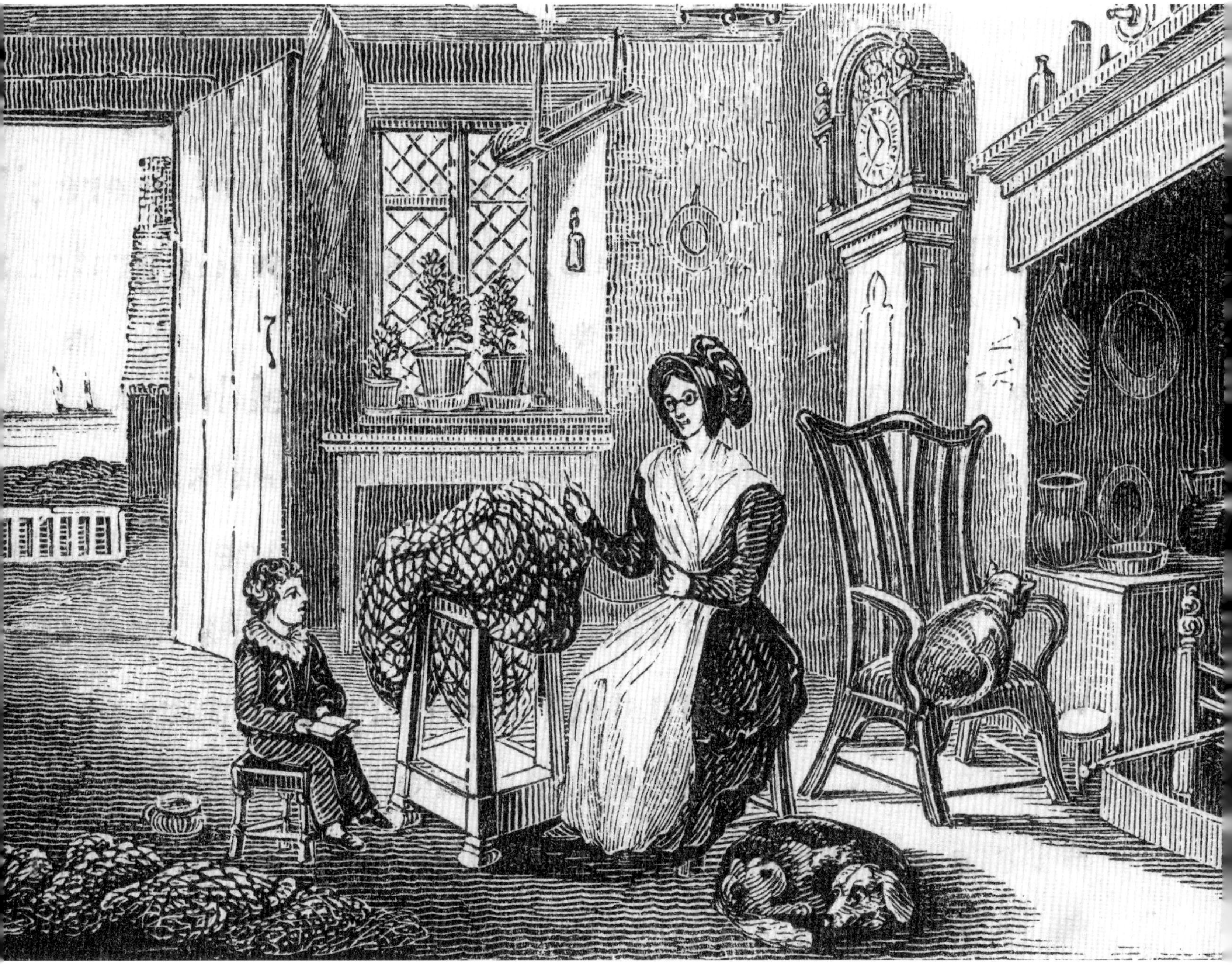

4.1
East Union Live-Work Lofts
Seattle, USA
The Miller/Hull Partnership

FOR those urbanites who demand to live and work right in the middle of the city, few developments declare their credentials more robustly than this dramatic seven-storey scheme in Seattle, by architect David Miller of local firm The Miller/Hull Partnership.

The live-work project at 1310 East Union, in the authentically bohemian Capitol Hill neighbourhood, presents eight loft-style condominium units as full-height glazed boxes within a raw-steel brace structure. This design strategy creates the immediate effect of progress, lightness and transparency, and has led one commentator to suggest admiringly that the development had an industrial-size garage door instead of a front wall. It also allowed the project to be constructed rapidly on a constricted site.

The developer, Liz Dunn of Anemone, is well known in Seattle for her innovative commercial projects. She liked the result so much that she moved into an 149-square-metre (1,600-square-foot), top-floor unit with her partner. She also chose all of the interior furnishings, using modern design to unify the functions of living and working in one light-filled space.

The architects built right up to Seattle's 20-metre (65-foot) high zoning limit to achieve units from 65 square metres (700 square feet) to 149 square metres (1,600 square feet), with great city views. Despite being hemmed in by buildings on three sides, the East Union Live-Work Lofts offer residents an excellent aspect. To ensure that the best is made of this view, the large aluminium-frame doors on the outer wall can be pushed up and out of the way, thus opening the indoor live-work space right up to the outside. There is also a public roof deck for all residents, and the top two floors have west-facing balconies, mezzanines and shared access to a private rooftop garden. This is a scheme that reaches out to the city while integrating living and working in a pattern of architectural discipline and order.

Above Façade of the development shows the robust adherence to modernist principles within a steel brace framework.
Opposite and overleaf Interior views of urban live-work lofts, reaching out to the city.

Location Seattle, USA
Client Anemone
Completed 2001
Total Floor Space 1,565 square metres (16,850 square feet)
Accommodates 16

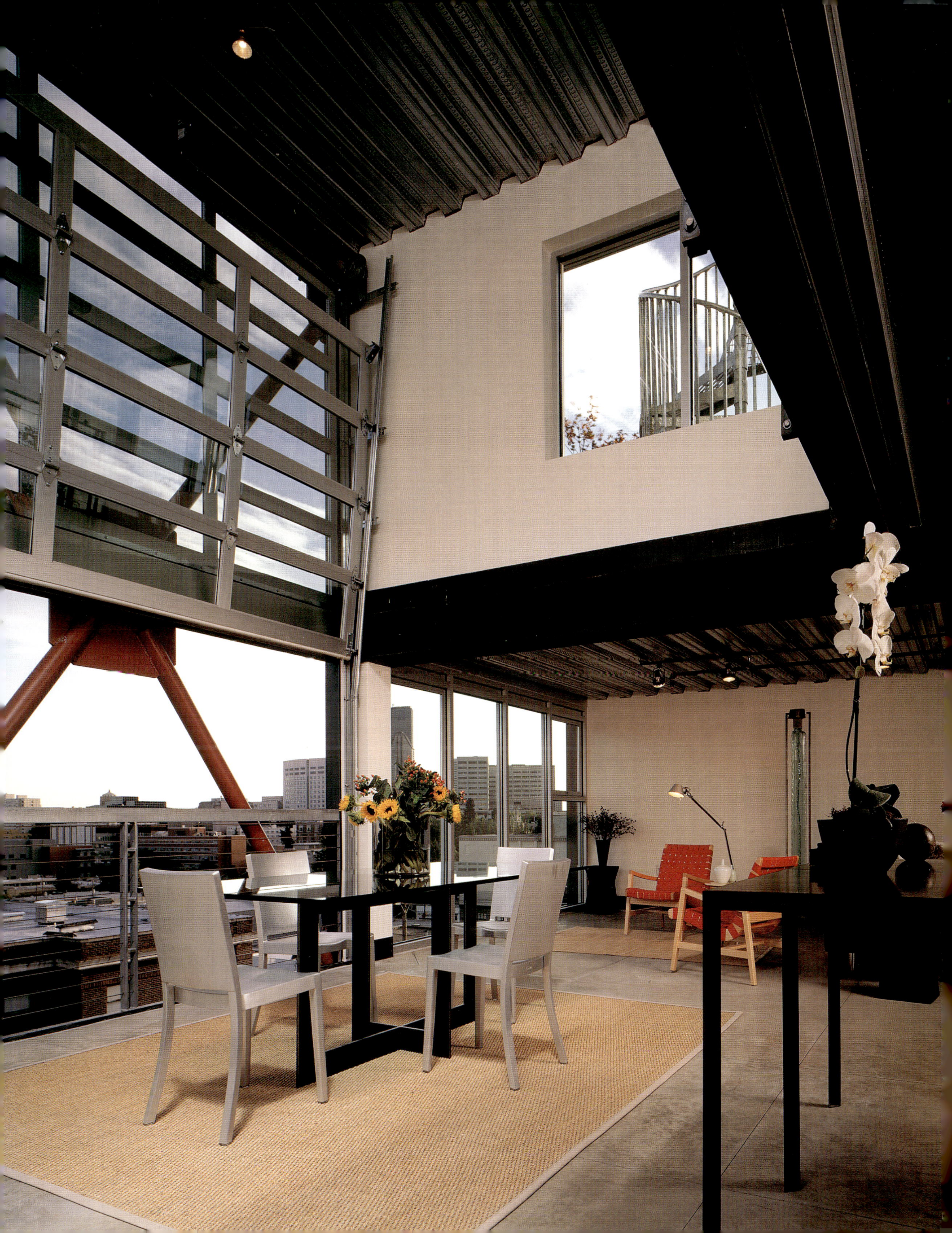

'It was only a modest success financially but it was a big success in every other way I care about.'
Liz Dunn, Developer, Anemone

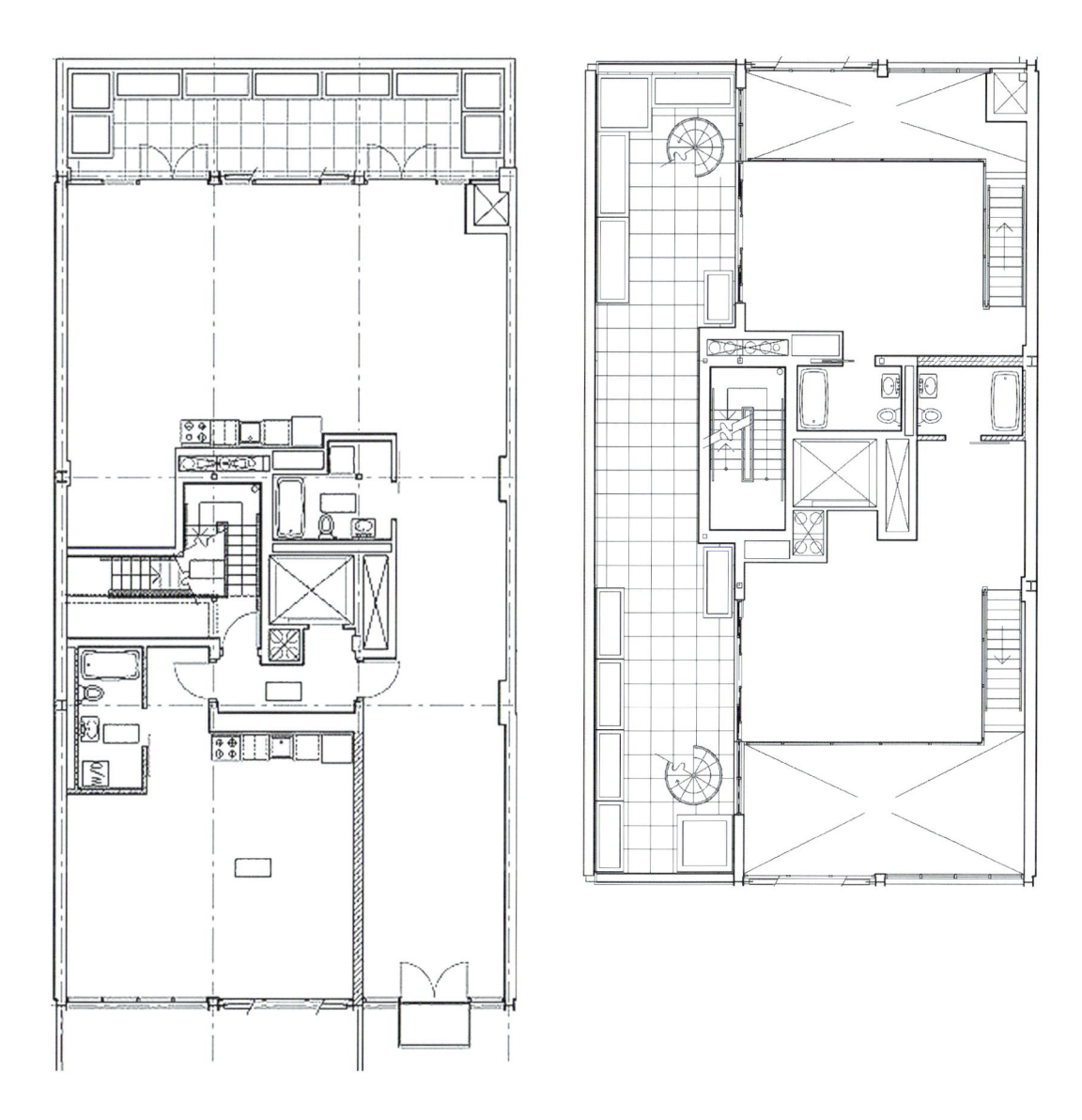

Above Floor plans show layout of a typical unit with mezzanine level.

4.2
Creative Lofts
Huddersfield, UK
Brewster Bye Architects

LOCATED in a handsome Grade II listed building on the edge of Huddersfield town centre in West Yorkshire, UK, this project has transformed the derelict Mechanics' Institute into 21 modern live-work units that offer an attractive place to do both.

Creative Lofts combine a domestic space with an 'office' studio environment. A prominent traditional façade hides an array of modern interior spaces that include double-height living rooms with floor to ceiling windows, wooden floors, exposed brickwork and structural columns, as well as wrought iron spiral staircases. These spaces reflect all that is best about loft living: great natural light, generous volumes and a tone that reflects the heritage of the building they are set in.

The units are provided on a short, one-year lease for those who are setting up their own businesses. Like the incubators and innovation centres that have proliferated in recent years in European cities, these units aim to bring together young entrepreneurs, so that they can benefit from the energy and vitality of a community of like-minded people. They are also situated adjacent to the Media Centre, which is run by an organization of the same name. Residents are encouraged to use the Centre's business services and to attend networking and cultural events. By encouraging short-term tenancies, the project aims to be a staging post for businesses to develop, rather than a long-term accommodation environment.

Funded by a mix of public and private sector finance as part of the social and business regeneration of West Yorkshire, this Lodge setting provides all the facilities needed for a twenty-first-century home worker. It also takes the concept a stage further by locating engaged entrepreneurs in an environment that encourages collaboration and allows access to first class business facilities in the adjacent Media Centre. Little wonder, then, that this live-work success story is set for further expansion, in order to build on the momentum generated by small media and IT businesses sharing their expertise.

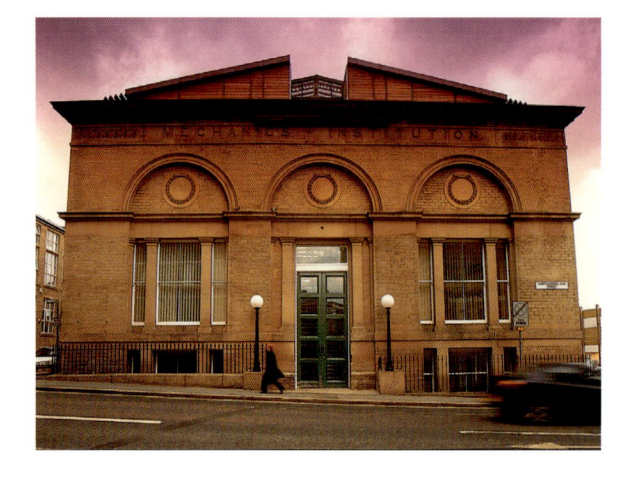

Above The former mechanics institute that now houses 21 modern live-work units.
Opposite Interior of a typical loft, where domestic and work space are blended together in one open environment.

Location Huddersfield, UK
Client Places for People Group (North British Housing)
Completed 2002
Total Floor Space 1,730 square metres (18,620 square feet)
Accommodates 54

163

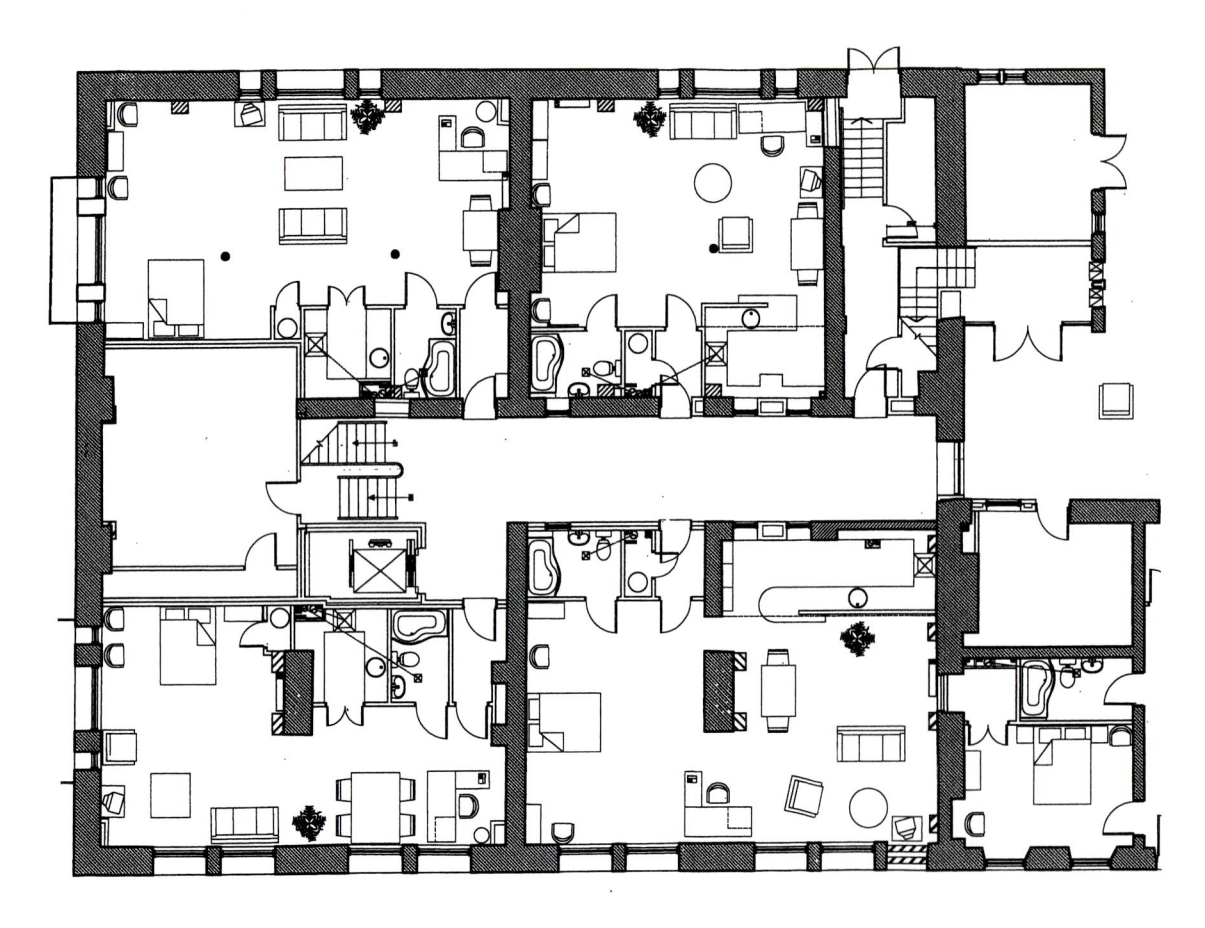

Above Typical floor plan showing four live-work loft spaces.
Right This lodge environment aims to encourage its entrepreneur occupants by providing free access to business facilities in the adjacent Media Centre.

'The time and energy we have saved not having to travel to work is a major factor for us.' *Rakesh Sinha, Fulcrum Logic, and Creative Loft Occupant*

Creative Lofts 165

4.3
Designer's Loft
Tokyo, Japan
Toshihiko Suzuki/Hirota Design Studio

WHEN space is at a premium functionalism usually has to be compromised, but this carefully considered interior for a product designer leaves nothing to chance. Indeed, it functions as a clever product in its own right. The one-room studio, based in an old mansion house near the centre of the city, has been used efficiently through the creation of a stage set that can be reconfigured as necessary. The architect has integrated mobile and interchangeable furniture into a multi-purpose space that morphs between a variety of uses.

As a live-work environment, it was important for the interior to provide a functional work setting, as well as a home and a place to entertain. The main surface, a table, used for work, conceals a kitchen that glides out to create the domestic sphere.

Every dual-function detail has been thought through. A flat screen display on a pivoting arm, for example, can be used for work or for watching television while cooking. Even the wardrobes are on wheels and can be used as impromptu partitions to subdivide the space when needed.

The designers have used the ceiling as the grid for cabling, lighting and power, resulting in a free-form space that connects upwards for its services. A series of ceiling-mounted stainless steel bars complements the service grid, providing a place for special lighting, hanging washing or even functioning as a place to put coats during parties. The interior as a whole combines the warmth of wood, such as white oak, with the coolness of stainless steel, in a minimalist space that creates a sense of illusion through its metamorphosis from work to leisure.

Location Tokyo, Japan
Client Naoko Hirota
Completed 2003
Total Floor Space 48 square metres (520 square feet)
Accommodates 1

Above This tiny studio apartment has been carefully designed to create a flexible live-work environment.
Right Bespoke furniture that changes use allows the space to function as a place for working, entertaining and living.

Lodge

Designer's Loft **167**

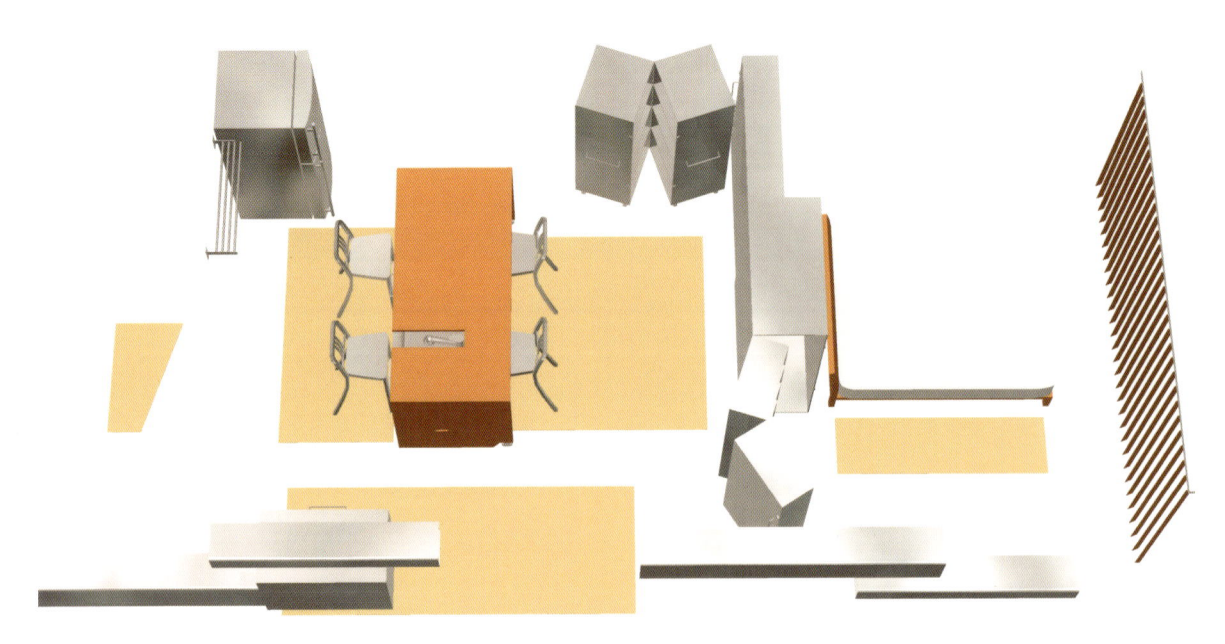

Above Visual showing the space in work mode, with a central table and chairs.
Below Morphing into the domestic sphere, as a kitchen glides out from underneath the central work table.
Opposite Everything in the space has a dual use, from the wardrobe on wheels that is used for subdivision to the exposed service grid on the ceiling that can be used for hanging coats during parties.

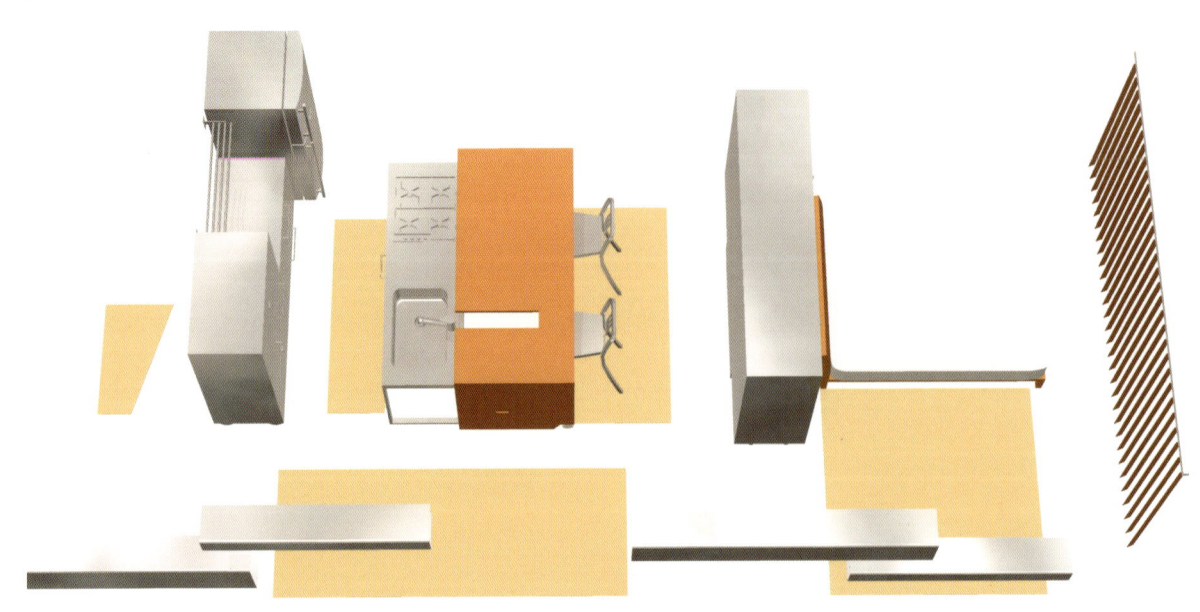

'The main character of the "furniture-like facilities" is mobility and interchangeability.' *Naoko Hirota*

4.4
Mann Residence
Sonoma County, USA
Fernau & Hartman Architects Inc.

PERCHED on a plateau that overlooks the famous Sonoma Valley in California, this Lodge scheme is an inspiring setting for work as well as a great family home. Accommodating a family of three, the residence has to function as a well-provisioned house, but with both an artist and writer in residence, it also has to provide inspirational space for an artist's studio and an effective office for a writer.

Both the house and the separate outbuilding are based around an L-shaped plan, defining a central courtyard that unifies the site. The main office and studio are housed in the outbuilding to provide separateness and privacy, while a smaller office and study is located within the main house.

Externally, other spaces such as the pergola and observation tower are linked by a granite walkway that leads to the kitchen. The materials and external finishes have been carefully chosen to stand out, from a small manicured lawn to the coloured wood façades. Vibrant yellow, red and green cladding defines the buildings, and the architect has made use of the entire site to create a variety of indoor and outdoor spaces. The 'meandering courtyard' achieves an effect that emphasizes the unexpected around every corner, and plays to the temperamental North Californian climate.

Internally, both the living and working spaces have a distinctive quality, enhanced by the extensive glazing that creates both wonderful light and dramatic vistas. The materials that have been used are warm, with extensive use of wood, such as bamboo, that contrasts with the white walls. The architect was keen to preserve a 'modernist spatial flow' and has left many spaces interconnected. The effect is that no one room has a boundary and each blurs into the next.

With vineyards in the foreground and mountains in the distance, this lodge makes the most of its natural surrounds to create an exemplary and innovative set of spaces in which to work and live.

Location Sonoma County, USA
Client Frederic and Kitty Mann
Completed 2002
Total Floor Space 307 square metres (3,300 square feet)
Accommodates Variable

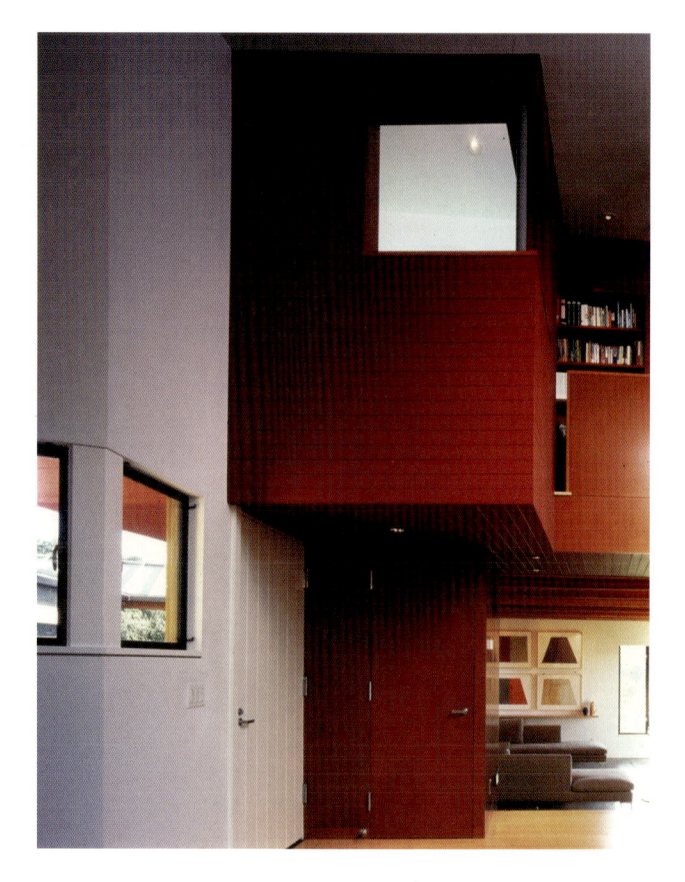

Above The interior spaces merge into each other so that there are no boundaries, with the double-height hall providing a focal point.
Below A series of outdoor courtyards provides a 'meandering effect', and bold colours contrast with the North Californian landscape.
Opposite above The artist's studio provides an inspirational setting with views across the Sonoma Valley.
Opposite below Section showing the main residence and living spaces.

170 Lodge

'Although the overall space of the house would be modest, interior spaces needed to interconnect, each borrowing from the other.' *Richard Fernau and Laura Hartman*

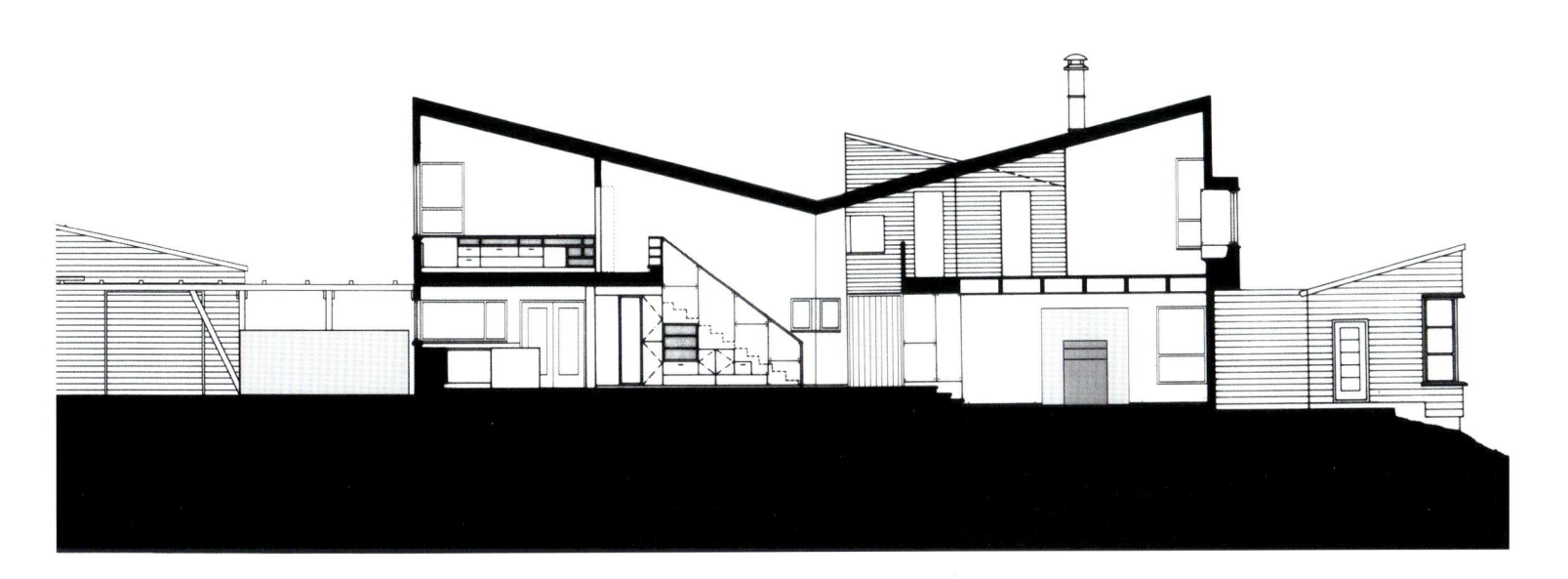

4.5
Katsan Office Building
Stockholm, Sweden
White Architects

OVER time, some city districts shift their image and function between living and working. The North Hammarby Docks in Stockholm, for example, were once bustling industrial docklands and a place of toil and labour. These days they form an essential part of the city's new residential precinct, Hammarby Sjöstad, their quays, locks and lakes creating a desirable place for people to live. Within this reborn waterfront landscape of leisure living, White Architects, one of Scandinavia's largest practices, has built its headquarters – an exercise in domestic planning on a large workplace scale.

A conventional office block would have looked out of place in a setting such as Hammarby Sjöstad, but White still needed the requisite environment to accommodate teams of architects working on big projects. To solve this problem, they set about creating an uncomplicated Lodge-style scheme that is sensitive to its site – so much so that its modest rectangular glass box reflects the flowing waters all around in a myriad of patterns at different times of the day and night.

The entrance to the long and narrow building is through a puncture in its glazed façade at quay level, or via a pedestrian bridge three storeys up. Once inside, the strict order of glass and steel is softened by the untreated timber panelling that forms the partitions between smaller offices and meeting rooms. The inventive juxtaposition of wooden floor joists and glazed elements also helps to soften the environment.

The architects have managed to re-create the simplicity of the traditonal dockside warehouse in a new, low-key context, but have also added something extra. An undeniable residential quality to the office space has been achieved through intimate-looking conference rooms and a restaurant with clear views of the piers and canals that the building overlooks. The architects liken the unobtrusive work areas to the light, relaxed setting of an artist's studio, and you can see why. By reducing what could have been a monumental block to human scale, without sacrificing their commitment to modern forms and materials for dockside pastiche, White has created a home for its staff that simultaneously acknowledges the area's past industry and present lifestyle.

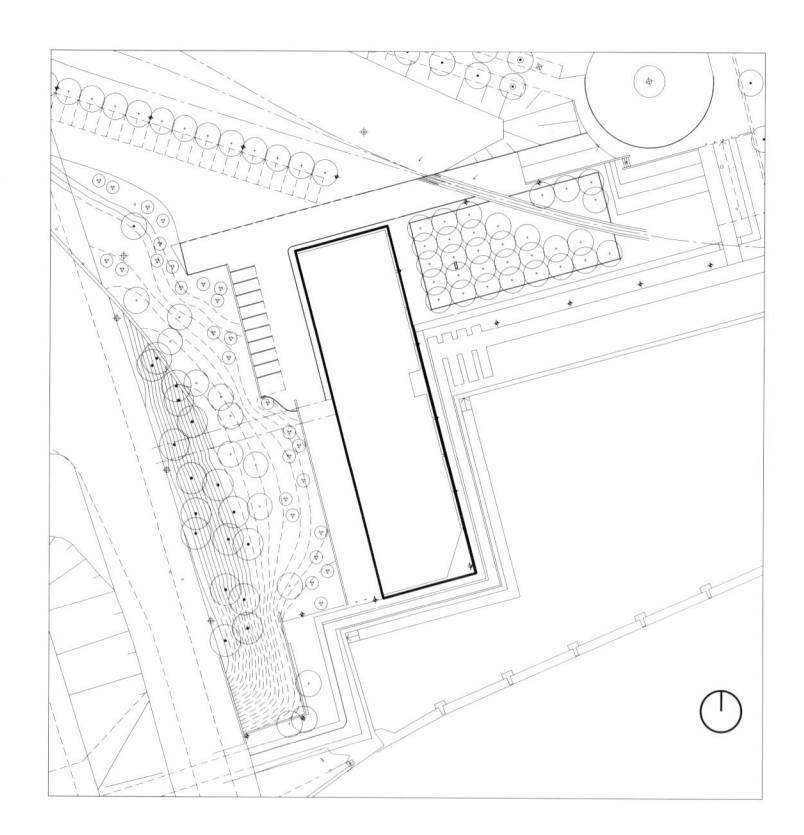

Above Site plan and external view of the building set the project in its context: regenerating an industrial docklands area to create a new residential quarter of Stockholm.
Opposite View of stairwells punctuated by lounge-style seating areas.

Location Stockholm, Sweden
Client White Architects
Completed 2003
Total Floor Space 3000 square metres (32,290 square feet)
Staff 130

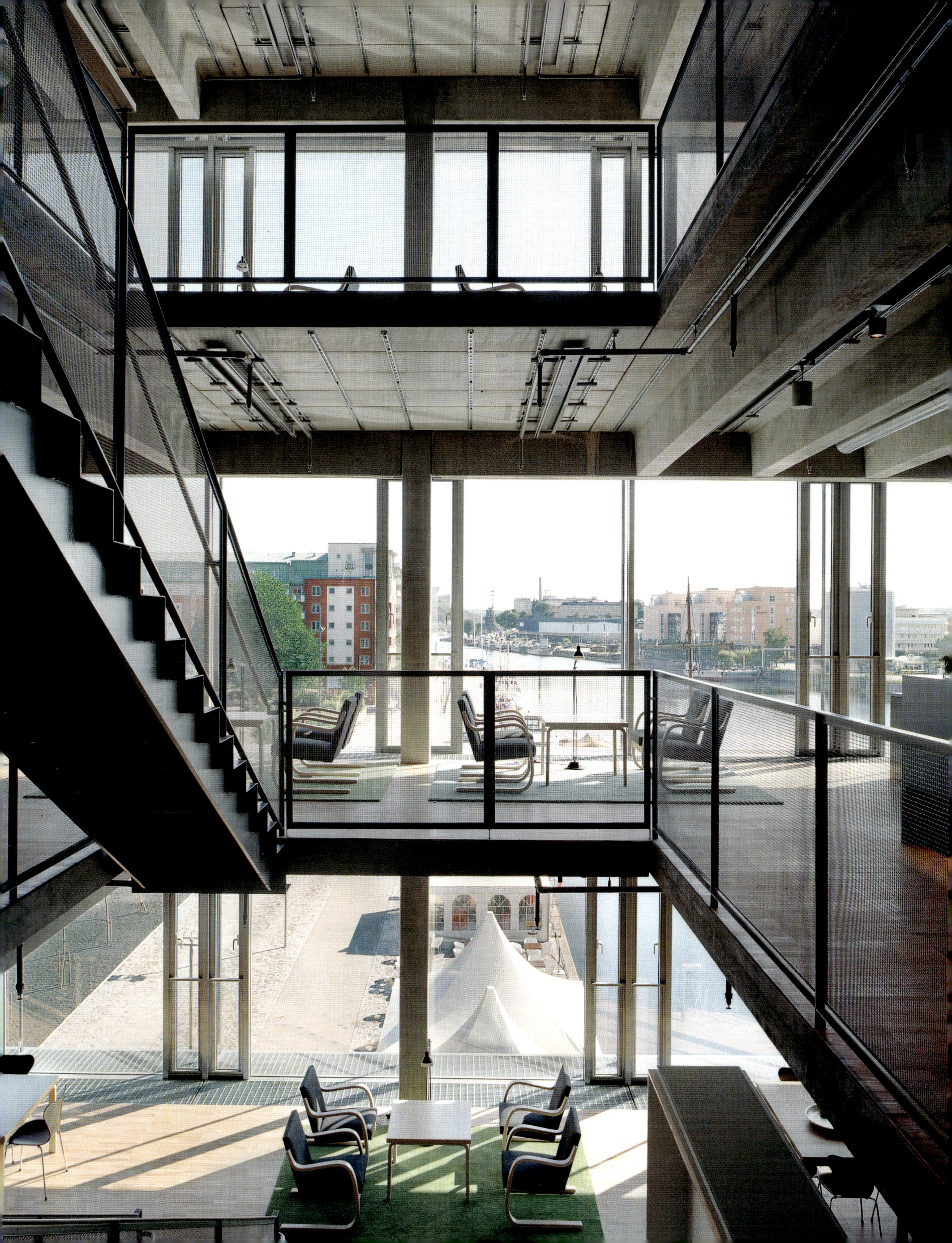

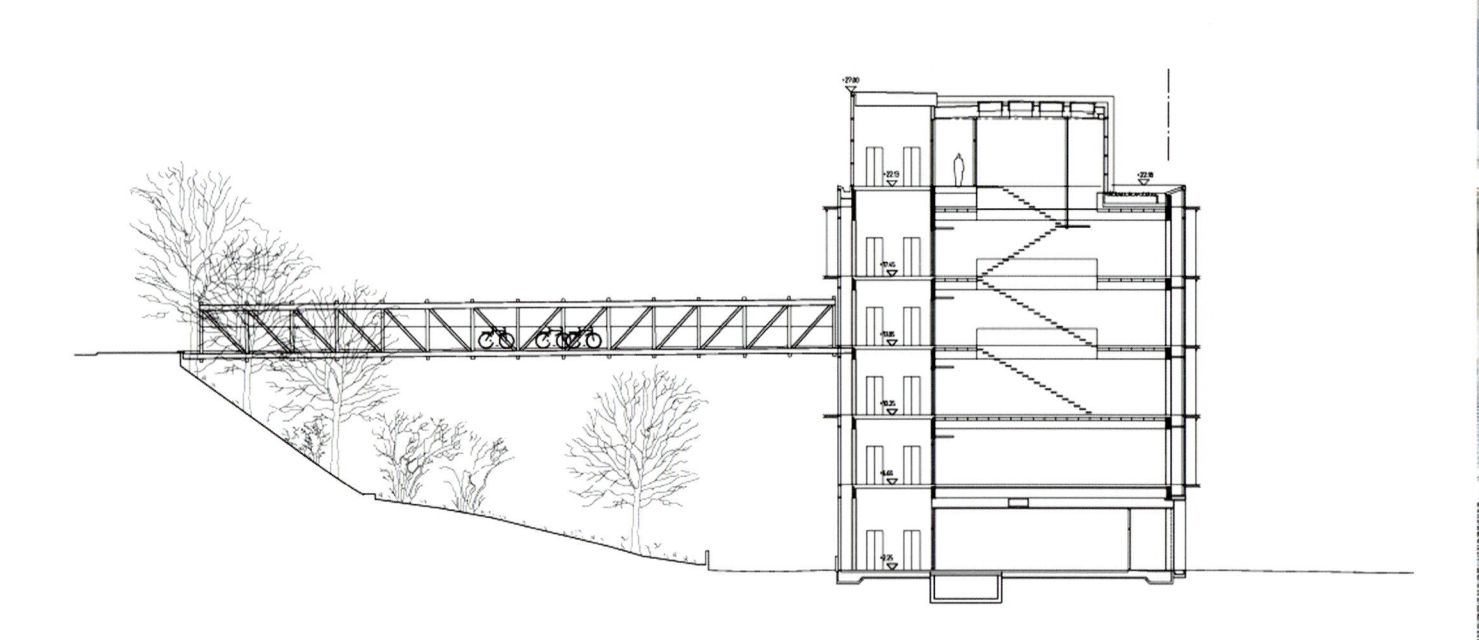

'Being able to recline comfortably and watch a newly restored yacht glide past adds real zest to everyday office life.' *Bengt Svensson and Linda Mattsson, White Architects*

Opposite Section shows the pedestrian bridge creating an upper-level entrance to the building.
Above Perimeter kitchen-dining area close to architects' workstations gives the scheme a domestic flavour, which is enhanced by wooden flooring.

4.6
Home/Office
New York, USA
Roger Hirsch Architect and Myriam Corti

ROGER Hirsch's interior for the New York graphic designer Wing Chan is a good example of the 'less is more' model, in a typical Manhattan space of modest proportions. With only 56 square metres (600 square feet) of floor space, the apartment has to function as office, living/dining room and bedroom. Miesian design ingenuity was called for here.

To avoid a permanent subdivision of space, which would have created a cramped environment, a flexible dividing wall was constructed that allows the room to be transformed according to the function and time of day. In this way, the space can literally metamorphose between the spheres of work and leisure.

Two workstations or desks are accommodated in a 'work' position that allows the living space to be transformed into an office, with a cantilevered sofa that glides away as the bi-folding panels are opened. In the evening the structure is moved, so that all the paraphernalia of work – computers, printers and files – is hidden away, and the room becomes a living space in the 'home' position, complete with bench, sofa and dining table.

The flexibility of this small apartment proves that it is possible to create a live-work space that allows for the separation of 'work' and 'home' environments and yet provides all the benefits of a fully functional home office.

Location New York, USA
Client Wing Chan
Completed 2001
Total Floor Space 56 square metres (600 square feet)
Accommodates 1

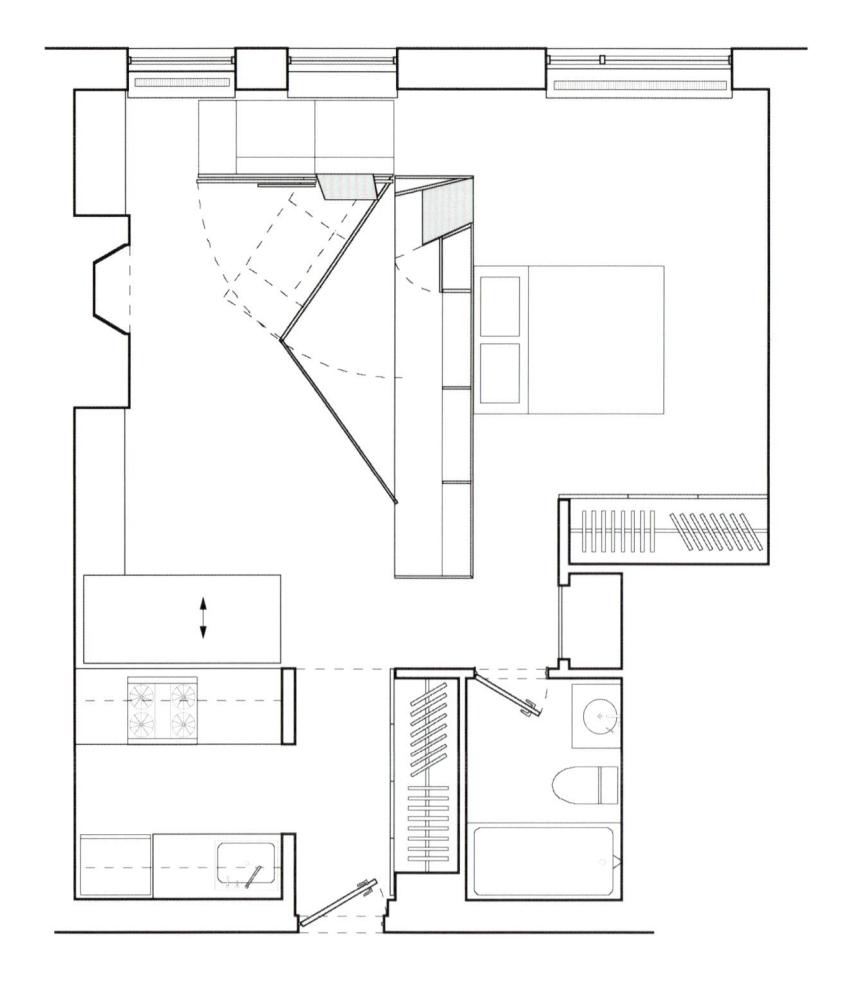

Above Plan showing the flexible dividing wall that changes the function of the room.
Right Separating the spheres of activity: the wall in transition between its 'home' and 'work' position.

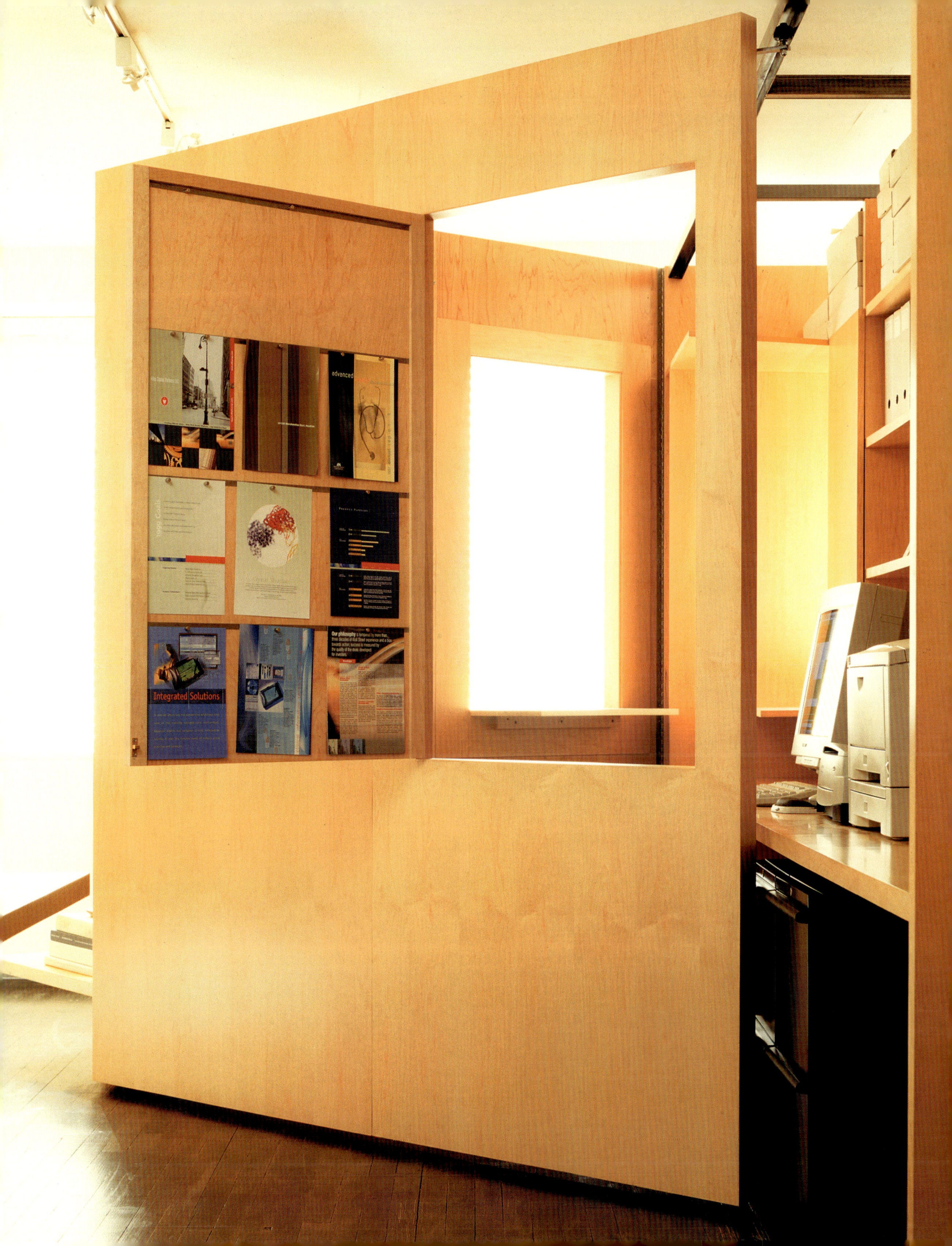
advanced
Integrated Solutions

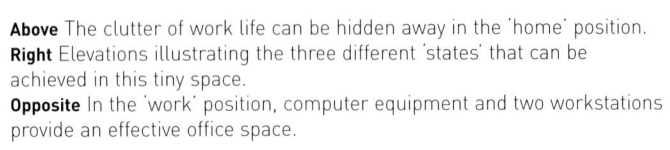

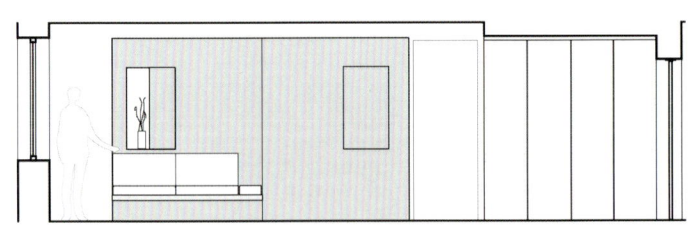

Above The clutter of work life can be hidden away in the 'home' position.
Right Elevations illustrating the three different 'states' that can be achieved in this tiny space.
Opposite In the 'work' position, computer equipment and two workstations provide an effective office space.

Office unit closed

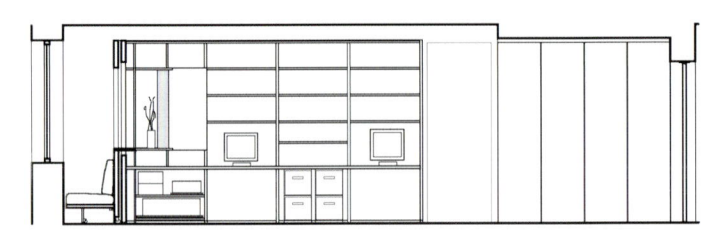

Office unit open

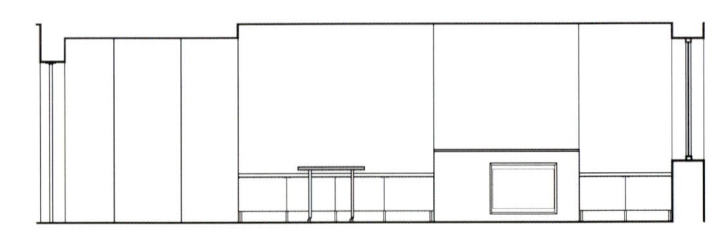

Built-in cabinet with sliding table

'The goal in this project was to create an interior that functioned as both home and office.'
Roger Hirsch

4.7
Apartment
Orio, Spain
Zómad Arquitectos

CONCEALED in a traditional narrow street of an old town centre, this project to create a modern apartment with integrated office skilfully balances history and modernity, home and work.

Externally, the refurbishment is respectful of its ancient surroundings: the exposed plaster-covered masonry walls and the woodwork of eaves and balconies blend in with what has gone before. The radical transformation is internal. To create a modern apartment-cum-workspace flooded with natural light, architect Jaime Ábalos organized the four floors of the building in such a way as to create a more fluid approach to living and working.

The lower floors are used mainly for bedrooms and bathrooms; the upper floors for open-plan living, lit naturally from above by three giant skylights in the roof structure. A staircase weaves down from the upper levels, demarcating spaces including a stylish dining area on the second floor and a neat study slotted in directly beneath the roofline.

Spain's tall and thin traditional houses do not normally lend themselves to modern conversions of this kind in which Lodge-style work areas can be inserted, but this scheme manages the transformation deftly, opening up the space while maintaining the authenticity of the building.

A sandstone wall provides vertical continuity up through the interior; steel rails and structures painted white offer another consistent element. Beech parquet flooring further brightens a space in which the narrow constraints of the site did not impede the architect's vision of an exemplary live-work project.

Location Orio, Spain
Client Private
Completed 2002
Total Floor Space 150 square metres (1,614 square feet)
Accommodates 4

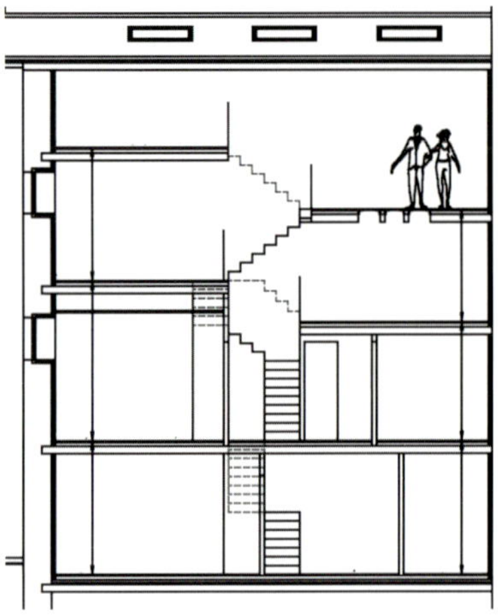

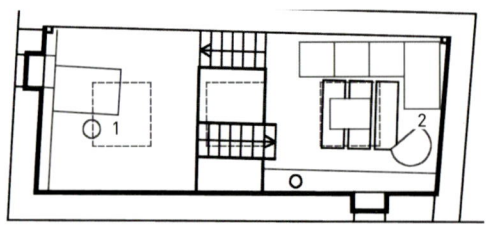

Top floor

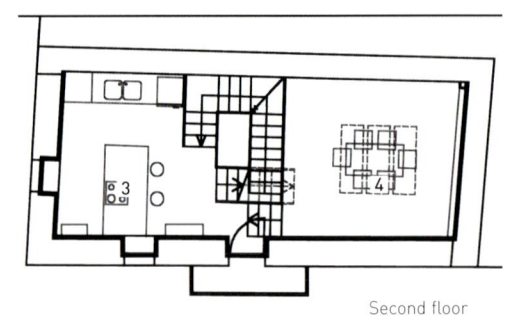

Second floor

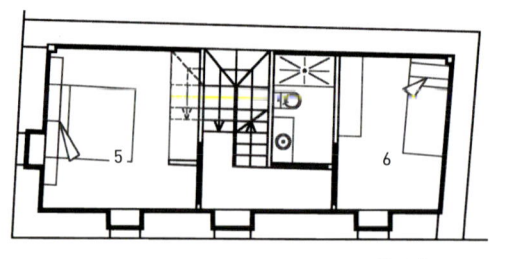

First floor

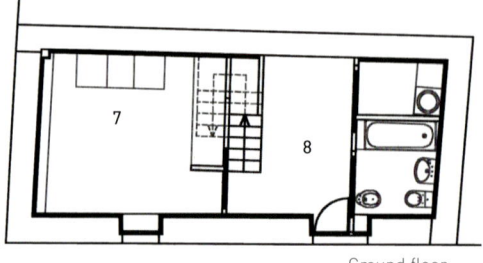

Ground floor

Left and above Plans and section for the remodelled scheme.
Opposite Interior views reveal dramatic skylighting.

1 living area
2 study
3 kitchen
4 dining area
5 bedroom
6 bedroom
7 bedroom
8 entrance hall

'The initial idea was to create a contrast between the traditional exterior and the contemporary interior.'
Jaime Ábalos, Zómad Arquitectos

4.8
Hemingways' Outdoor Office
London, UK
Hemingway Design

THE final project in this book is, rather fittingly, the furthest removed from a conventional office building. This space to work, a two-level 'tepee' structure built from ten recycled telegraph poles, is the summer workplace of British design duo Wayne and Gerardine Hemingway, inspirational founders of the Red or Dead fashion chain. Tired of spending too many hot days sitting at their desks while running their multi-disciplinary design firm, they decided to get out under the blue skies and create an office amid the rhododendrons in their lush English back garden.

The Hemingways share a communal desk on the ground floor of the structure, which has seating built into the decked floor. A wireless network enables them to collaborate with clients and colleagues all over the world. As conventional broadband was not available, they connect to broadband services via satellite. In fact, the Red Indian-style shape of their home office accommodates a host of high technology features, including a plasma TV to review digital imagery. The Hemingways, who are vocal critics of conservative British house-builders, worked closely with Sony to realize their high-tech Lodge setting. A project pow-wow may never be the same again.

Location London, UK
Client Hemingway Design
Completed 2002
Total Floor Space 45 square metres (484 square feet)
Accommodates 2, with up to 5 others

Above The Hemingways at work in their garden office.
Right View of the tented structure.

'I can't wait to get out and work in the garden – I can even do a spot of weeding when I am in need of creative inspiration.' *Gerardine Hemingway*

182 Lodge

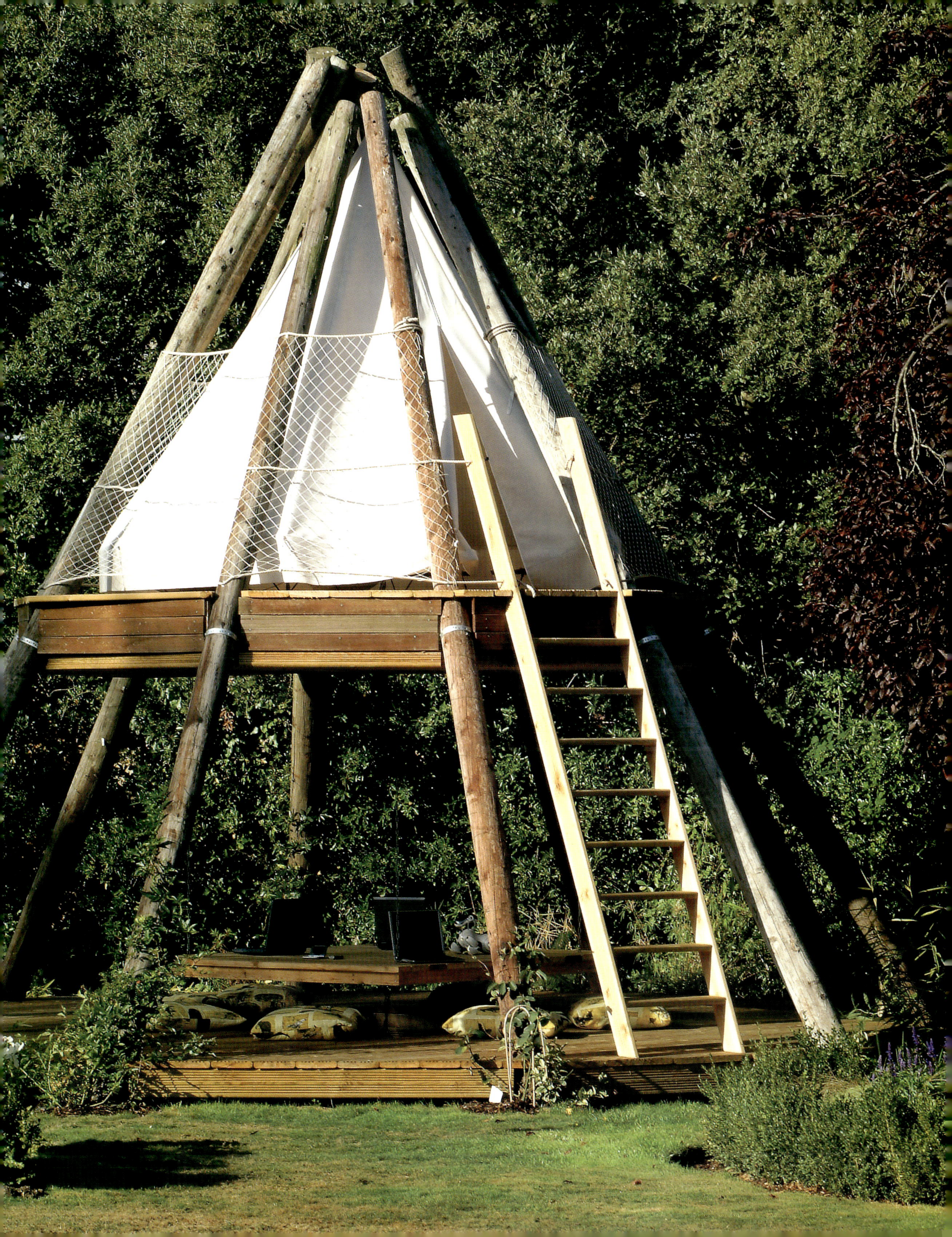

Credits

30 St Mary Axe, London, UK
Architect: Foster and Partners
Riverside Three
22 Hester Road
London SW11 4AN
UK
Website: www.fosterandpartners.com

Project team: Norman Foster (principal-in-charge), Stefan Behling, Grant Brooker, Michael Gentz, Rob Harrison, Paul Kalkhoven, Robin Partington, Paul Scott, Ken Shuttleworth, Hugh Whitehead (project architects), Sara Fox (building director), Francis Aish, Gamma Basra, Geoff Bee, Aike Behrens, Ian Bogle, Thomas Brune, Julian Cross, Joel Davenport, Ben Dobbin, Chris Kallan, Jürgen Küppers, Paul Leadbeatter, Stuart Milne, Jacob Nørlov, Tim O'Rourke, Jason Parker, Ben Puddy, Simon Reed, Narinder Sagoo, Sebastian Schoell, Michael Sehmsdorf, John Small, Robbie Turner, Neil Vandersteen, John Walder, Tim Walpole-Walsh, Richard Wotton, Helen Yabsley.
Client: Swiss Re
Main contractor: Skanska Construction UK Ltd
Project management: RWG Associates
Construction management: Kontor GTCM
Planning consultants: Montagu Evans
Urban design and conservation consultants: The Richard Coleman Consultancy
Structural engineers: Arup
Mechanical and electrical engineers: Hilson Moran Partnership Ltd
Environmental engineers: BDSP Partnership
Cladding consultant: Emmer Pfenninger
Façade access: Reef UK
Lighting: Speirs and Major
Acoustics and AV consultant: Sandy Brown Associates
Landscape architects: Derek Lovejoy Partnership
Planning supervisor: Osprey Mott Macdonald

Academyhills Roppongi Library, Tokyo, Japan
Architect: Kengo Kuma & Associates
2-24-8 Minami Aoyama
Minatoku
Tokyo 107.0062
Japan
Website: www.kkaa.co.jp

Project credits unavailable at time of going to print.

Apartment, Orio, Spain
Architect: Zómad Arquitectos
Po Bizkaia, 4 Bajo
20010 San Sebastián
Spain

Project Team: Jaime Ábalos
Client: Adriana Campoy
Main Contractor: Empresa Constructora
Wood Structure and Masonry: Construccines Kexka
Electricity and Lighting: Txangurro Elektrizitatea SL

Plexiglass: Benegas Industrias Plásticas SL
Tiling and Flooring (bathroom and kitchen): Cerámicas Callejo
Bathroom Fittings: Cabo Bacalao
Dada Kitchen (Molteni), Sofa and Chaise Longue: Coop Mueble
Blue Ekstrem Armchair: Stokke Mobiliario SL

BBC Media Centre, London, UK
Architect: Allies and Morrison/DEGW
85 Southwark Street
London SE1 0HX
UK
Website: www.alliesandmorrison.com

Project Team: Bob Allies and Graham Morrison (senior partners), Joanna Bacon, David Amarasekera, Chris Bearman (project partners), Jason Syrett (project architect for BBC restaurant), Simon Fraser (project architect for Broadcast Centre), Miles Leigh (project architect for Media Centre), Kasia Buguslawska, Nicholas Champkins, Jason Cully, Oliver Heywood, Ewan Morrison, James Parkin, Adam Parkyn, Jonathan Schwinge, Ian Sutherland, Mark Taylor, Miranda Webster, Miles Wilkinson
Client: Land Securities Development (developer), BBC and the BBC Media Village (occupier)
Main Contractor: Bovis Lend Lease
Landscape Architect: Christopher Bradley-Hole Landscape
Interior Designers: DEGW
Project Manager: Gleeds Management Services
Structural Engineer: Buro Happold
Services Engineer: Buro Happold
Quantity Surveyor: Gleeds
Fire Engineer: Buro Happold
Planning Consultants: Nathaniel Litchfield
Access Consultants: David Bonnett Architects Studio

BMW Plant, Central Building, Leipzig, Germany
Architect: Zaha Hadid Architects
Studio 9, 10 Bowling Green Lane
London EC1R 0BQ
UK
Website: www.zaha-hadid.com

Project Team: Zaha Hadid, Patrick Schumacher (design), Lars Teichmann, Jim Heverin (project architects), Jan Huebener, Matthias Frei, Cornelius Schlotthauer, Fabian Hecker, Wolfgang Sunder, Manuela Gatto, Anette Bresinsky, Anneka Wegener, Achim Gergen, Robert Neumayr, Christina Beaumon, Caroline Anderson, Markus Planteau
Client: BMW Group AG, Munich
Landscape Architects: Max Gross
Project Architect Landscape: Daniel Reiser
Main Contractor: Wates Interiors, Arge Rohbau
Project Manager: ARGE Projektsteuerung, Faithful & Gould

Designers and Communications Consultants: BDG Workfutures
Quantity Surveyors: Faithful & Gould
M&E Consultants: GW Building Services Consulting Ltd, AGP Arge Gesamtplanung, Anthony Hunt Associates
Structural Engineers: Faithful & Gould, AGP Arge Gesamtplanung, Anthony Hunt Associates
Cost Consultant and Coordination: AGP Arge Gesamtplanung
Acoustic Engineer: PMI
Civil Engineer: AGP Arge Gesamtplanung
Lighting: Equation Lighting
Steelworks: Max Bögl Bauuntemehmung
Fit-out and Interior Glass: Jaeger Akustik GmbH + Co.
Façade: Radeburger Fensterbaus, Schneider Fertigbau

Coblentz, Patch, Duffy & Bass LLP, San Francisco, USA
Architect: Aston Pereira & Associates
Westlake Building
909 Montgomery Street, Suite 101
San Francisco CA 94133
USA
Website: www.aston.com

Architects of the Ferry Building: SMWM, BCV, Page & Turnbull
Aston Pereira Project Team: Aston Pereira, Eileen Pereira, Ken Eng, Koji Okamura, Melissa Van Zee
Client: Coblentz, Patch, Duffy & Bass LLP
General Contractor: Webcor Builders
MEP Engineer: Mazzetti & Associates
Structural Engineer: Rutherford & Chekene
Acoustic Consultant: Charles M. Salter Associates
Nework Cabling: Access Communications
Electrical Subcontractor: Rosendin Electric
Glass, Glazing, Handrails: Walters & Worl
Handicap Lift: McKinley Equipment Corporation
Operable Partitions: Chaix Company
Millwork, Wood Panelling & P-LAM Cabinets: Wood Connection
Drywall: California Drywall Co.
Mechanical, Sprinkler, Plumbing: Anderson, Rowe & Buckley
Structural Steel, Window Walls: Delta Steel
Acoustic Ceiling: Spacetone Acoustics
Stone Flooring & Walls: D&J Tile
Carpet and VCT Flooring: R. E. Cuddie Co.
Painting and Wallcovering: George E. Masker Inc.
Appliances: McPhails Appliances Inc.
Italian Stucco: Frey Plastering
Millwork Furniture: Dependable Furniture Manufacturing
Furniture Dealer: Vanguard Legato

Creative Lofts, Huddersfield, UK
Architect: Brewster Bye Architects
5 North Hill Road
Headingley
Leeds LS6 2ED
UK
Website: www.brewsterbye.co.uk

Project Team: Chris Austin, Michael Rushforth
Client: Places for People (also known as North British Housing Association)
Client's Agent: Faithful & Gould
Main Contractor: Termrim Construction
Structural Engineers: Doyle Partnership
Facilities Management: Media Centre Network Ltd

Designer's Loft, Tokyo, Japan
Design: Hirota Design Studio
Tuttle Bldg 4F-B
2-6-5 Higashi Azabu
Minato-ku 106-0044
Tokyo
Japan
Website: www.hirotadesign.com

Architectural Collaboration: Toshihiko Suzuki
Client: Naoko Hirota

East Union Live/Work Lofts, Seattle, USA
Architect: The Miller/Hull Partnership
71 Columbia, Sixth Floor
Seattle WQ 98104
USA
Website: www.millerhull.com

Project Team: David Miller (partner), Lene Copeland (project manager)
Client: Dunn & Hobbs, Anemone LLC
General Contractor: Turner Construction Company SPD
Structural Engineer: Peter Opsahl
Steel Fabricator and Detailer: Standard Steel Fabricating Co. Inc.
Steel Erector: International Steel

EMI London Headquarters, London, UK
Architect: MoreySmith Design and Architecture
24 Marshalsea Road
London SE1 1HF
UK
Website: www.moreysmith.com

Project Team: Linda Morey Smith, Andrew McCann, Graeme Montague
Client: EMI Group
Main Contractor: ISG InteriorExterior
Project Manager: Rowney Sharman
Cost Consultant: David Langdon & Everest
M&E Contractor: Cameron Taylor Brady
Quantity Surveyor: Davis Langdon
Structural Engineer: Sinclair Knight Merz

Enjoy, Paris, France
Architect: Edouard François Workshop
136 rue Falguière
75015 Paris
France
Website: www.edouardfrancois.com

Project Team: José Reis de Matos, Caroline Witendal, Jean Baptiste Fontanarosa, Enzo Renard, Camille Bernard
Client: Enjoy
Contractor, Consultant and Manufacturer: Edouard François Workshop

Ericsson North American Headquarters, Texas, USA
Interior Architecture: Lauckgroup
2828 Routh Street, Suite 200
Dallas, TX 75201
USA
Website: www.lauckgroup.com

Design Architects: Thompson Vaivoda & Associates, Gideon Toal
Lauckgroup Project Team: Alan Lauck, Anne Kniffen, Brigitte Preston, Carrie Bobbett, Craig Anderchak, Debra Kolb, Jennifer Griesbaum, Julie Holbert, Rick Hibbs, Sherrie McElroy, Sonia Kidman, Ted Kollaja
Client: Ericsson Inc.
Research Consultants: BOSTI
Engineering: Purdy-McQuire
Wetland: Halff Associates
Landscape: Mesa Design Group
Lake: Waterscape Consultants
FPE: Schirmer Engineering
Geotechnical: GMC Consulting Service
Lighting: Randy Burkett Lighting Design
Technology: TechKnowledge
Acoustical and Audio Visual: Wrightson, Johnson, Haddon & Williams

ESO Hotel, Cerro Paranal, Chile
Architect: Auer+Weber+Architekten
Georgenstrasse 22
80799 Munich
Germany
Website: www.auer-weber.de

Project Team: Philipp Aier (project architect), Dominik Schemkirz, Robert Giessl, Michael Krüger, Charles Martin
Client: ESO European Southern Observatory
Outdoor Facilities: Gesswein, Henkel + Partner
Engineering: Mayr + Ludescher (structural), HL-Technik AG (mechanical), HL-Technik AG (electrical), Schneidewendt (kitchen)
Lighting Design: Werner Lampl, Diessen

Future Centre, Innsbruck, Austria
Architect: Peter Lorenz
Maria-Theresien-Strasse 37
A-6020 Innsbruck
Austria
Website: www.peterlorenz.at

Project Team: Peter Lorenz, Martin Franzmair
Client: Association of Employees/Workers
Electrical Engineer: Herrn Ing. Dieter Eidelpes
Acoustics: Herrn Dipl. Ing. Dr. techn. Karl Bernd Quiring, Ars Electronica (new media)
Site Management: Herrn Baumeister Ing. Georg Malojer

Genzyme Centre, Massachusetts, USA
Architect and General Planner, Building and Interior: Behnisch, Behnisch & Partner
Gorch-Fock-Strasse 30
70619 Stuttgart
Germany
Website: www.behnisch.com

Project Team: Stefan Behnisch, Christof Jantzen, Günther Schaller, Martin Werminghausen (design architect), Maik Neumann (design architect)
Clients: Lyme Properties LLC, Genzyme Corporation
Executive Architects: House & Robertson (base building), Next Phase Studios (tenant improvement)
General Contractor: Turner Construction Company
Master planning: Urban Strategies
Environmental Consultancy, Structural and MEP Engineers: Buro Happold,
MEP Engineers: Laszlo Bodak Engineers
Green Building/LEED® Consultant: Natural Logic
Gardens: LOG ID
Natural and Artificial Lighting Consultancy: Bartenbach LichtLabor GmbH
Workplace Consultancy: DEGW
Colour Concepts, Ceiling Mural, Workstations and Chandelier Design: Behnisch, Behnisch & Partner
Acoustic Consultant: Acentech Inc. with McKay Conant Brook
Water Feature Consultant: Crystal Fountains, Manufacturer: Carbone Metal Fabricators
Filigree System and Components: Mid State Filigree Systems
Curtain Wall: Karas & Karas
Green Roof: Roofscapes Inc.
Photovoltaic Panels: Powerlight Corporation
Prism Skylight: Bomin Sola GmbH
Chandeliers: Behnisch, Behnisch & Partners (design), Bartenbach LichtLabor (engineering), Bomin Solar GmbH (manufacture)
Light Wall: Contract Shading Systems
Reflective Panels: Karas & Karas
Reflective Perimeter Blinds: Bomin Solar GmbH
Millwork: Modern Industries Co.
Lobby and Office Furnitue: Office Environment
CEO Suite: Creative Office Pavilion manufactured by VS – Vereinigte Spezialmöbelfabriken Tauberbischofsheim

Hemingways' Outdoor Office, London, UK
Design concept: Wayne Hemingway
15 Wembley Park Drive
Wembley
Middx HA9 8HD
UK
Website: www.hemingwaydesign.co.uk

Home/Office, New York, USA
Architect: Roger Hirsch Architect and Myriam Corti
91 Crosby Street
New York NY10012
USA
Website: www.rogerhirsch.com

Client: Wing Chan/Wing Chan Design
Metalwork: Art & Design Works
Woodwork: Timehri Studios

Interpolis, Tilburg, Holland
Consultancy WorkConcept: Veldhoen + Company
Meerssenerweg 166B
6222 AK Maastricht
Holland
Website: www.velhoen.nl

Client: Piet Lambrechts, MD Group Facility Management Unit, Interpolis
Architect Exterior: Bonnema Architecten, Hardegaryp
Architect Interior/Supervisor: Nel Verschuuren, Buro Kho Lang Li
Project Management: Interpolis Bouwburo
Designer, House in the Wood: Piet Hein Eek, Eek & Ruygrof vof, Geldrop
Designer, Stone House: Marcel Wanders, Studio Wanders, Amsterdam
Designer, Station House: Irene Fortuijn, Studio Fortuijn-O'Brien, Amsterdam
Designer, Weaver's Hut: Bas van Tol, Studio Muller en van Tol, Amsterdam
Designer, Sea House: Ellen Sander, Sander Architecten, Amsterdam
Designer, House of Light: Mark Warning

Designer, Garden House: Joep van Lieshout, Atelier van Lieshout, Rotterdam
Designer, Living room eatery: Jurgen Beij, Rotterdam

Katsan Office Building, Stockholm, Sweden
Architect: White Architects
Östgötagatan 100
Box 4700
SE-116 92 Stockholm
Sweden
Website: www.white.se

Project Team: Åke Willén (project manager) Bengt Svensson, Linda Mattson, Per Wikfeldt, Mikael Sewon, Sara Grahn (architecture), Kjell Jensfelt, Åke Haremst, Lotta Holmgren.
Client: White Architects (HB Katsan)
Environment Management: White Architects – Marie Hult, Marja Lundgren, Anders Lood
Main Contractor: Peab Sverige AB.
Major Contractors: Strängbetong AB (precast manufacture), Flex fasader AB (glass façade)
Major Consultants: Scandiakonsult/Ramböll (structural engineer), Ångpanneföreningen (mechanical engineer), Elkonsult Lennart Goldring (electrical engineer)

Kennispoort, Eindhoven, Holland
Architect: Koen van Velsen
Spoorstraat 69 a, 1211 GA
Postbus 1367, 1200 BJ Hilversum
Holland

Project Team: Marco van Zal, Marcel Steeghs, Gero Rutten, Chris Arts, Gideon de Jong, Tom Bergevoet, Merihn de Jong
Client: Technische Universität Eindhoven (TH/e)
Main Contractor: Heijmans IBC Buw BV
Construction: D3BN
Cabinetmaker: Peter Vocking Meubelmakers

Kirshenbaum Bond & Partners West, San Francisco, USA
Architect: Jensen & Macy Architects
55 Sumner Street
San Francisco CA 94103
USA
Website: www.jensen-macy.com

Project Team: Mark Jensen & Mark Macy (principals), Dean Orr, Nana Kim, Frank Merritt, Balz Mueller
Client: Chuck Maggio CFO
Contractor: Johnstone & McAuliffe
Lighting Designer: Jensen & Macy Architects
Suppliers: Flos, Zumtobel (lighting), Flex Tray (raceways), Hufcor (operable partitions), Eurotex (carpet), AFCO USA (coir matting), Jasper Seating (library chairs), Herman Miller (conference room chairs), Knoll (dining counter stools/café chairs), C&H Distributors (dining counter and park benches)

Less Limited, Hong Kong, China
Architect: Dou Design
Room 601
6/f Hoseinee House
69 Wyndham Street
Central Hong Kong
China

Project Team: Lambert Ma, Bill Price, Joshua So, Michael Valenzuela
Client: Less Limited
Main Contractor: Sprout (Design and Collaborative) Limited

Madrid Regional Documentary Centre, Madrid, Spain
Architect: Mansilla + Tuñón
Rios Rosas 11, 6º
28003 Madrid
Spain
Website: www.mansilla-tunon.com

Project team: Luis M. Mansilla, Emilio Tuñón, Matilde Peralta, Ainoa Prats, Oscar F. Aguayo, Jaime Gimeno, Andrés Regueiro, Fernando Garcia-Pino, Maria Linares, David Nadal, Robert Rininger
Client: Madrid Regional Government
Principal Engineer: J. G. Asociados,
Alfonso Gómez Gaite
Graphic Design: Gráfica Futura
Furniture and Equipment: Oscar F. Aguayo
Civil Engineers: Santiago Hernán and Juan Carlos Corona
U-Glass: Alferglas
Façade Restoration: Artemón
Portuguese Basalt Pavement: Const. Joanino
Exterior Doors: Dacin
Aluminium Shades and Sign Panels: Entorno
Windows: Gravent
Woodwork: La Navarra
Electricity: Cymi
Plumbing: Eralia
Electrical Systems: Gúdulo
HVAC Heating Ventilation and Air Conditioning: Nordes
Lighting: Erco

Maison de l'Architecture, Paris, France
Architect: Chartier-Corbasson Architectes
3 rue Ambroise Thomas
75009 Paris
France
Website: www.chartier-corbasson.com

Project Team: Karine Chartier, Thomas Corbasson, Joseph Grappin, Alexander Cloekner
Client: Conseil Régional de l'Ordre des Architectes d'Ile de France
General Contractor: SNCE, AMG-Féchoz
Scenography: Ducks Scéno
Acoustics: Jean Paul Lamoureux
MEP Engineering: Cotec
Graphics: LM Communiquer

Mann Residence, Sonoma County, USA
Architect: Fernau & Hartman Architects, Inc.
2512 Ninth Street No. 2
Berkeley CA 94710
USA
Website: www.fernauhartman.com

Project Team: Richard Fernau, Laura Hartman (partners in charge), Jeff Day (house design project architect), Aaron Thornton (pool project architect, bunker architect), Alexis Maznick
Client: Frederic & Kitty Mann
House Contractor: Jeff F. Nimmo
Pool Contractor: Jess Janssen
Consultants: Richard Hartwell, Jon Brody
Mechanical Consultant: Madcon
Electrical Consultant: O'Mahoney & Myer
Surveyor: Ray Carlson & Associates Inc. Land Surveying
Cooling: Davis Energy Group
Plumbing: Dry Creek Plumbing
Landscape and Soils: Bauer Associates
Pool Engineer: Endres/Ware

Max Planck Institute of Molecular Cell Biology and Genetics, Dresden, Germany
Architect: Heikkinen-Komonen Architects
Kristianinkatu 11-13
00170 Helsinki
Finland
Website: www.heikkinen-komonen.com

Project Team: Mikko Heikkinen and Markku Komonen (partners in charge), Janne Kentala (project architect)
Architect of Record: HENN Architekten Ingenieure
Project Team: Gunter Henn, Rudolf Röglin (project architect), Frank Gebler
Client: Max-Planck-Gesellschaft zur Förderung der Wissenschaften e.V.
Engineers: Ingenieurbüro Prof. Dr. Ing. G. Scholz und Partner (construction engineer), Jaeger, Mornhinweg + Partner Ingenieurgesellschaft (HVAC)
Façades: Radeburger Fensterbau
Exterior Cladding: Lichtgitter (metal mesh)
Staircase: Metallbau Söll
Acoustic Ceilings: Lidner AG
Furnishings: Mebel Oy (wood chairs), Avarte Oy (lounge chairs)
Upholstery: Schäfer Ausstattung-Systeme (instrument cupboards)
Landscape Architect: Landschaftsarchitektur Petzold
Electrical Consultant: Müller+Bleher GmbH
Structural Consultant: PMI Peter Mutard Ingenieurgesellschaft mbH

Momentum, Science Park, Hørsholm, Denmark
Architect: Bosch & Fjord
Sølvgade 11
DK-1307 Copenhagen K
Denmark
Website: www.bosch-fjord.com

Project Team: Rosan Bosch, Rune Fjord Jensen, Maria Keinicke Davidsen, Janne Raahauge, Helene Øllgaard
Client: Momentum and SCION/DTU (finance)
Consulting engineer: Dines Jørgensen & Co.
Carpentry: Uvelse Maskinsnedkeri
Electrician: John Hoeberg El ApS
Painting: Malermester Claus Mattsson
Plumber: Fredensborg VVS
Lighting: Flos
Mezzanine: Handler A/S
Flooring: Chris Coating A/S
Spiral staircase: Sundby Trapper A/S
Tarpaulin/canvas: August Olsens Eftf. A/S
Cabinetmaker: Totalproduktion ApS
Furniture: Paustian
Stair construction calculations: By & Byg

Mother, London, UK
Design Architect: Clive Wilkinson Architects
101 S. Robertson Blvd, Suite 204
Los Angeles CA 90038
USA
Website: www.clivewilkinson.com

Project Team: Clive Wilkinson, Richard Hammond
Client: Mother Advertising Agency
Developer and Landlord: Simon Silver
Real Estate Broker: David Rosen, Pilcher Hershman
Executive Architect: AHMMA (Allford Hall Monaghan Morris Architects)
Main Contractor: Dragados Obras Y Proyectos SA
Project Management: Jackson Coles
General Contractor: SAMES plc
Plastic Curtains: Safety Screens

Marimekko Covers: Marj Abela
Millwork: Roger Hynam (walls of doors and white leather ottomans), David Hall (stainless reception desk and bar)
Floor Finish: Thortex (polyurethane paint)

Munich Re, Munich, Germany
Architect: Baumschlager & Eberle
Lindauer Strasse 31
A-6911 Lochau
Austria
Website: www.baumschlager-eberle.com

Project Team: Christian Tabernigg, Echkehart Loidoit (project architects), Bernhard Demmel, Marc Fisler, Elmar Hasler, Alexia Monauni, Marlies Sofia, Daniela Weber
Client: Munich Re Group
Construction Supervision: BIP Beratende Ingenieure für das Bauwesen VBI GmbH
Civil Engineering: CAE Ingenieurbüro für Haustechnik
Acoustic Consultant: ZP Zumbach & Partners
Corporate Art and Architecture consultant: Dr. Susanne Ehrenfried
Graphics: PI Project Innovations
Landscape Architects: Vogt Landschaftsarchitekten
Electrical Engineers: OvM Oskar von Miller/Beratende Ingenieure
Mechanical Engineer: GMI Gasser & Messner Ingenieure
Structural Engineer: FSIT Friedrich Strasse Ing. Büro Tragweksplanung
Façade: Dobler Metallbau GmbH

Norddeutsche Landesbank, Hanover, Germany
Architect: Behnisch, Behnisch & Partner
Gorch-Fock-Strasse 30
70619 Stuttgart
Germany
Website: www.behnisch.com

Project Team: Günter Behnisch, Stefan Behnisch, Günther Schaller (partners), Martin Haas, Jörn Genkel (project leaders), Alexandra Burkard, Martin Gremmel, Dominik Heni, Bettina Maier, Klaus Schwägerl, Jorg Usinger with Dirk Anhorn, Chiara Baccarini, Volker Biermann, Andrea Croé, Willy Haberer, Michael Huiss, Eckart Krüger, Birgit Mannsdörfer, Maik Neumann, Severin Rüssmann, Alex Sargeson, Ann Katrin Schilling, Noa Shatzmiller, Wolfgang Sterr, Roland Zimmerman
Client: Norddeutsche Landesbank
Project Management: NILEG
Engineers: Arge Tragwerksplanung, Wetzel & von Seht, Pfefferkorn.
Consultants: Transsolar Energietchnik (energy), Christian Kandzia (colour), Becker & Becker, Lindhorst, Grabe, Taube/Goerz/Liegat (environmental)
Landscape: Behnisch, Behnisch & Partner

One Omotesando, Tokyo, Japan
Architect: Kengo Kuma & Associates
2-24-8 Minami Aoyama
Minatoku
Tokyo 107.0062
Japan
Website: www.kkaa.co.jp

Client: Riso Kagaku Corporation
General Contractor: Constructor: Ando Corporation
Structural Engineers: Oak Structural Design
Mechanical Engineer: P.T. Morimura & Associates Ltd

Pallotta TeamWorks, Los Angeles, USA
Architect: Clive Wilkinson Architects
101 S. Robertson Blvd, Suite 204
Los Angeles CA 90038
USA
Website: www.clivewilkinson.com

Project Team: Clive Wilkinson, Ian Macduff (design director), Alexis Rappaport (project manager), Bill Beauter (project architect), Philippe Pare, Vance Ruppert, Jonathan Chang, Catherine Garrison, Merideth Waltzeck
Client: Pallotta TeamWorks
Client Representative: Dan Pallotta
General Contractor: Turelk Inc.
Structural Engineer: Nabih Youssef & Associates
Design/Build Mechanical: ACCO
Design/Build Electrical: Accord Electric Corporation
Tent Fabrication: J. Miller Canvas
Rubber Flooring: Johnsonite
Custom Dyed Carpet: Designweave
Steel Shipping Containers: Mobile Mini
Millwork: Jeff Trott Industries
Exposed Wood Framing: Kincaid
Reception Desk: Ilan Dei Studio
Metalwork: Washington Ironworks

Parliamentary Annexe, Helsinki, Finland
Architect: Helin & Co Architects
Mannerheimplatsen 1B
Helsinki
Finland
Website: www.helinco.fi

Project Team: Pekka Helin (project management), Peter Verhe (project director), Mariitta Helineva (interior design management), Tarja Hildén, Seija Ekholm, Jaana Saarelainen, Lasu Aura, Sanna Siltala, Kirsi Pajunen, Jonni Laitto, Jukka Björn, Terhi Manninen, Jyrki Rihu, Kai Makkanen, Tatu Korhonen, Johanna Nordman, Petteri Lautso, Harri Kemppainen, Mika Vesterinen, Minna Partti, Satu Jaatinen, Kirsi Wass, Ari Sahlman
Client: Parliament of Finland
Main Contractor: YIT Corporation, YIT Construction Services
Foundation Engineering: JP-Transplan Oy
Structural Engineering: WSP ConsultingKORTES Ltd
HVAC Engineering: Niemi Group, Insinööritoimisto Niemi & Co. Oy
Electrical Engineering: Lausamo Consulting Ltd, Insinööritoimisto Lausamo Oy
Stone Façade Structures: OK Graniitti Oy Ltd
Double Façade, Glazed Roof structures: Teräselementti Oy
HVAC and Electrical Systems: YIT Huber Oy Ltd

Pixar Animation Studios, Emeryville, USA
Architect: Bohlin Cywinski Jackson
733 Allston Way
Berkeley CA 94710
USA
Website: www.bcj.com

Project Team: Peter Q. Bohlin (design principal), Jon C. Jackson (principal-in-charge), Karl Backus (Principal and project manager), Rosa Sheng, Sean Pulsifer, Can Tiryaki, Kruti Majmudar, Charles Cwenar, David Senft, Sara Snyder, Amy Nradac, Peter Streibig, Josh Keller, Maria Danielides, Theresa Bucco, Mary Beth Coyne, Doug Speckhard
Client: Pixar
General Contractor: DPR Construction

Landscape Architect: Peter Walker & Partners
Structural Engineer: Rutherford & Chekene
Structural Engineer, Glass Specialities: Dewhurst MacFarland & Partners Inc.
Mechanical Engineer: Flack & Kurtz Inc.
Civil Engineers: Brian Kangas Foulk
Acoustic Consultants: Design West Partnership
Communications Consultants: Connectin Communications
Security Consultants: Tomasi-Dubois & Associates

Porta22, Barcelona, Spain
Design: Interiors Disseny
Plaça Reial 18 2on 1º
08002 Barcelona
Spain
Website: www.mbmarquitectes.com

Project Team: Lluis Pau, Josep Martorell, Oriol Bohigas, David Mackay
Client: Barcelona Activa/Ajuntament de Barcelona/Associació Pla Estratègic Metropolità de Barcelona/Department de Treball de la Generalitat de Catalunya/Fons Feder de la Commissió Europea
Main Contractor: Llorenç Querol
General Carpentry: Ritortell SL
Technical Pavement: Irme SA
Acoustic Walls and Ceilings: Grupo Tecnologias 2000 SA
Metal Structure: Aluminium and Glass: Aplicaciones Inox 2000 SA
Painting: Decoración y Pintados
Furniture/Carpentry: Creaciones Capellades
Furniture equipment: Berna Disseny
Equipments: Instalaciones Higuera Castillo SL
Audio visual: Cibionte
Fire Detection: Siemens Cerberus SA
Lighting: Philips Ibérica SA
Lighting: Iguzzini Illuminazione España SA
Sign paintings and system of signs: Signes

PricewaterhouseCoopers, Birmingham, UK
Architect: BDGworkfutures
33 St John Street
London EC1M 4PJ
UK
Website: www.bdgworkfutures.com

Project team: Lydia New (director), Victor Spouge (senior associate)
Client: PricewaterhouseCoopers
Main Contractor: Wates
Consultant: ZZA
Project Manager/QS/Structural Engineer: Faithful & Gould
M&E Consultant: GW Building Services Consultants
Furniture: TSK

Rafineri, Istanbul, Turkey
Design Group: Erğinoğlu & Çalislar
Bestekar Sevki Bey Sokak 26/2
Balmumou 80700
Istanbul
Turkey
Website: www.ecarch.com

Project team: I. Kerem Erğinoğlu, Hasan C. Çalislar Elvan Çaliskan, Berke Hatipoglu, R. Mete Sönmez, Basak Çolakoglu, Emin Balkis
Client: Rafineri Advertising Agency
Main Contractor: Erginoglu & Çalislar (accents)
Electrical Contractor: Bilisim Electric
Mechanical Contractor: Step Engineering

Carpentry: Bahadir Carpentry
Construction: Eksper steel Construction
Graphics: Rafineri
Lighting: Has & Koen
Furniture: Koleksiyon

Rotterdam Chamber of Commerce, Rotterdam, Holland
Consultancy WorkConcept: Veldhoen + Company
Meerssenerweg 166B
6222 AK Maastricht
Holland
Website: www.velhoen.nl

Architect: Kraaijvanger Urbis, Rotterdam
Client: Ton Geerts, Managing Director, Chamber of Commerce
Project Management: BOAG, Rotterdam

The Royal Society, London, UK
Architect: Burrell Foley Fischer LLP
York Central
70-78 York Way
London N1 9AG
UK
Website: www.bff-architects.co.uk

Project Team: Stefanie Fischer (partner-in-charge), Helen Grassly (associate and project architect), Trevor Perkins (site supervisor), Tosin Trim (assistant architect)
Client: The Royal Society
Main Contractor: Interior plc
Quantity Surveyor: James Nisbet & Partners
Structural Engineer and Planning Supervisor: Price & Myers
Services Engineer: FHP Consulting Engineers
Acoustic Consultant: Paul Gillieron Acoustic Design
Lighting Designer: Light & Design Associates
Asbestos Consultant: Adams Environmental Ltd
AV Installations: Whitwam
Electrical Subcontractor: Trilectric Ltd
Mechanical Subcontractor: Mala Engineering
Joiners: Task Joinery Installations Ltd
Display Cases: Click Systems Ltd, Glasbau Hahn
Office Furniture: Unifor by Ergonom Ltd
Conference Room Equipment: Cerdan
Marble and Stone: Keystone Restoration Ltd, Natural Purbeck Cap.
Ceramic Flooring: Granitogres
Ironmongery: Allgoods plc, Glass, Ize, Elite Architectural Ironmongery
Timber Doors: Leaderflush Shapland
Metal-framed Glazed Doorsets: Pollard Fyrespan, Bassett & Findley Ltd
Secondary Glazing: Selectaglaze Ltd
Blinds: CBS Curtain and Blind Specialists
Atrium Roof: Birchdale Glass
Glass Floor and Atrium Light Sculpture: Arc Lighting Ltd, Rankins (Glass) Company Ltd
Glazed Screens: Charles Henshaw and Sons Ltd, Optima Architectural Glass, Pilkington plc
Stainless Steel: Steel Arts Fabrications Ltd

Scottish Parliament Building, Edinburgh, Scotland
Architect: Enric Miralles Benedetta Tagliabue Embt Arquitectes/RMJM
Addresses:
Enric Miralles, Benedetta Tagliabue
Ptge.pau 1o bis, Pral
08002 Barcelona
Spain
RMJM

10 Bells Brae
Edinburgh EH4 3BJ
Scotland
Websites: www.mirallestagliabue.com, www.rmjm.com

Client: Scottish Parliament Corporate Body
Structural Engineer: Ove Arup
Landscape Architects: Embt/RMJM
Cost Consultant: Davis Langdon Everest
Furniture Design: Ben Dawson
Fit Out and Specialist Joinery: Mivan

Sedgwick Rd., Seattle, USA
Architect: Olson Sundberg Kundig Allen Architects
159 South Jackson Street, 6th Floor
Seattle WA 98104
USA
Website: www.olsonsundberg.com

Project Team: Tom Kundig (principal in charge), Janice Webb (project manager), Alan Maskin, Kristen Becker, Kirsten Murray, Stephen Wood
Client: Sedgwick Rd., Manning Family (builder/owner)
Main Contractor: Schuchart
Engineers: Holaday Parks (mechanical), Haaland & Associates (electrical)
Consultants: The Seneca Group (owner's representative and project manager), Mike Stanley
Steel Stairs and Rail: Standard Steel Fabricating (drawings), Big Doors (fabricators), CHG Buildings Systems (installation)
Glazing: Emerald Glass
Window Coverings: Iris Window Coverings
Doors: All New Glass (steel pivot doors), Tangent Associates (wood doors)
Workstations: Schubert
Fabric Walls: Koryn Rolstad Studios
Cabinetwork and Custom Woodwork: Master Millwork
Steel Floor: Schuchart

Telenor, Oslo, Norway
Architect: NBBJ in collaboration with HUS, PKA and Dark Design
The Clove Building
4-6 Maguire Street, Butler's Wharf
London SE1 2NQ
UK
Website: www.nbbj.com

Project Team: Scott W. Wyatt, FAIA (Partner-in-Charge), Peter Pran, FAIA, MNAL (Design Principal/Design Leader), Jonathan Ward (Design Principal/Team Leader), Jin Ah Park (Design Principal/Team Leader), William J. Nichols (Principal/Project Executive), Thomas J. Morton, AIA, RIBA (Principal/Project Executive), Erik Lind, MNAL (Architect/Team Leader)
Architectural Team: Nils Inge Aarholt, Robert Anderson, Sten Bisgaard, Benedicte Bjercke, Ron Bolstad, Ola Bratset, Lasse Brogger, Craig Brookes, Nich Charles, Ivar Christensen, Torhild Dahl, Guillermo Diaz, Anne Droyli, Phu Duong, Beate Eikrem, Edwin Fajardo, Per Fossen, Duncan Griffin, Kelly Griffin, Urs Gutknecht, Gry Haddeland, Jay Halleran, Alf Haukeland, Joseph Herrin, Christopher James, Wiggo Karoliussen, Zenul Aberdin Khan, Ditlef Knudsen, Ali Kousha, Hans I. Kjaerem, Aud Kristoffersen, John Erik Kvam, Patrik Larsson, Mette Lie, Nazare Lillebo, Jon Meland, Hans Petter Mittet, Hans Kristian Moen, Joey Myers, Steffen Norang, Sigurd Refsnes, Lars Ribbum, Lena Simes, Michael Soubotin, Carsten Stinn, Agata Suchecka, Christian Sundby, Oddvar Svartdal, Alec Vassiliadis, Gunn Vesterli, Kjell Winsvold, Rukad Yousif

Client: Telenor AS
3D Visualization: Knut Ramstad (Director 3D Design, Telenor Property Fornebu AS), Henrik Th. Strom (Computer Graphics Manager, Telenor Expo, Telenor AS)
HUS: Bjorn C. Sorum, MNAL (Partner-in-Charge), Tom Forsberg, MNAL (Partner),
Lars Christian Koren Hauge, MNAL (Partner), Annema Selstrom (Architect/Team Leader)
PKA: Per Knudsen, MNAL (Partner-in-Charge), Jan Storing, MNAL (Design Principal/Lead Planner)
Structural Engineer: Scandiaconsult AS
Mechanical Engineer: Techno Consult
Electrical Engineer: Alfacon Nielsen og Borge
Acoustics Engineer: Inter Consult Group ASA
Traffic Consultant: SCC Trafikon
Civil Engineer: SCC Bonde & Co.
Landscape Architect: Asplan Viak AS, Hang Kjaerem AS
Project Group Leader: PTL Loken AS
Interior Architect: Spor Dark Design AS
Lighting Designer: Vesa Honkonen and Julle Oksanen

VAA Clubhouse, Johannesburg, South Africa
Architect: W1 Studio
70 Charlotte Street
London W1T 4QG
UK
Website: www.w1-studio.co.uk

Project Team: Patrick Hegarty
Client: Virgin Atlantic Airways
Main Contractor: VG Shopfitters
Quantity Surveyors: Mahlati Ntene Liebetrau
Electrical Engineers: BFBA Consultants
Structural Engineers: Tony Smith Associates
Mechanical Engineers: Richard Pearce and Partners
Food Service Equipment Consultants: Vulcan
Audio Visual Consultants: Active Audio
Furniture Consultants: Invoke

Index

Academyhills Roppongi Library, Tokyo, Japan 152–5
Allies and Morrison 76–81
apartment, Orio, Spain 180–1
Auer+Weber+Architekten 100–1
Austria 86–9

Baumschlager & Eberle 146–51
BBC Media Centre, London, UK 76–81
BDGworkfutures 30–3
Behnisch, Behnisch & Partner 40–3, 64–5
BMW Plant, Central Building, Leipzig, Germany 44–9
Bohlin Cywinski Jackson 106–9
Bosch & Fjord 90–3
Brewster Bye Architects 162–5
Burrell Foley Fisher LLP 102–5

Chartier-Corbasson Architectes 138–41
Chile 100–1
China 120–1
Clive Wilkinson Architects 36–9, 50–3
Coblentz, Patch, Duffy & Bass LLP, San Francisco, USA 116–19
Corti, Myriam 176–9
Creative Lofts, Huddersfield, UK 162–5

Dark Design 22–5
DEGW 76–81
Denmark 90–3
designer's loft space, Tokyo, Japan 166–9
Dou Design 120–1

East Union Live-Work Lofts, Seattle, USA 158–61
Embt Arquitectes Associates SL 94–9
EMI HQ, London, UK 68–73
Enjoy, Paris, France 66–7
Erğinoğlu & Çalislar 34–5
Ericsson North American HQ, Plano, USA 54–7
ESO Hotel, Cerro Paranal, Chile 100–1

Fernau & Hartman Architects Inc. 170–1
Finland 82–5
Foster and Partners 124–9
France 66–7, 138–41
François, Edouard 66–7
Future Centre, Innsbruck, Austria 86–9

Genzyme Center, Cambridge, USA 64–5
Germany 40–3, 44–9, 110–13, 146–51

Heikkinen-Komonen Architects 110–13
Helin & Co Architects 82–5
Hemingway Design 182–3
Hemingways' Outdoor Office, Middx, UK 182–3
Hirota Design Studio 166–9
Hirsch, Roger 176–9
Holland 58–63, 132–5, 142–3
home/office project, New York, USA 176–9

Interiors Disseny 122–3
Interpolis, Tilburg, Holland 58–63

Japan 136–7, 152–5, 166–9
Jensen & Macy Architects 16–21

Katsan Office Building, Stockholm, Sweden 172–5
Kennispoort, Eindhoven, Holland 132–5
Kirshenbaum Bond & Partners West, San Francisco, USA 16–21
Kuma, Kengo 136–7, 152–5

Lauckgroup 54, 56
Less Limited, Hong Kong, China 120–1
Lorenz, Peter 86–9

Madrid Regional Documentary Centre, Spain 130–1
Maison de l'Architecture, Paris, France 138–41
Mann Residence, Sonoma County, USA 170–1
Mansilla + Tuñón 130–1
Max Planck Institute of Molecular Cell Biology and Genetics, Dresden, Germany 110–13
The Miller/Hull Partnership 158–61
Miralles, Enric 94–9
Momentum, Hørsholm, Denmark 90–3
MoreySmith Design and Architecture 68–73
Mother, London, UK 50–3
Munich Re, Munich, Germany 146–51

NBBJ-HUS-PKA 22–5
Norddeutsche Landesbank, Hanover, Germany 40–3
Norway 22–5

Olson Sundberg Kundig Allen Architects 26–9
One Omotesando, Tokyo, Japan 136–7

Pallotta TeamWorks, Los Angeles, USA 36–9
Parliamentary Annexe, Helsinki, Finland 82–5
Pereira, Aston 116–19
Pixar Animation Studios, Emeryville, USA 106–9
Porta22, Barcelona, Spain 122–3
Price, Bill 120–1
PricewaterhouseCoopers, Birmingham, UK 30–3

Rafineri, Istanbul, Turkey 34–5
RMJM 94–9
Rotterdam Chamber of Commerce, Holland 142–3
The Royal Society, London, UK 102–5

Scottish Parliament Building, Edinburgh, UK 94–9
Sedgwick Rd., Seattle, USA 26–9
South Africa 144–5
Spain 122–3, 130–1, 180–1
Suzuki, Toshihiko 166–9
Sweden 172–5

Tagliabue, Benedetta 94–9
Telenor, Oslo, Norway 22–5

30 St Mary Axe, London, UK 124–9
Thompson Vaivoda & Associates 54–7
Turkey 34–5

UK 30–3, 50–3, 68–73, 76–81, 94–9, 102–5, 124–9, 162–5, 182–3
USA 16–21, 26–9, 36–9, 54–7, 64–5, 106–9, 116–19, 158–61, 170–1, 176–9

van Velsen, Koen 132–5
Veldhoen + Company 58–63, 142–3
Virgin Atlantic Clubhouse, Johannesburg, South Africa 144–5

W1 Studio 144–5
White Architects 172–5

Zaha Hadid Architects 44–9
Zómad Arquitectos 180–1

The publisher would like to thank the following sources for permission to use their images.

Peter Aaron/ESTO (107-109), Susana Aréchaga (180-181), Richard Barnes (16-21, 116), Ali Bekman (34-35), Benjamin Benschneider (160-161), Tim Bies (28), Courtesy BMW (45, 47), Benny Chan (36-39), Darren Chatz (144-145), Peter Cook/VIEW (76, 79 top, 80), Corbis (74-75), H. G. Esch (46, 49), Mitsumasa Fujitsuka (137), Chris Gascoigne (68-73, 79 bottom, 81), Chris Gascoigne/VIEW (63), Dennis Gilbert (102-105), Anton Grassl (65), Tim Griffith (117-119), Grundy & Northedge (10), Nick Guttridge/VIEW (78, 125 bottom 128), Roland Halbe/artur (40-43, 100-101, 130-131), Wayne Hemingway (182-183), James F. Housel (158-159), Eduard Hueber (147, 148-149, 151), Hufton & Crow (30-33) Hufton & Crow/VIEW (129), Thomas Jantscher (86-89), Natasja Jovic (173-175), Lachenmann/Bruchhaus (146, 150), John Linden (170-171), Ake E:Son Lindman (172), Duccio Malagamba (132-135), Mary Evans Picture Library (14-15, 114-115, 156-157), Minh+Wass (176-179), Voitto Niemelä (82, 84 right, 85), Lluìs Pau (122-123), Michael Perlmutter (83, 84 left) Marco Prozzo (27, 29), Paul Raftery/VIEW (66-67, 94-99), Christian Richters (22-25), Sharon Risedorph (106), Philippe Ruault (138-141), Sadamu Saito (166-169), Sas Savik (162-165), Shinkenchiku-sha (136), Jean Simons for Veldhoen + Company (59-61), Grant Smith/VIEW (126-127), Richard H. Strode (54-57), Edmund Sumner/VIEW (77), Jussi Tiainen (110-113), Graham Uden (120-121), Elsje van Ree (90-93), Courtesy Marcel Wanders (62), Adrian Wilson (50-53), Nigel Young (124-125 top), Kim Zwarts for Veldhoen + Company (142-143) Picture credits for pp152-155 unavailable at time of going to print.

Authors' acknowledgements

Jeremy Myerson would like to thank Wendy Smith, Matthew Myerson and Nathan Myerson for their support and encouragement in writing this book.

Philip Ross would like to thank Katy Manuel, Oliver Ross and Joshua Ross for their inspiration, understanding and help during the research and writing of Space to Work.

E-mail: info@workplaceinnovation.co.uk